THE ILLUSTRATED BOOK OF
HERBS

THE ILLUSTRATED BOOK OF
HERBS

Barbara Hey

CRESCENT
BOOKS
New York

This 1996 edition is published by Crescent Books,
a division of Random House Value Publishing, Inc.,
201 East 50th Street, New York, N.Y. 10022.

Crescent Books and colophon are trademarks of
Random House Value Publishing, Inc.

Random House
New York • Toronto • London • Sydney • Auckland
http://www.randomhouse.com/

✠

EDITOR: Thea Coetzee
DESIGNER: Odette Marais
DESIGN ASSISTANT: Lellyn Creamer
PICTURE RESEARCHERS: Arlene de Muijnk and Michelle Downey
INDEXER: Sandie Vahl
PROOFREADER: Tessa Kennedy

✠

Printed and bound in Malaysia

A CIP catalog record for this book is available
from the Library of Congress.

ISBN 0-517-18473-7

8 7 6 5 4 3 2 1

✠

PLEASE NOTE

*Throughout this book, we have tried to select only those herbs which are not very easily confused with others.
You should, however, always make absolutely sure that you are indeed using the correct plant, because there are many highly
toxic herbs which have the same appearance as some of the useful herbs.
Every effort has been made to verify all the facts and to present clear and accurate instructions for using the herbs. Therefore,
the authors and publishers can accept no liability for any injury, illness or damage which may inadvertently be caused to the
user while following these instructions.*

GLOSSARY OF MEDICAL TERMS

ABORTIFACIENT — causes abortion

ANALGESIC — reduces pain

ANAPHRODISIAC — reduces sexual libido

ANTI-INFLAMMATORY — helps to reduce inflammation

ANTIOXIDANT — a substance that protects cells from damage by oxidation and free radicals

ANTISEPTIC — prevents infection

ANTISPASMODIC — relieves spasms or cramps

AROMATIC — having a strong aroma

ASTRINGENT — contracts tissue and reduces secretion

BITTER — bitter substance that stimulates digestion

CARMINATIVE — reduces colic and flatulence

DEMULCENT — soothes and protects mucous membranes

DIAPHORETIC — encourages perspiration and excretion of toxins

DIURETIC — encourages the kidneys to secrete more urine

EMMENAGOGUE — stimulates menstruation

EXPECTORANT — helps expel mucus from the respiratory system

FEBRIFUGE — reduces fever

FLATULENCE — digestive tract gas

GALACTOGOGUE — stimulates milk production

HEMOSTATIC — stops bleeding

HEPATIC — stimulates the liver

HYPNOTIC — induces sleep

HYPOGLYCEMIC — lowers blood sugar

HYPOTENSIVE — lowers blood pressure

LAXATIVE — aids bowel evacuation

MUCILAGE — soothing slippery substance that coats and protects mucous membranes

NERVINE — strengthens the nerves

NUTRITIVE — with nourishing properties

SEDATIVE — calming

STIMULANT — energises the body

STYPTIC — stops bleeding

TONIC — improves vitality

VERMIFUGE — expels worms

VULNERARY — speeds up the healing of wounds

PHOTOGRAPHY

ILLUSTRATIONS

CONTENTS

I

THE
HISTORY OF
HERBS

"An herb is a friend of physicians and pride of cooks."

THE
HISTORY OF
HERBS

GENERALLY, HERBS ARE PLANTS WITHOUT WOODY TISSUE AND SPICES ARE WOODY PLANTS. FOR THE
PURPOSES OF THIS BOOK, HOWEVER, HERBS ARE DEFINED IN THE BROADER SENSE AS BEING PLANTS
WHICH ARE USED FOR CULINARY AND MEDICINAL PURPOSES, WHETHER THEY ARE WOODY OR NOT.
IN THIS SENSE, THE DEFINITION OF HERBS INCLUDES SPICES, TOO.

THERE IS MUCH FOLKLORE, superstition and ceremony surrounding herbs. This is not surprising, as they have been part of our lives since the time of Neanderthal man. Fossils of mallow, rose petals and yarrow pollen have been found in caves inhabited by early man.

HERBS AND ARCHAEOLOGY

Herbs and spices were and, to some extent, still are used for embalming and in funeral rites, as they have proved to be efficient preservatives. When archaeologists opened up ancient Egyptian tombs, traces of rosemary and basil were found laid on and around the bodies. An interesting find was made in Siberia, when a Pazyryk burial site dating back to 400 B.C. that had been covered by a layer of permafrost, was opened. Next to the very well-preserved body of a woman was a bowl of perfect coriander seeds. Coriander and cumin have also been found in ancient Egyptian graves. In Bahrain mint was found in 4,000-year-old Sumerian burial grounds. Sumerian clay tablets of cuneiform inscriptions show that they cultivated nearly a thousand different plants, many for culinary and medicinal use, among which were coriander, fennel, marjoram, mint, thyme and caraway. Writings on Egyptian papyrus also list anise, mustard, wormwood, cinnamon and cassia. In biblical times mint, thyme and anise were so valuable that they were used to pay tithes.

HERBS AND TRAVEL

People's desire for herbs and spices other than those easily obtained or grown was one reason for very early travel and exploration. By 2000 B.C. the Phoenicians included spices in their cargo. Arab traders sailing to and from the Malabar coast and along the coasts of East Africa and the Mediterranean carried valuable spices such as turmeric, cloves, cinnamon, myrrh and ginger, thereby creating a market for them. Arabian camel caravans also crossed the Middle East from India to Egypt. As the herb and spice business was lucrative, trading posts were set up along the Mediterranean coast for wider distribution into Europe and North Africa. Around 300 B.C. conquering armies such as those of Alexander the Great ranged from Greece to India and carried hitherto unknown spices and herbs for medicinal purposes and food preservation. The Romans introduced herbs such as chervil, land cress, lavender, lemon balm and rosemary to Britain.

Just as armies opened up trade as they advanced, it was the opposite when they retreated. When the Roman armies withdrew from Britain and Western Europe, certain herbs and spices became quite scarce and the knowledge of their cultivation and use declined.

THE MONASTERIES

Monastic communities seemed best able to survive the lack of law and order which followed the withdrawal of the Roman armies. The monks had the knowledge to use spices and grew herbs for culinary and medicinal uses from as early as 600 AD. Some of this knowledge must have come down to them by word of mouth, as the Saxons and others also made use of herbs. The monks of some orders became well known for the highly sought-after, herb-based liqueurs they produced. As the sale of these bottled elixirs was lucrative, the recipes were kept a closely guarded secret. An example is chartreuse — made by blending herbs grown in the Swiss Alps with fine spirits.

The Emperor Charlemagne was one of the first rulers to introduce cultivated herb growing outside the monastic gardens. In the 9th century, he ordered that all plants grown in St. Gall's monastery in Western Europe — listed in old manuscripts as 76 in number — were to be grown on his Royal Estates stretching from Germany to Spain. Soon herbs were found growing wild in the countryside and were cultivated in the gardens of wealthy property owners and also those of more humble people. Herb gardens only really became popular in Britain and Europe in the 14th century, when people became aware of the benefits of herbs.

SUPERSTITIONS

The ancient Egyptians set great store by the health-giving properties of onions and garlic and included them in the diet of the slaves who built the pyramids. Garlic was also incorporated into the Greek and Roman army rations. Strangely enough, the officers and upper classes did not partake of it.

The writings of the Greek Hippocrates and later also of Theophrastus and the Roman Pliny give us an insight into the many superstitious beliefs of their time and how the herbs

then available were used for culinary, cosmetic and medicinal purposes. Another writer, Dioscorides, advised that excessive eating of basil would weaken the eyesight and cause indigestion. Many other myths have grown up around this herb. Nicholas Culpeper, author of *Complete Herbal* (1653), states: "Basil being applied to a place bitten by venomous beasts or stung by a wasp or hornet, it speedily draws the poison out." It was also believed that the constant smelling of basil would cause scorpions to grow in the head! To this day, basil is placed across doorways and on windowsills in some parts of India to deter snakes. Because Indians regarded it as a sacred plant, they also used it in their funeral rites. Sacred basil is often found growing around houses and temples.

HERBS IN CEREMONIAL RITES

Rosemary played an important part in the ceremonial life of the Greeks and Romans. Wreaths of rosemary adorned the heads of household gods and, when students were studying or being tested for their knowledge, they wore rosemary in their hair for memory retention. Wearing rosemary wood combs was said to ward off insanity. This herb was also used by the Elizabethans in wedding and funeral ceremonies.

Another significant herb in ceremonial rites was celery, which was eaten at funeral feasts and also made into wreaths laid on graves to placate the gods of the underworld. The Greeks regarded parsley as a sacred symbol of joy and fame, and therefore did not use it for culinary purposes. A bay tree in the garden was said to keep witches away. The leaves of bay *(Laurus nobilis)* were woven into wreaths to be worn as a mark of honor by poets (hence the title poet laureate) and the winners of marathons. A strange way of rewarding the winner of the four-horse chariot (quadriga) race was to

proffer him a drink of wormwood (which is extremely bitter) to ensure his future good health. Another snippet of folklore about herbs is quoted from the ancient herbal, *Hortus Sanitatus*: "The pleasant, scented smoke of southernwood drives snakes out from the house."

HERBS THROUGH THE AGES

Most communities had a wise person, usually a woman, who dispensed potions made from plants either grown in or harvested from fields, forests and hedgerows. One of the earliest comprehensively written records of recipes and prescriptions was the 10th-century *Leech Book of Bald*.

Chinese herbalists, who have written records going back 5,000 years, have contributed much to our knowledge. In the 11th century, Marco Polo entered China and eventually opened up a trade route to Europe — besides silk, herbs and spices also formed an important part of his cargoes.

While Marco Polo was making his journeys, the Crusades or Holy Wars (1095–1291) were being fought in Palestine. The Crusaders, mainly from France, Italy, Germany and Britain, became used to different kinds of food in which herbs and spices were used. On returning home, some of these plants were included in their baggage in the form of roots and seeds, many of which were later grown successfully in cooler climates. The borage flower also played a part in these wars. Known as the "herb of courage," this simple blue flower was embroidered on the knights' tunics by their womenfolk to sustain them in battle.

For many years Venice had been the center of the European herb and spice trade and in the late 14th century cooking became an art as a wider variety of flavorings and foods became available. This created an even greater demand

for supplies, resulting in the search for sea routes to the East. The Venetian and Arab hold on the spice trade was broken when the Portuguese seafarers found their way to India and the East Indian islands. Later this trade was captured by the Dutch, who in turn kept the price artificially high on spices such as cloves and nutmeg by forcing restrictive planting. It was only with the decline of Dutch power that the spices and certain herbs could be afforded by less wealthy people. They were still so valuable that they were kept in small locked wooden boxes, to be opened only by the lady of the house.

A search for a spice route was planned, but, as charts were inadequate, Columbus turned west and arrived in America in 1492. Later new plants, including herbs, were brought to Europe from this side of the world. As Europeans traveled west to settle, they took roots and seeds of familiar herbs with them and many plants became naturalized. These early settlers learned through necessity from indigenous inhabitants, who also had a long history of herbal lore. Archaeological digs in Central and South America have revealed remains of what was a very efficient system of agriculture, maintained for thousands of years by the Inca and Maya people. They also cultivated herbs — some of the earliest ideas on sowing by the moon came from their cultures. It is believed that root crops grow best when planted at the waning of the moon, and that the seeds of plants that are harvested above ground should be sown at the rising of the new moon. The Native Americans, being mainly nomadic, relied on herbs from the wild rather than those which were cultivated.

From the mid-17th century, with explorers and botanists bringing back new plants, the interest in gardening increased and those that could afford to — mainly in Britain and Europe — had knot and walled gardens laid out, and much later orangeries and hothouses were built. These enabled people to grow a wide variety of fruits, vegetables and herbs. Many of these gardens have since been lovingly restored and are now on view to the public.

In the more affluent households, the still room was of great importance. This was where the women of the house used herbs to make medicines, lotions and creams. We owe much of our knowledge about the plants grown in these gardens, as well as those found in the countryside at this time, to herbalists such as Turner, Gerard, Parkinson and Culpeper. Shakespeare referred to many herbs in his writings and as a result it became fashionable to have a garden in which only Shakespearean herbs were grown.

In a similar vein there are also gardens containing only herbs mentioned in the Bible. Reading about the plantings in these gardens may be confusing, as some herbs are now known by different names. Hyssop, for instance, bears no relation to that which we grow today — it was more likely to have been a form of origanum.

HERBS TODAY

In our ongoing quest for knowledge, people in many countries are now taking the opportunity to find out more about their indigenous plants. Aborigines, Maoris, Central and South Americans, Native Americans and Africans, among others, have in the past (and, to some degree, today) used many plants which nature has provided for healing, health and comfort. We have much to learn from our elders, with their unwritten but instructive knowledge. Much of our environment is being destroyed, taking a lot of its indigenous plant life with it. Time is running out: we should all start becoming aware of our environment and doing something positive to preserve it for future generations.

II

A
DIRECTORY OF
HERBS

*" Talke of perfect happinesse or pleasure,
and what place was so fit for that as the garden place
where Adam was set to be the Herbalist."*

(JOHN GERARD)

A
DIRECTORY OF
HERBS

LIKE ALL PLANTS, HERBS NEED CARE AND ATTENTION. BEAR IN MIND THAT CLIMATE AND SOIL CAN AFFECT GROWTH; THEREFORE THE GIVEN SIZE OF A PLANT IS ONLY APPROXIMATE. SOME HERBS MAY BE HARVESTED FROM HEDGEROWS AND MEADOWLANDS IF THEY ARE FREE FROM CHEMICAL AND TRAFFIC POLLUTION. FOR MORE INFORMATION ON GROWING HERBS, PLEASE REFER TO CHAPTER 3.

Achillea millefolium

YARROW

ORIGIN
Caucasus and China

DESCRIPTION
Height 12–24 in (30–60 cm), depending on variety. It has a spreading root system, producing many low-growing, dull green, feathery leaves. A firm, furrowed, sparsely leafed stem bears an umbel of dense, small white flowers. The foliage varies in color among many shades of yellow. Red-, pink- and cream-flowered yarrows are also available.

CULTIVATION
Yarrow is an undemanding plant. It does best in a sunny position with good drainage and light soil. Propagate by root division or from semihardwood cuttings taken in autumn or spring.

DISEASES
Mildew (*see* page 87)

MEDICINAL USES
See page 130

SIMPLE REMEDY
Crush the leaves and apply to a wound to stop bleeding.

OTHER USES
Yarrow gives color to a herbaceous border. Use the flowers for fresh or dried arrangements. Cut the flower stems at the base of the plant when they are at the height of their color, before the sun bleaches them. Bunch loosely and hang to dry. Yarrow flowers make a pretty, fragrant addition to potpourri. Dig out the surplus plants and use them for the compost heap — this also helps to curb the root spread.

YARROW

Acorus calamus

SWEET FLAG

ORIGIN
Northern India

DESCRIPTION
Height 3 ft (1 m). Sweet flag is similar to an iris, though it is not of the same family. It is grown for its thickly rooted,

SWEET FLAG

creeping rhizome. The narrow, light green lanceolate leaves are ribbed on both the upper and undersides and they give off a warm, spicy aroma when they are crushed. In summer an upright, triangular stem produces a cylindrical head of tiny, scented, greenish-yellow flowers. This flower head is unusual in that it protrudes at an angle about a quarter of the way down the stem. There is also a variegated variety which has cream stripes running down the leaves.

CULTIVATION
This plant is a perennial grown by rhizome division or from cuttings of the rhizome, 2–4 in (5–10 cm) long, with roots. This is best done in spring and autumn. Sweet flag's natural habitat is shallow water or marshy ground. If this plant is grown in the garden, a sunny position in damp, rich soil is required. It may also be grown in a large container in a pond.

HARVESTING
Lift rhizomes in the second or third year. If they are left longer than this, they tend to become hollow. Wash well and remove the roots, then spread out to dry. Lightly bunch the leaves and hang to dry. The fragrance intensifies during the drying process.

MEDICINAL USES
The rhizome is used to alleviate acidity in the stomach.

CULINARY USES
The leaves may be used as a substitute for vanilla pods. Cut up the leaves and add them to the containers in which dry foods are stored. This will prevent any infestation by weevils.

OTHER USES
Use the dried rhizomes as well as the foliage in potpourri.

ROUND BUCHU

Agathosma betulina

ROUND BUCHU

Agathosma crenulata

OVAL BUCHU

ORIGIN
South Africa

DESCRIPTION
Height 3–6½ ft (1–2 m). A woody shrub, producing slender stems of small, dark green, shiny, oval or round leaves. Oil glands, which give off a strong, bitter, astringent aroma and taste, are clearly visible on undersides of leaves. The small, star-like flowers are white or pink. *Coleonema* is another member of the family and this shrub, with its small, perfumed, white or pink flowers, is an attractive addition to the garden.

CULTIVATION
Buchu is a perennial propagated either from seed or cuttings. In some countries, plants can be obtained from specialist herb nurseries or botanical garden shops. Grow established plants in a well-drained, sunny, hot position. Minimum care is needed. Water during very hot, dry weather. Give the plants some extra shelter and care in areas where frost occurs. Buchu also benefits from an occasional mulch of well-rotted compost. Do not use any fertilizers. In the wild, buchu grows in rough ground in hot, dry conditions.

HARVESTING
Cut short stems of foliage before flowering and hang to dry.

MEDICINAL USES
See page 130

OTHER USES
Use the dried leaves and flowers in potpourri.

Agrimonia eupatoria

AGRIMONY

ORIGIN
Britain

DESCRIPTION
Height in flower 20 in (50 cm). The hairy, serrated leaves are divided into leaflets which have white undersides. The plant has upright, slender stems with smaller leaflets. The simple, fruit-scented, sulfur-yellow flowers cluster on these long tapering stems. The seeds are contained in burr-like cases.

CULTIVATION
This herb is a perennial. Try sowing seed in late winter, as it germinates best under cool conditions. Agrimony is a plant of the hedgerows and grows in well-drained soil in full sun.

AGRIMONY

HARVESTING

Cut the flowers when the plant starts to bloom. Cut the leaves as required and then hang them up to dry.

MEDICINAL USES

See page 130

OTHER USES

Agrimony is a decorative plant when grown in a herbaceous border.

Alchemilla vulgaris

LADY'S MANTLE

ORIGIN

Europe, North Asia, Greenland and mountainous areas like the Himalayas

DESCRIPTION

Height 2–20 in (5–50 cm). Leaf stems grow from a fibrous root clump. Large, soft, grayish-green, serrated, kidney-shaped leaves are neatly gathered at the stem joint where a gleaming drop of moisture is often to be seen. Small, yellow-green flowers are borne in soft, loose clusters. *A. mollis* is a more robust

---

plant, commonly grown in flower beds for its decorative qualities.

CULTIVATION

Sow seed of this perennial in moist, rich alkaline soil. It may be propagated by root division in spring and autumn. In the wild it is found in damp meadows, open woodlands and mountain edges. It does not thrive in a hot climate.

HARVESTING

For drying, gather leaves at the height of summer while the plants are still flowering, or cut as required.

CULINARY USES

Very young leaves may be torn into a salad to impart a slight bitterness.

MEDICINAL USES

See page 131

HEALTH AND COSMETIC USES

See page 167

Allium cepa

ONIONS

Allium sativum

GARLIC

Allium schoenoprasum

COMMON CHIVES

Allium tuberosum

GARLIC CHIVES (CHINESE CHIVES)

ORIGIN

Europe, Asia, Siberia and regions of North America

DESCRIPTION

There are several varieties of *Allium*, both culinary and ornamental.

A. cepa

Height could reach 3 ft (1 m), depending on the variety and the climate. The onion is made up of layers of flesh forming a bulbous whole, with a firm, circular base producing a cluster of fine, straight roots. The flesh may be any

---

color from white or green to reddish purple, depending on the variety. There are also several variations in the shape of the bulb. The stems are erect and hollow, topped from midsummer to autumn with rounded clusters of white flowers. The gray-green leaves are smooth, hollow and slightly indented on one side.

A. sativum

Height 24 in (60 cm). Long, flat, gray-green leaves grow from a segmented bulb. The central stem carries long, pointed buds from which a rounded cluster of mauve-white flowers breaks. The cloves of garlic are individually covered in a thin, smooth skin, forming a tight head with a cluster of dense roots. The color of the head may vary from white or green to deep purple.

A. schoenoprasum

Height 10–12 in (25–30 cm). This is a small, onion-like bulb which has long, fine roots, and it grows in clumps. The foliage of this variety is in the form of hollow, gray-green, grass-like shoots.

LADY'S MANTLE

GARLIC

COMMON CHIVES

Soft, pinkish-mauve flower heads are produced on the firm, straight stems.

A. tuberosum

Height 12–14 in (30–35 cm). It consists of loose clumps of small rhizomes with short roots and flat, narrow, dark green foliage. Heads of small, star-like, white flowers grow on stiff, upright stems.

CULTIVATION

A. cepa

Propagate by sowing in trays or rows directly. It is often easier to buy small plants or sets from a professional grower. Onions require rich, well-drained and cultivated soil in a sunny position. Unless you need flowers for seed or arrangements, nip out the stem shoots close to the ground. When the foliage is brown and droopy, lift the onions, tie them into bundles and hang up or leave spread out to dry. For salads, formed onions may be lifted green as required.

A. sativum

Seed may be sown, but it is usually easier to buy a head of garlic from a nursery, break off cloves and plant them

about 2 in (5 cm) deep in well-drained, loose, alkaline soil which has been given a good dressing of well-rotted manure. Garlic requires sunshine. It needs to stay in the ground for eight months and should therefore be planted early in autumn for harvesting the following summer. Remove flowering stalks as they appear. Lift plants when the foliage begins to droop and either spread them out to dry or plant the cloves.

A. schoenoprasum and *A. tuberosum*

Both of these varieties can be grown from seed sown in trays. They are, however, easier to propagate by dividing clumps into six to eight plants in spring and autumn. It is necessary to do this every two or three years. Grow them in full sun, in a good soil which has been enriched with bone meal and used coffee grounds. Chives may also be grown in a container. In some areas the plants die back, only to shoot up again as the weather warms. When harvesting chives, use a sharp pair of scissors and cut only half of a clump, leaving about 2 in (5 cm) of growth. This way the plants recover quickly.

DISEASES

Rust (*see* page 88) can attack chives. Cut down to approximately 2 in (5 cm), then remove all the other foliage and burn it. Feed the plants well. A copper spray may also be applied if the attack is particularly severe.

CULINARY USES

It is usually the onion bulb and the garlic head that are used for culinary purposes. The foliage of common and garlic chives is used raw as a garnish or to give an onion or garlic flavor to egg dishes, salads, herb butters, herb cheeses, stews and soups. Chives are also particularly good with raw tomato as well as in any number of pasta dishes.

A. tuberosum is used freely in Chinese cooking. Vinegars and oils are made using the flowers and the foliage. The

flowers of *A. schoenoprasum* are edible and, when separated from the head, make a decorative and tasty garnish.

MEDICINAL USES

See page 131

OTHER USES

For either dried or fresh arrangements, flower heads of *Allium* are remarkably decorative, especially the flowers of the common chive which, when dry, are a pretty, silvery mauve.

Aloe ferox

CAPE ALOE

Aloe vera (= A. barbadensis)

ALOE

ORIGIN

South Africa

DESCRIPTION

A. ferox

Height 6½–13 ft (2–4 m). This plant is a succulent with an erect stem which bears several large, fleshy leaves. The

ALOE

A. vera

Propagate from small, rooted offshoots at the base of the parent plant. It may be grown from seed. It requires a rough, gritty growing medium and a well-drained, sunny position. It is sensitive to frost. In cooler climates it is grown as an indoor pot plant, in a position with plenty of sun. Do not overwater.

HARVESTING

A. ferox

The resinous, milky sap is drained from cuts in the leaves throughout the year and then dried, preferably in the sun.

A. vera

Cut leaves as required from mature plants.

MEDICINAL USES

See page 131

by planting it in a sheltered area. Plant it near a door or path, as the fragrance is strong when you brush against it. The plant requires full sun and average alkaline soil. Prune back hard in autumn. Save all the leaves for drying, in order to have a sufficient supply until the new leaves appear. The shrub does not stay bare for long.

HARVESTING

Cut leaves as required. Small branches may be cut in summer for drying.

PESTS

Red spider mites and, when conditions are dry, stinkbugs (*see* page 88).

CULINARY USES

This herb has a strong lemon fragrance and flavor. The finely chopped young leaves may be added to any dish where a lemon flavor is indicated. You could sprinkle them over fruit or vegetable salads or stir them into herb butter and cottage cheese. Lemon verbena makes a refreshing tea when made with mint, other herbs or on its own. It is ideal served cold on a hot summer day. For a

long leaves are almost triangular in shape, and they have rough, spiky, reddish margins and upper surfaces. These leaves form a rosette towards the top of the stem. The many firm stems bear dense clusters of long, tubular, red or orange flowers in late spring.

A. vera

Height 12–16 in (30–40 cm). A fibrous root system produces long, tapering, stemless, succulent leaves. These light green leaves have spiky margins and are blotched with cream. The firm, upright stems bear several bell-shaped, fleshy, yellow-orange flowers.

CULTIVATION

A. ferox

This perennial is propagated from offsets at the base. It needs well-drained, coarse, sandy soil and full sun. In cool climates, grow under glass as it is sensitive to frost.

Aloysia triphylla
(= Lippia citriodora)

LEMON VERBENA

ORIGIN

Chile, Argentina and Mexico

DESCRIPTION

Height 2–4 ft (60–130 cm). In hot climates it can reach an astonishing 14½ ft (4.5 m). This shrub has a slender, woody trunk and branches, and tender stems of thin, slightly sticky, lanceolate, pointed, light green leaves which are shiny on top and dull on the undersides. Small, pale mauve flowers grow in spikes from summer to autumn.

CULTIVATION

Propagate from pencil-sized cuttings, heeled if possible, taken any time except midwinter. Protect the plant from frost

LEMON VERBENA

reduced salt diet, crush the dried leaves and then mix in the proportion of one part salt to three parts lemon verbena. It also combines well with dried celery and lovage leaves to make a salt-free seasoning.

OTHER USES

Lemon verbena is ideal for potpourri, as the dried leaves can retain their oils for two or three years. Cut mature flowers for fresh arrangements. Place a handful of the leaves in the bag of your vacuum cleaner to scent the house.

Althaea officinalis

MARSH MALLOW

ORIGIN

Europe, Britain, North Africa and Central Asia

DESCRIPTION

Height 36 in (90 cm). It has a strong, thick, tapering, creamy yellow root. The light green stem is sparsely branched and covered in a coarse down. The short-stemmed leaves are rounded, with pointed tips and serrated edges, gray-green in color and downy on both upper and undersides. In late summer, panicles of soft pink flowers appear from the leaf axils. As the flowers fade, round, flat green seed capsules form. These are commonly known as "cheeses."

CULTIVATION

This plant is a perennial, grown from seed sown in autumn or late winter. Take cuttings in spring, or propagate by taking offsets in autumn. It likes damp, rich soil in a sunny position. It dies back in winter — remove old growth.

HARVESTING

Cut the leaves and flowers as required. Collect green seeds when plump. Lift the root in autumn — do not wash it, but brush clean before drying.

MEDICINAL USES

See page 131

CULINARY USES

Scatter the nutty flavored "cheeses" in salads. In the past, the root was the basis for marshmallow candy.

MARSH MALLOW

Anethum graveolens

DILL

ORIGIN

Unknown

DESCRIPTION

Height 24 in (60 cm). A hollow main stem grows from a long taproot. Dill has loose, feathery, blue-green leaves with umbels of fine yellow flowers. The flat, oval seeds are pale brown with a dark rib down the center. There is a dwarf variety which is suited to hot climates, as it does not go to seed so quickly.

CULTIVATION

Dill is an annual. Sow directly, as the seedlings do not transplant well. Cover the seeds lightly — germination takes approximately one to two weeks. Sow continuously, except in winter. Allow to grow in fairly close clumps for support, in a position with sun or semi-shade where the soil is well drained, light and slightly acid. Do not grow dill near caraway, fennel or angelica.

PESTS

Caterpillars (*see* page 87)

CULINARY USES

The mild, spicy leaves of dill taste of caraway, while the seeds are strongly pungent and aromatic. Freshly cut and lightly chopped leaves enhance the flavor of dips, cottage cheese, herb butters, soups, salads and all fish dishes. When the seeds are a pale brown in color, dry them using the bag method (*see* page 104). The seeds of dill are used to make pickled cucumber and cabbage and they also improve the taste of roasts, stews, cooked vegetables and potato and cucumber salads. They are very good sprinkled on breads, rolls and fruit pies. Grind the seeds and use this as a salt substitute in the diet. Use the flowering heads as well as the seeds to make dill vinegar (*see* page 104).

DILL

ANGELICA

ORIGIN
Far northern Europe

DESCRIPTION
Height 24 in (60 cm) or much more. Spread 24 in (60 cm). Angelica has hollow, ribbed stalks with branching stems of bright green basal leaves which divide into finely serrated, oval leaflets. Leaves are smooth and grayish on the underside. Large umbels of greenish-white or yellow flowers appear on the upright stems. Seeds are ribbed, and green to light brown when ripe.

N.B. Not to be confused with Angelica pachycarpa, *which has crinkled, shiny, dark green leaves and is a purely ornamental plant, having no medicinal or culinary uses.*

CULTIVATION
Propagate angelica from seed, which should be sown in trays or directly as soon as possible after removing them from the plant. If this is not practical, seal the seed in a plastic container and store it in the refrigerator, as it soon loses its viability. Annual sowing is advisable in order to ensure continuity.

Choose the coolest part of the garden. The soil needs to be deep, rich, slightly acid and moist, but at the same time well drained, as soggy soil will cause dieback. Protect plants from the wind. Angelica does not seem to do well under trees, so a position against a fence or wall with some morning sun is best. To perpetuate the plant, you should cut out the flowering stem, which usually shoots up in the second year and may be used for crystallizing. Allow to flower in the third or fourth year, when the plant will need to be replaced. Plant out the seedlings when they have four to six leaves. Do not leave them too long before transplanting, as they have long taproots.

HARVESTING
Cut the stems during late spring. The leaves are at their best a little later. Lift mature roots in autumn.

PESTS
Red spider (*see* page 88). Water undersides of the leaves, especially in hot, dry weather, as a preventative. At the first signs of yellowing and silvering of the leaves, dust with sulfur dust. To make it stick, apply early in the morning when leaves are still slightly damp.

CULINARY USES
Angelica has a sweet and refreshing fragrance. The leaves may be chopped for fruit salads and also added to fish dishes and cottage cheese in smallish quantities. Cook the leaves and stems with sour fruit such as apricots, plums and rhubarb to neutralise their acidity. Boil the stems with jams to improve the flavor, but remove these stems when the jam is done. Steam the stems as a vegetable. Young stems may be used as a substitute for salad celery. The strong-flavored seeds are added in small quantities to breads, cookies and cakes. Stems may be crystallized (*see* page 104). Certain liqueurs, such as chartreuse, contain extract of angelica seed.

MEDICINAL USES
See page 132

OTHER USES
For a refreshing bath, add leaves and stems to the water. Leaves and seeds may be dried for potpourri.

ANGELICA

CHERVIL

ORIGIN
Eastern Europe

DESCRIPTION
Height 12–20 in (30–50 cm). It has soft, lacy, light green foliage growing on upright stems and bears umbels of white flowers.

CULTIVATION
This annual herb may be sown throughout the year, depending on climatic conditions (except in very hot areas), directly or in containers. It self-sows and it does not transplant well. To germinate, seed needs to be fresh. Germination is rapid and takes seven to twelve days. Soil needs to be light, composted and well drained. Water seedlings often, especially during hot weather. In hot areas, chervil prefers to grow in the shelter of larger plants, but it does not thrive in the drip area of trees.

CHERVIL

CULINARY USES

It has a pleasant, sweet, slightly resinous flavor and is one of the herbs used to make *fines herbes*. This delicate herb, which should be snipped with scissors from the outside edge of the plant and chopped finely, enhances the flavor of chicken, fish, herb butter, vegetables, cottage cheese, salads and all egg dishes. The leaves are used fresh, except in *fines herbes* for which they may be dried.

Apium graveolens
CELERY

ORIGIN
Mediterranean coastal area
DESCRIPTION
Height 16 in (40 cm). Celery consists of a cluster of crisp, overlapping, fluted stems, which branch towards the top, bearing several pairs of shiny, bright green and deeply indented leaves. The plant bears umbels of creamy green flowers in the second year.

CULTIVATION
Celery is a biennial, grown from seed sown directly or in trays in spring and autumn. It self-sows freely, depending on climatic conditions. Plant it in full sun in rich soil and keep well watered. Harvest some seed as it ripens for later sowing. For blanched stems for salad, plant *A. graveolens* var. *dulce* in trenches and heap up soil around stems as they grow, or place cloches over the plants.
HARVESTING
Remove the foliage from the stems and dry them on a rack. Cut stems of seed heads and dry using the bag or tray method (*see* page 104).
CULINARY USES
The leaves and stalks of celery are cut from the outside of the plant, chopped and cooked in stews and soups. Celery stalks may also be cooked with root vegetables such as carrots or turnips. The tender, crisp, blanched stalks are eaten raw in salads and as crudités. The seeds are often used as a flavoring in pickles. Finely ground dried celery

CELERY

seeds combined with salt make a good celery salt. Grind equal parts of dried lemon verbena leaves and celery seed and use this in salt-free diets.
MEDICINAL USES
See page 132

BURDOCK

Arctium lappa
BURDOCK

ORIGIN
Europe, Asia, North America
DESCRIPTION
Height 3–6½ ft (1–2 m). The deep roots of burdock produce several thick, furrowed, branched stems. These stems bear large, wavy, heart-shaped lower leaves, which are a dull light green with a hairy surface and downy underside. Leaves become progressively smaller the higher up the stem they grow, where they also become more ovate and less downy. The rounded heads of deep maroon flowers are encased in hooked scales. As these dry, they form burrs.

ARNICA

leaves which form a rosette at the base of the plant. It bears daisy-like yellow-orange flowers throughout the summer.

CULTIVATION
Arnica is a perennial which is difficult to grow in temperate areas. It requires a light, acid, well-composted soil in full sun. Seed is sown in spring, but can be slow to germinate. Propagation by root division is done in spring. Its natural habitat is woodland and mountain pasture.

HARVESTING
Cut flowers throughout summer and well into autumn. Roots are lifted after all autumn leaves have died back.

MEDICINAL USES
See page 132

HARVESTING
This herb is usually harvested from wasteland and from areas of alkaline soil. Roots are lifted in autumn while leaves are cut in midsummer. Dry single leaves on wire mesh and turn occasionally.

MEDICINAL USES
It cleanses the liver and eliminates toxic build-up. It also helps arthritis.

Arnica montana
ARNICA (MOUNTAIN TOBACCO)

ORIGIN
Central Europe

DESCRIPTION
Height 12–24 in (30–60 cm) when it is in flower. A rhizome with matted roots produces stems with pairs of oval, hairy

Artemisia abrotanum
SOUTHERNWOOD

ORIGIN
Southern Europe and Middle East

DESCRIPTION
Height 24 in (60 cm). Southernwood is a woody subshrub with sprigs of fine, feathery, dull gray-green leaves and insignificant flowers.

CULTIVATION
Propagate southernwood from semi-hardwood cuttings in the spring and autumn. It requires a light, well-drained soil in a position with either full sun or semishade. Keep southernwood well pruned to prevent the plant looking leggy. Remove the flower heads as they appear. Well-shaped plants are suitable for a large container.

HARVESTING
Hang prunings in bunches to dry out or cut fresh as required.

USES
Southernwood has an aromatic, slightly bitter aroma. It is quite a potent moth-repellant which the French call *garde-robe*. Add to potpourri or use on its own. Southernwood is one of the herbs used in a lover's posy or tussie mussie. When the plant is kept well clipped, it makes a suitable low hedge for a formal herb garden. It has been said that it prevents baldness and also makes young men's beards grow. There is, however, no evidence to prove this.

Artemisia absinthium
WORMWOOD

ORIGIN
Temperate areas of Europe and Asia

DESCRIPTION
Height 24 in (60 cm). Wormwood is a perennial with branched, leafy, ridged stems which grow from a woody base.

SOUTHERNWOOD

WORMWOOD

The deeply indented leaves are covered in fine hairs. The leaves are gray-green with silver undersides and they are approximately 4 in (10 cm) long.

In the heat of summer, this herb gives off very potent volatile oils which can be tasted on one's lips when passing by.

CULTIVATION

It is an undemanding perennial which does best in a sunny position with good drainage and light soil. Propagate by root division or from semihardwood cuttings taken in autumn or spring.

CULINARY USES

The volatile oils have a very bitter taste and aroma. At one time wormwood was used to flavor drinks such as absinthe, vermouth and tonic water. This practice was, however, made illegal when it was found that this herb, if taken often, will adversely affect both the nervous system and eyesight. Wormwood should therefore not be used for culinary purposes.

MEDICINAL USES

See page 132

OTHER USES

Dry the foliage of wormwood and use it in moth-repellant bags for the storage of clothes. The dried leaves, scattered wherever ants are a problem, act as a deterrent. Grow wormwood under fruit trees in order to discourage codling moths. It is also used to make an anti-caterpillar spray (*see* page 88).

Artemisia dracunculus

TARRAGON

ORIGIN

Southern and Central Europe

DESCRIPTION

Height 24 in (60 cm). Tarragon has a creeping, fibrous root system from which grow the thin, fibrous stalks. The long, narrow, glossy leaves have oil glands on the undersides. The growth is quite dense and bushy. From midsummer spikes of insignificant yellow flowers appear.

CULTIVATION

Tarragon is a perennial. Propagate in late spring from 6 in (15 cm) semi-hardwood cuttings, or by root division. Grow it in a sheltered, sunny position, either in the ground or else in a container. The soil must be rich and well drained, otherwise the roots will rot. Lift and divide the plant about every two or three years. Tarragon dies back completely in winter; therefore you should mark the place and protect the roots with a thick mulch. New shoots will appear in early spring. In some climates, it is not the easiest herb to grow. Another variety, *A. dracunculoides* (Russian tarragon), grows much more freely, but the flavor of this variety is slightly bitter and not very aromatic.

HARVESTING

Cut the leaves as required. For drying, cut in early autumn.

CULINARY USES

This herb has a warm, aromatic taste. Good tarragon has a slightly numbing after-effect on the tongue. It is one of the ingredients of *fines herbes*. Strip the tips and leaves from the mature stems. Finely chopped, fresh tarragon enhances the flavor of poultry, mayonnaise, vegetables (especially green beans), cream and butter sauces and salad dressings. Tarragon is an ideal herb to use for

TARRAGON

making flavored vinegars and oils (*see* page 104). Use it sparingly in butters and cottage cheeses. To freeze tarragon, chop the leaves and add to a little water in an ice cube tray. Tarragon does not dry very well, so use it fresh, cutting the stems approximately 6 in (15 cm) above the base of the plant.

Avena sativa

OATS

For medicinal, culinary and cosmetic use, purchase organically grown oats.

MEDICINAL USES
See page 133

Barbarea verna

LAND CRESS (AMERICAN CRESS)

ORIGIN
North America

DESCRIPTION
Height about 6 in (15 cm). The plant becomes taller when it is in flower. It grows close to the ground in the form of a rosette with short-stemmed, shiny green lobed leaves. In the second year, the tall stems are topped with heads of bright yellow flowers.

CULTIVATION
Propagate from seed throughout the year. Land cress self-sows well if seed is allowed to set. If no commercial seed is available, buy a plant and allow seed to set for sowing or allow to self-sow. Seedlings will transplant.

This herb is suitable for growing in containers. Land cress requires a rich soil, occasionally mulched with well-rotted manure. It will grow in a position with full sun or semishade. The plants provide good eating for two years, after which the leaves tend to become rather bitter. Land cress is frost sensitive.

CULINARY USES
It has a strong, peppery, mustard-like flavor. Cut leaves from the outer edge of the plant and use sparingly in salads, sandwiches, cottage cheese, herb butters and sauces. You should either tear or cut the leaves — do not chop them.

Berberis vulgaris

BARBERRY

ORIGIN
Europe, Middle East, North Africa

DESCRIPTION
Height 6½–16 ft (2–5 m). Barberry is a shrub with a thick rootstock which tends to form suckers. A characteristic yellow flesh is revealed when the thin, many-branched, spiny stems are cut or scraped. The leaves are elliptical, dark green and leathery, with small, rather vicious spikes at the base of the short stems. The tiny yellow flowers hang in clusters along the stems. They in turn become dark red berries.

CULTIVATION
It is a perennial which may be grown from seed, although cuttings or rooted suckers produce better results. It grows

OATS

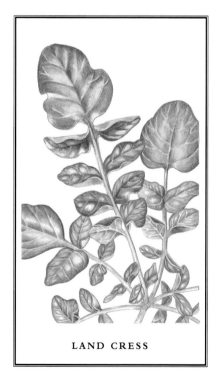

LAND CRESS

BARBERRY

almost anywhere and is not very fussy about growing conditions, but it seems to do better in alkaline soil in the sun.

HARVESTING

Lift roots and cut stems for bark as required. Pick berries when ripe.

CULINARY USES

Use the berries for jams and jellies.

MEDICINAL USES

See page 133

OTHER USES

It is ornamental in a large garden.

Betula pendula

SILVER BIRCH

ORIGIN

Europe and Asia Minor

DESCRIPTION

Height 60 ft (18 m). The silver birch is an erect, graceful tree. When it is young, the bark is a shiny reddish brown, ageing to silvery white blotched with black diamond-shaped markings. The bole may become blackened,

SILVER BIRCH

rough and fissured. The bright green, rounded triangular leaves, with finely serrated edges, hang from drooping branches. Both male and female catkins appear on the same tree in spring.

CULTIVATION

The silver birch is a deciduous tree which is usually planted in groups of three, five or more in gardens. As these trees take approximately four years from sowing to planting out, it is sensible to purchase young trees from a garden center or an arboretum rather than trying to grow them yourself.

MEDICINAL USES

See page 133

Borago officinalis

BORAGE
(HERB OF JOY)

ORIGIN

Southern and southwestern Europe

DESCRIPTION

Height 32 in (80 cm). The thickish, hollow stem grows from a rosette of dimpled, hairy, oval dark green leaves which have pointed tips. As the stem grows longer, the leaves become much smaller and looser. These stems bear sprays of bright, true blue, star-shaped flowers which have pointed black stamens. These stamens are circled in white. Varieties with pink and white flowers do exist, as well as varieties which have variegated foliage, but they are comparatively rare.

CULTIVATION

Borage is an annual. It is not a fussy plant, but the better the soil, the more lush the growth will be, especially if it is planted in a sunny, sheltered position. Sow the seed directly throughout the year, except in very wet conditions. Borage self-sows freely. Transplant the seedlings when they are young, placing them fairly close together so that the

BORAGE

plants can support each other, as the growth tends to be lax.

CULINARY USES

Borage is cucumber-flavored. The flowers and young leaves are added to salads, dips and cucumber soup. For a very attractive addition to summer drinks, carefully place the flowers in ice cube compartments, slowly pour water over them and freeze. Chop up borage leaves and add them to soups and stews during the last few minutes of cooking. Improve the appearance and flavor of pale, uninteresting cabbage by cooking one part borage leaves with two parts cabbage. The leaves can also be cooked like spinach and then served as a separate vegetable. The hairiness of the leaves eventually disappears with the chopping and the cooking. The flowers make a pretty garnish. Borage is not really suitable to be dried for cooking purposes, but one may crystallize the flowers (*see* page 104) and keep them to decorate cakes and desserts when fresh flowers are not available.

OTHER USES

Borage makes an excellent facial steam for improving very dry, sensitive skin. Dry the flowers of borage face down on paper to add some extra color to a pot-pourri mixture.

MEDICINAL USES

See page 133

Bulbine frutescens

BULBINE

ORIGIN

Southern Africa

DESCRIPTION

Bulbine is a low-growing herb, with leaves which are firm, narrow, slightly flattened and succulent, appearing directly from the crown. These leaves contain a mucilaginous sap. The slender stems of bulbine bear small, cone-like heads of orange and yellow flowers.

CULTIVATION

Bulbine is a perennial which grows in full sun in average to poor soil. A plant grown in a pot near the kitchen door is a good idea in case of urgent need. It is ideal for very hot, dry places where nothing else will grow. Grow it from a rooted section taken from a mature plant, or an unrooted section which will soon root when potted. Plants will need water in very hot, dry weather. When a plant looks dense and overcrowded, lift, divide and plant out.

SIMPLE REMEDIES

Because the sap of bulbine has similar properties to that of *Aloe vera*, it is used to relieve the pain of insect bites and bee-stings. In some cases of shingles it will soothe the itch. When applied to chapped lips, cold sores and mouth ulcers, healing will take place.

CALENDULA

BULBINE

Calendula officinalis

CALENDULA (POT MARIGOLD)

ORIGIN

Southern Europe

DESCRIPTION

Height 12–20 in (30–50 cm). Calendula has brittle, branching stems bearing bright green, stalkless, oval to oblong leaves which, like the buds, are covered with slightly sticky, fine hairs. Of the daisy family, the large double and single flowers come in shades of pale yellow to deep orange. In some of the varieties the firm centers of the flowers are dark brown. There are also dwarf varieties suitable for edging and for containers. In its wild state the flowers are smaller, single and bright orange.

CULTIVATION

Sow this annual directly or in trays. Germination is rapid — transplant at four- to six-leaf stage. Sow from early autumn into winter in the southern hemisphere, where it flowers in winter. Sow in spring and summer in the northern hemisphere, where it flowers most of the year if the weather is mild. It needs a good, well-drained soil and a sunny position. Water during hot spells.

HARVESTING

Cut flowers as soon as they open. For medicinal use, cut the whole plant at ground level and then discard the root.

PESTS AND DISEASES

Remove caterpillars by hand. Spray the plants with sulfur dust at the first sign of mildew, which is usually caused by insufficient sunlight (*see* page 87).

MEDICINAL USES

See page 134

CULINARY USES

Calendula is mainly used for eye appeal, as the spicy, tangy flavor is mild. Carefully separate the petals from the flower heads (they bruise easily) and use as a substitute for saffron. Use the petals in rice dishes, stews, soups, custards, salads and cheese dips.

OTHER USES

Calendula flowers steeped in boiling water make a brightening rinse for fair hair. The flowers are also decorative, both in the garden and as a cut flower in floral arrangements. To brighten pot-pourri, carefully remove petals from the flower heads, spread out to dry and then add them to potpourri when ready.

Capsicum frutescens

CAYENNE

ORIGIN

Central, South America and Zanzibar

CAYENNE

DESCRIPTION

Height 24 in (60 cm). Cayenne is a shrublike plant which has a woody stem with angular branches. The leaves are elliptical, slightly leathery, dark green and quite smooth. The small, starry, yellow-centered white flowers produce pods of flat, white, very pungent seeds. The pods, depending on the variety, could be any color ranging from purple to red, orange or yellow when ripe. There are some dwarf varieties which are suitable for growing in containers.

CULTIVATION

Cayenne is a perennial plant when it grows in its natural tropical habitat, but it is treated as an annual when it is grown in gardens or under glass. Propagate it from seed and plant in a sheltered, sunny position. Cayenne requires quite a rich, well-composted soil to which a smallish quantity of potassium has been added.

HARVESTING

Pick the pods when the color has developed fully and hang them up to dry until they are required. The pods may also be used fresh.

CULINARY USES

Use the fresh or dried whole pods. Grind the seeds and use as spice.

MEDICINAL USES

See page 134

Carum carvi

CARAWAY

ORIGIN

Europe, Siberia and as far east as India, also North Africa

DESCRIPTION

Height 20 in (50 cm) when the plant is mature. Caraway is a deep-rooted herb with soft, feathery, light green leaves which are similar in growth to those of a carrot, only the foliage tends to droop

CARAWAY

more. Caraway takes approximately two years to mature and to bear flowers. The stems of delicate white flowers produce the seed cases, each containing two crescent-shaped ribbed seeds.

CULTIVATION

Caraway is a biennial plant. Sow the seed in a sunny situation in spring. It is rather slow to germinate. It will usually self-sow readily and can also be transplanted successfully. It is not fussy about soil, provided it has been well dug, as it is a deep-rooted plant.

HARVESTING

Cut the young leaves when they are required. When the seed turns light brown, cut the whole plant off at ground level. Use the bag method to dry the seeds (*see* page 104).

CULINARY USES

Use the young shoots of this plant for both garnishing and flavoring, and use the seeds for seasoning. Cook the root as a vegetable.

MEDICINAL USES

See page 134

*Chamaemelum nobile
(= Anthemis nobilis)*

ROMAN OR LAWN CHAMOMILE

Matricaria recutita

GERMAN OR ANNUAL CHAMOMILE

ORIGIN
Europe and areas of Asia

DESCRIPTION
C. nobile
Height 4–12 in (10–30 cm). It is a perennial ground cover with feathery, apple-scented foliage. It bears white, daisy-like flowers. The single variety has a prominent yellow center and down-turned petals, the double variety has a tight head of cream petals.

M. recutita
Height 20 in (50 cm). This herb has an upright growth with fine, feathery foliage. It has branching stems with small, single daisy-like flowers with a greenish-yellow center. It is not quite as highly perfumed as *C. nobile*, as the flowers are scented but the leaves are not.

CULTIVATION
Chamaemelum nobile is usually propagated by root division or cuttings. *Matricaria recutita*, which is annual, is sown directly in the early spring. The soil needs to be sandy and slightly acid and the position sunny, except in hot, dry climates when shading from the midday sun is necessary. Grow *C. nobile* as an edging and allow it to spread through paved paths. The fragrance of the plant rises when it is walked on and slightly bruised. It is, however, not suitable for areas with heavy traffic.

ROMAN CHAMOMILE

Chamomile can often be used most effectively to soften the edge of a large container of other herbs. After the flowering period, cut the plants right back to the main growth. Before you put the annual variety on the compost heap, either shake the seeds into the garden for the following year or otherwise save them to sow later.

HARVESTING
For drying, cut the flowers from the stems with sharp scissors or pruning shears and then spread them out on muslin-covered racks to dry.

CULINARY USES
The foliage of Roman chamomile has a fresh, apple-like fragrance. Stir a few flowers into sour cream and use the flavored cream for serving over baked potatoes. Try adding a few flowers to a white sauce or herb butter.

GERMAN CHAMOMILE

MEDICINAL USES
Although *Matricaria recutita* and *Chamaemelum nobile* have similar medicinal properties, *M. recutita* is the variety more commonly used for medicinal purposes (*see* page 140).

SIMPLE REMEDIES
Chamomile tea made from the single or double flowers of *Chamaemelum nobile* or *Matricaria recutita* is a calmative and also helps to induce sleep.

OTHER USES
Chamomile leaves and flowers make a refreshing bath and foot bath. To lighten and condition fair hair, make a rinse by simmering about 2 tsp (10 ml) dried flowers in 8 oz (250 ml) water for 15 to 20 minutes. The flowers are dried face down for potpourri. Dried leaves and flowers are also added to the stuffing for a sleep-pillow.

Cichorium intybus

CHICORY

ORIGIN
Europe, Asia

DESCRIPTION
Height 12–50 in (30–125 cm). A strong taproot produces an erect, grooved, hairy, branching stem. The base leaves are mid-green, broad and lanceolate, with roughly serrated edges. They grow in the form of a rosette. The stems have smaller leaves. Bright blue, daisy-like clusters of flowers grow from the axils of the upper leaves. A purple-foliaged variety of chicory is also available.

CULTIVATION
This perennial is grown from seed in a well-composted, alkaline soil in full sun. For white-leaved crowns (whitloofs or chicons), choose a variety like 'Witloof.' Dig up roots in autumn, remove the leaves and replant in sand boxes. Cover to exclude light. The new leaves that grow will be soft and creamy white and less bitter than those grown in the open.

CHICORY

BLACK COHOSH

HARVESTING
Cut the young leaves and the chicons as they are required. The roots can be lifted in autumn.

CULINARY USES
Use ground chicory roots for adding to coffee blends. Include the leaves and flowers in salads. The chicons can be used as a vegetable.

MEDICINAL USES
See page 134

Cimicifuga racemosa

BLACK COHOSH

ORIGIN
Northern North America

DESCRIPTION
Height 5 ft (1.5 m). A black, fleshy rhizome is surrounded by wiry roots which tend to creep. Slender, angular stems bear sharply toothed, bright green leaves in threes. Fluffy cream flowers grow as drooping racemes and have a most unpleasant smell.

CULTIVATION
Black cohosh is a perennial which is propagated by root division or seed sown in late winter or early spring. It requires moist, rich soil in light shade. It dies back in winter.

HARVESTING
Lift the ripe rhizomes in autumn. Clean and slice to dry.

MEDICINAL USES
See page 135

Cinnamomum zeylanicum

CINNAMON

ORIGIN
Southeast Asia

DESCRIPTION
Height 33 ft (10 m). Cinnamon is an evergreen tree with pairs of large, shiny, leathery leaves which are about 6½ in (16 cm) long. The flowers are simple, waxy and creamy yellow, growing in loose sprays. These flowers in turn become dark blue berries.

CINNAMON

CULTIVATION

This plant is grown in plantations in Sri Lanka. For harvesting purposes, the whole tree is cut down to ground level. The new shoots grow quite rapidly to approximately 6½ ft (2 m) when they in turn are also cut down.

HARVESTING

The bark is stripped from the trees and the younger shoots. The outer bark is then removed to expose the more tender inner bark, which is then dried. As the bark dries, it forms curls. The best flavor comes from the bark which is taken from the younger shoots.

CULINARY USES

Ground or whole curls of the bark of cinnamon are used to flavor a wide variety of fruit, cakes, cookies, desserts and also mulled wine.

MEDICINAL USES

See page 135

Citrus limon

LEMON

ORIGIN

Warmer regions of China and Asia

DESCRIPTION

Height 10–16 ft (3–5 m). The lemon has quite a stumpy trunk bearing many branches of densely growing, glossy, oval, pointed green leaves which have slightly crinkled, serrated edges and dull green undersides. The leaves have small glands containing a rich, highly fragrant oil. The waxy, white or pale pink, perfumed flowers grow directly from the branches or from the leaf axils. The fruit is glossy and yellow with fine dimpling on the skin. These dimples are minute oil glands which give off a sharp, crisp aroma. The insides of the fruit are pithy, pulpy and acidic in taste.

CULTIVATION

Lemons can be grown from seed, but the trees are usually purchased, as good varieties have been grafted onto sturdy rootstock. Grow trees in well-drained, fertile soil in a sheltered, sunny position. In cooler climates they may be grown in a greenhouse or conservatory. Do not prune like other fruit trees, unless for formal planting when they should be clipped accordingly. Remove deadwood and unsightly, protruding growth.

HARVESTING

Pick the fruit and the leaves as required. In a more temperate climate, some varieties of lemon will bear fruit almost all year-round.

CULINARY USES

There are endless culinary uses for the leaves, the fruit and the juice of the lemon. The leaves are used to flavor and garnish various curry dishes. The fruit, cut into slices or wedges, is used as a garnish, especially with fish dishes. It is also used to make marmalade. Lemon juice and zest are used to flavor desserts, cakes and pies.

MEDICINAL USES

See page 135

LEMON

Coriandrum sativum

CORIANDER (CHINESE PARSLEY OR CILANTRO)

ORIGIN

Eastern Mediterranean

DESCRIPTION

Height 20 in (50 cm). The first leaves of coriander are dark green, finely scalloped or round. The secondary leaves are fine, light green and feathery, borne on slender stems. The flowers are umbels of dainty pink or mauve, and they become clusters of round, green seeds. Leave seeds on the plant until brown and ripe.

CULTIVATION

Coriander is an annual herb, grown from seed which is usually sown directly. Germination takes approximately ten days and sowing is continuous for most of the year. (Do not sow the roasted seed of coriander.) The plants need to be grouped in fairly close clumps in order to support each other.

CORIANDER

ECHINACEA

Very small seedlings will transplant. These are most suitable for planting in an average-sized container. A well-composted, light soil is required. Do not allow the plant to dry out in hot weather. For a constant supply of young leaves, nip out the young center stems to retard the secondary growth. Do not sow coriander near dill or fennel.

HARVESTING
Cut foliage as needed. Cut stems of seed heads and dry using bag or tray method (*see* page 104).

CULINARY USES
The green seeds have a revolting smell, and should therefore only be used when they have turned pale brown on the plant. When dried, they have a sweet, pungent flavor and aroma. Roast them lightly for an even better flavor. Keep some in a pepper grinder for easy flavoring of cakes, cookies, breads, gingerbread and some preserves like marmalade and tomato jam. Use in marinades, and also to flavor dried meat and sausages (charcuterie). The whole seeds are an ingredient in pickling spice and they are also added to herb vinegars and oils. The young, flat leaves can be roughly chopped and added to salads or to curries and stews during the last few minutes of cooking time. The leaves are also an important ingredient in Mexican cuisine.

OTHER USES
The whole, dried seeds included in potpourri act as a form of fixative for the volatile oils. The pretty flowers cut well for fresh arrangements.

Echinacea purpurea

ECHINACEA (CONE FLOWER)

ORIGIN
North America

DESCRIPTION
Height 2–4 ft (60–120 cm). A rhizome sends up a strong, erect, smooth stem. The lower leaves are toothed, oval and rough to the touch, while the upper leaves are spear-like. The flower head is made up of a circle of loose, crimson, daisy-like petals which surround a mahogany-red, cone-like center.

CULTIVATION
Echinacea is a perennial plant which is usually propagated either by root division or by sowing seed. When it becomes necessary to divide the roots, it will transplant easily. The production of flowers increases if the plants are not disturbed too often. The soil for this plant should ideally be well composted and deeply dug. Echinacea prefers a sunny position and flowers from mid-summer onward.

HARVESTING
Cut the leaves and the flowers as they are required. Lift the roots in late autumn or in early spring.

MEDICINAL USES
See page 135

OTHER USES
Echinacea is a most decorative plant in the garden when it is in flower. The flowers may also be used for indoor floral arrangements.

Equisetum arvense

HORSETAIL

ORIGIN
Britain and Europe

DESCRIPTION
Height 8–20 in (20–50 cm). A creeping rhizome produces the brownish-yellow, jointed stems. These stems have sheaths from which whorls of small, slender, bright green branches grow. The stems terminate in catkin-bearing spores.

CULTIVATION
Horsetail is a perennial plant which is usually propagated from the catkin-bearing spores or by root division. This plant prefers a damp, shady spot and it will also grow in an exposed position, provided that it is near water.

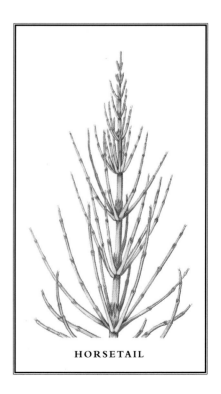

HORSETAIL

HARVESTING

Cut stems in midsummer for drying. It is usually harvested from the wild.

MEDICINAL USES

See page 136

Eruca sativa

ROCKET

ORIGIN

Southern Europe and western Asia

DESCRIPTION

Height 20 in (50 cm). It starts as a loose rosette of smooth, dark green, deeply indented leaves, about 8 in (20 cm) long. The purplish stems bear leaves which become smaller and slightly pointed towards the flowering tips. The purple-tinged buds produce yellow and white flowers. Seed pods are 2 in (5 cm) long, turning a pale tan color before opening to scatter round black seeds.

CULTIVATION

This annual is sown directly. As the plants mature quickly, sow continuously during the year, except in areas of frost or intense heat. Grow these plants in clumps so that they can support each other — single plants always tend to straggle. Transplant the seedlings when four leaves appear. The trans-plantings tend to bolt early. Grow in the sun in well-composted soil. If seed is unavailable, obtain a plant from a nursery or friend and collect seed. Sow some immediately. Established plants tend to self-sow.

CULINARY USES

It has a nutty, mustard-like flavor, good for salads and sandwiches. Buds and flowers may be stirred into cottage cheese or used as a garnish. Leaves are used as a basil substitute in pesto. Braise greenery to serve as a vegetable.

Euphrasia officinalis

EYEBRIGHT

Eyebright is mainly a plant of the hedgerows. It is difficult to cultivate, because it is a semi-parasite on certain kinds of grasses.

MEDICINAL USES

See page 136

Filipendula ulmaria

MEADOWSWEET

ORIGIN

Europe, Asia, China and some parts of North America

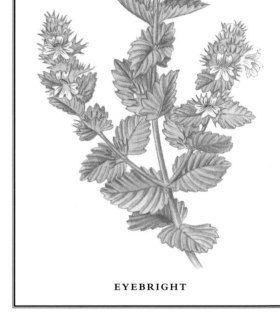

EYEBRIGHT

ROCKET

DESCRIPTION

Height 2–4 ft (60–120 cm). It has a spreading, reddish rhizome with hairy roots which produce angular, furrowed, erect, red-tipped stems bearing dark green, indented leaves with grayish undersides. The fluffy, creamy white flowers grow in sweetly scented clusters. The roots as well as the flowers of meadowsweet are fragrant.

CULTIVATION

This perennial plant is grown from seed. It needs a sheltered spot with very rich, damp ground. In the wild, it is usually found near marshes, swamps, wet woodlands, meadows and next to rivers.

HARVESTING

Pick flowers when they are fully open.

MEDICINAL USES

See page 136

MEADOWSWEET

Foeniculum vulgare

COMMON FENNEL

Foeniculum vulgare
'Purpurascens'

BRONZE FENNEL

Foeniculum vulgare var. *dulce*

FLORENTINE FENNEL

ORIGIN

Mediterranean (fennel has also been known to the Chinese, the Indians and the Egyptians since ancient times)

DESCRIPTION

Common fennel may reach a height of 10 ft (3 m). A thick, perennial rootstock produces the strong, erect, cylindrical, smooth, bright green stems. Branches grow from the sheaths on the stems. The sprays of feathery foliage are a lush green when young, later maturing to a dull green. The plant bears flat umbels of bright yellow flowers. The greenish-brown seeds are curved and ribbed.

Bronze fennel only grows to about 3 ft (1 m) and it has distinct bronze foliage. The flowers are golden.

Florentine fennel grows to about 30 in (75 cm). Stalks are pale green and the umbels of yellow flowers are loose. It is grown especially for its bulb-like, swollen stem, delicious in a salad.

CULTIVATION

Fennel is propagated from seed sown directly, as the seedlings do not transplant very well. It also self-sows generously. Remove unwanted seedlings while they are still young. Owing to a long, sturdy taproot, mature plants do not uproot easily. Fennel grows in most soils and positions, but the richer the soil, the more tender the foliage. Florentine fennel is grown from seed sown in rows. It is treated as an annual, the "bulb" being lifted when it is mature. To blanch the bulb, heap soil around the stem. Do not plant fennel near coriander or dill. It requires a sunny position, good soil and adequate water. In order to promote the growth of the bulb, remove any flowering heads which are not wanted for seed.

HARVESTING

Cut the foliage as it is required. Cut the stems of seed heads when they are quite ripe and dry them completely, using the bag or the tray method (*see* page 104). Lift bulbs of Florentine fennel when they are approximately the size of a tennis ball.

CULINARY USES

Common fennel has a warm, sweet, aniseed-like flavor. Cook young leaves as a vegetable. Add chopped foliage to meat, chicken and fish. Wrap a whole fish in fennel before placing it on the barbecue coals. Flavor butters, cheeses, mayonnaise, vinegars, oils, egg dishes and salads with the young leaves. Allow the seeds to become almost dry, then remove the heads and give them the bag treatment (*see* page 104). Crushed or whole, fennel seeds add flavor to butters, cheeses, breads, rolls, sauces and fish dishes.

Cook the bulb of Florentine fennel gently and serve with a white sauce, or slice it thinly and serve it as a salad with a vinaigrette dressing.

MEDICINAL USES

See page 136

SIMPLE REMEDIES

A tea made with a few fresh sprigs of fennel or a flat teaspoonful of fennel seed will relieve indigestion.

COMMON FENNEL

Galium aparine

CLEAVERS (GOOSEGRASS)

ORIGIN

Britain, Europe and northern and the western parts of Asia

DESCRIPTION

Height can range from 6 in–4 ft (15–120 cm), depending on the growing conditions. The shallow roots produce many scrambling, square stems, which are covered in minute prickles, as are the leaves. These prickles enable the plant to cling to anything with which it comes into contact. Cleavers has narrow whorls of lanceolate leaves, light green in color. The small, greenish-white flowers are borne on short stems in pairs from the leaf axils. Globular capsules covered with hooked bristles contain hard, round seeds.

CULTIVATION

Cleavers is an annual grown from seed sown in well-composted soil in dappled shade. It will self-sow, but can overgrow other plants in the garden. In the wild, this herb is often found forcing its way up to the light in hedgerows.

HARVESTING

The leaves are at their best for cutting before the seed capsules set. Collect the seed when it is ripe.

CULINARY USES

The ground seeds may be used as a good coffee substitute.

MEDICINAL USES

See page 137

OTHER USES

The foliage of this plant makes an excellent poultry feed.

Gentiana lutea

YELLOW GENTIAN

ORIGIN

Central and southern Europe

DESCRIPTION

Height 36 in (90 cm). Yellow gentian has a very long, thick taproot. An erect stem, bearing leaves in opposite pairs at each stem joint, carries the large orange-yellow flowers in clusters which form whorls from the leaf axils, usually in the third year. The bright green lower leaves are borne on short stalks. These leaves are stiff and ovate, ending in points. There are five raised veins on the underside of the leaf.

N.B. This herb should not be confused with poisonous false hellebore (Veratrum album) which, although it looks similar, has longer, pleated mature leaves and small, green, star-shaped flowers and, unlike yellow gentian, grows in swamps and damp meadows.

CULTIVATION

This perennial is usually propagated from seed or by root division. The soil needs to be well dug with plenty of compost and also the addition of some bone meal. Plant yellow gentian in a sunny position but do not allow the soil to dry out completely. In the wild, yellow gentian is found on slopes and mountain pastures.

HARVESTING

Lift the roots in autumn. *Do not* wash them — clean them by brushing off the soil and then dry them slowly. Slice the roots to speed drying.

MEDICINAL USES

See page 137

OTHER USES

It may be planted as an ornamental plant for a herbaceous border.

Ginkgo biloba

MAIDENHAIR TREE

ORIGIN

China

DESCRIPTION

Height could reach 100 ft (30 m). Firm branches grow in threes from a central trunk covered in brown bark with corky fissures. As the tree ages, the bark becomes gray and crinkled. Light green leaves, like those of a maidenhair

CLEAVERS

YELLOW GENTIAN

MAIDENHAIR TREE

Hamamelis virginiana

WITCH HAZEL

ORIGIN
Eastern North America

DESCRIPTION
Height 10–14½ ft (3–4.5 m). This large shrub has many smooth-barked, gray trunks. The oval leaves have serrated, wavy edges and hairy undersides. Clusters of fragrant, loose, narrow-petalled, bright yellow flowers appear in autumn when the leaves drop. When the flowers fade, the black seed cases containing edible white seeds can take up to a year to ripen.

CULTIVATION
This deciduous tree is propagated by layering mature branches in autumn. It needs an acid soil, either in sun or in dappled shade. Its natural habitat is dry or moist woodland.

MEDICINAL USES
See page 137

COSMETIC USES
See pages 167–169

Harpagophytum procumbens

DEVIL'S CLAW

ORIGIN
Namibia

MEDICINAL USES
See page 138

Humulus lupulus

HOP

ORIGIN
Europe, Asia and North America

DESCRIPTION
Height 10–20 ft (3–6 m). This creeper's thick, fleshy root produces hairy, red-tinged stems which climb and twist in a clockwise direction. The coarse, dark green, deeply lobed, heart-shaped leaves have serrated edges. The leaves and stems are able to cling by means of small hooks. There are male and female vines. The female has light green, cone-like flowers which grow in clusters. These flowers later ripen into papery bracts.

fern, turn gold before dropping in autumn. Trees are male and female. The male produces small catkins, whereas the female has small, round, bright green flowers. These turn into green, plum-like, foul-smelling fruits. As the trees can withstand quite a lot of air pollution, they are often used for street-planting in big cities.

CULTIVATION
The maidenhair tree is a deciduous tree which grows slowly in the early years, after which the growth speeds up. Propagate from stem cuttings taken in spring. It grows in fertile, well-drained soil in either sun or dappled shade. It is advisable to plant only male plants, as the female plants drop their fruit and are therefore very messy.

HARVESTING
Cut leaves in early summer. These are best used when freshly picked.

MEDICINAL USES
See page 137

OTHER USES
This is a good tree for a large garden.

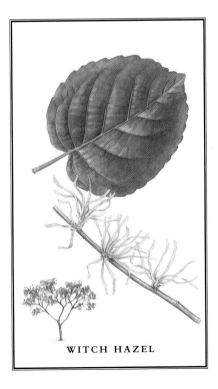

WITCH HAZEL

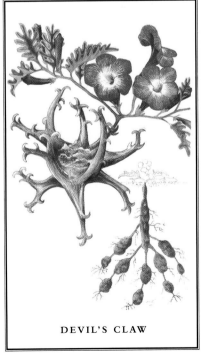

DEVIL'S CLAW

HOP

GOLDENSEAL

Hydrastis canadensis

GOLDENSEAL

As the root of this plant takes about eight years to mature, it is a good idea to purchase it from professional growers.

ORIGIN
North America

MEDICINAL USES
It is antimicrobial and a bitter tonic for the liver. It is also a uterine stimulant.

Hypericum perforatum

ST. JOHN'S WORT

ORIGIN
Southern Europe, North Africa and western Asia Minor

DESCRIPTION
Height 12–36 in (30–90 cm). St. John's wort is quite a tough, shrublike plant which grows from a short rhizome. It has several angular, reddish-brown stems. These stems have woody bases and they bear oblong, opposite pairs of dark green leaves, with oil glands which look like tiny perforations on their undersides. The simple, fragrant, five-petaled yellow flowers with clusters of feathery, gold stamens are borne in profusion all over the whole shrub.

CULTIVATION
St. John's wort is a perennial herb which is usually propagated from runners in the autumn or otherwise by seed which is sown early in the spring. This plant is

CULTIVATION
This plant is a deciduous, vine-like creeper. Propagate it by root division or from suckers in spring, preferably taken from the mature female rootstock. The plant dies down in winter, but the fast-growing shoots will appear again in spring. It requires a rich, deep soil, preferably in a sunny position, but it will also grow in semishade. It needs a thick mulch and good care should always be taken to keep it well watered in very hot weather.

HARVESTING
Cut the flowers in autumn when tinged with yellow.

MEDICINAL USES
See page 138

HEALTH AND COSMETIC USES
Use for a relaxing bath.

OTHER USES
Hop may be added to the stuffing of a sleep-pillow. It makes a decorative creeper. The dried flowers of this plant are used for arrangements. Hop is also used for making beer.

ST. JOHN'S WORT

usually at its best when planted in an average soil and it prefers a position in dappled shade or full sun.

HARVESTING

Cut the flowers when they are fully open. Pick the leaves as required. The harvesting is always best done before the heat of the day.

MEDICINAL USES

See page 138

Hyssopus officinalis

HYSSOP

ORIGIN

Southern Europe and east Asia

DESCRIPTION

Height 18 in (45 cm). A cluster of square, woody stems grows from the fibrous rhizomes of this plant. The lanceolate, slightly leathery, dark green leaves grow in whorls up the stems. The growth of hyssop is usually fairly dense. In midsummer the small, fluffy, purple, blue, pink or white flowers will bloom in whorls on the upper stems. Both the leaves and the flowers have a warm, spicy flavor. This is not the hyssop of biblical writings, which is believed to be a form of origanum.

CULTIVATION

Hyssop is a perennial which is grown from seed sown in spring. It germinates very rapidly, which means that the appearance of the new shoots is not anticipated, and before you know it, the plants can fall prey to slugs and snails. One should therefore be on the alert for these pests. Cuttings, as well as root division of the mature plants, are done in the spring and autumn. The soil for this plant should preferably be light, well drained and also in a sunny position. Cut back the stems after flowering in order to neaten the bushes.

HARVESTING

Cut the leaves as required. Cut flowers as they begin to open.

PESTS

Slugs and snails (*see* page 88)

CULINARY USES

A few hyssop leaves may be used to spice up savory dishes like rich stews and they are also good in marinades. Scatter the flowers over salads.

MEDICINAL USES

See page 138

OTHER USES

Dry both the leaves and the flowers and add to potpourri. Plant hyssop for use as a low hedge or as a clipped garden border. It is also a most suitable plant for container gardening.

HYSSOP

ELECAMPANE

Inula helenium

ELECAMPANE

ORIGIN

Britain and Europe

DESCRIPTION

Height 2–5 ft (60–150 cm). This plant has a succulent rootstock with large, fleshy roots. It has strong, straight, furrowed, hairy stems. Long, pointed, ovate leaves with serrated edges and down on the undersides grow in the form of a rosette. The leaves become smaller, stemless and more heart-shaped on the flowering stalks. The bright yellow flowers, like small, single sunflowers, grow in loose clusters.

CULTIVATION

Elecampane is a perennial plant which is usually grown from seed sown in the spring or by root division in spring or autumn. Make sure that each piece of the root has a budding shoot. Stake the plants and tidy up in autumn. In some areas, elecampane dies back in winter. Mulch the plants well. In the wild, it is sometimes found in hedgerows and damp meadows.

HARVESTING
Lift the roots in the second or third year. Slice them and then spread them out to dry. The dried roots have a violet-like fragrance.

MEDICINAL USES
See page 139

OTHER USES
Use the dried petals and minced dried root of elecampane for potpourri. The seed heads look lovely when used in dried flower arrangements. It is also very decorative when planted at the back of a herbaceous border.

JUNIPER

Juniperus communis

JUNIPER

ORIGIN
Northern Europe, southwest Asia and North America

DESCRIPTION
Height can reach 33 ft (10 m). Juniper is a shrublike tree which has reddish-brown, shredding bark. The blue-green leaves are narrow, pointed and rather leathery, and they grow stemless from the branches. The tree bears single, downy, blue berries.

CULTIVATION
As the seed of juniper is quite difficult to germinate, propagate it from semi-hardwood cuttings and protect them until they are well rooted. Plant them out into bags or pots with good soil and leave them until well established, then plant them in a sunny position. Juniper does well in poor soil, but the richer the soil, the more tree-like it will grow. For the forming of the berries, it is necessary to have both male and female plants.

HARVESTING
Pick the berries when they have turned black. This usually happens in the third year. Dry them on a flat surface in the open air, but protect them from the evening damp. Turn the berries frequently until they are quite shriveled.

CULINARY USES
Juniper berries are used in stuffings and marinades and are also an ingredient in gin.

MEDICINAL USES
See page 139

Lactuca sativa

LETTUCE

ORIGIN
Europe and Britain

DESCRIPTION
Quite a wide choice of lettuces are available, of which the loose-leafed varieties are the most interesting. These do not form heads. The outer leaves are plucked as required and the plants continue to grow for months, depending on climatic conditions. Nip out the centers occasionally to prolong growth. The plants will eventually bolt and self-sow. The leaves of some of the other varieties, for example 'Lollo Rosso,' 'Australian Yellow,' 'American Brown,' 'Oak Leaf,' 'Red Salad Bowl,' 'Rubin' and 'Round Leaf,' vary in color from lime green to deep red. Some of these leaves are quite deeply indented, while others have frilly edges.

CULTIVATION
Propagate these annuals by sowing seed in trays throughout the year, or sowing

'LOLLO ROSSO' LETTUCE

directly and thinning and transplanting seedlings at the four-leaf stage. The loose-leafed varieties self-sow readily. In hot weather, plant in semishade or protect from the midday sun. Lettuce requires a light, well-drained, composted soil. Keep well watered. When plants bolt and go to seed, leave seed to mature on plants, then lift, shake seed over the ground and cover lightly.

Nurseries sometimes have packs with two or three varieties of loose-leafed lettuce which are sufficient for the needs of one or two people. They are suitable for growing in containers.

PESTS
Slugs and snails (*see* page 88)

CULINARY USES
Lettuce must be fresh, preferably from garden to table. For salads, tear leaves for easier eating or leave whole. Do not cut or chop, as this causes bruising and discoloration. Cook mature leaves in chicken stock as a good summer soup. Steam young peas with a sprig of mint in a pot lined with mature lettuce leaves and very little water. Braise the leaves to serve as a vegetable. Dry the seed of mustard lettuce by using the bag method (*see* page 104). It is a good substitute for true mustard as a seasoning.

MEDICINAL USES
Proprietary cough mixtures containing lettuce are stocked by drugstores.

OTHER USES
Lettuce is used for color in the garden. It makes an excellent border plant, especially the more colorful varieties.

Laurus nobilis

BAY

ORIGIN
Mediterranean countries

DESCRIPTION
Height up to 33 ft (10 m) if not clipped. The bark of this tree is smooth and has a reddish-green color. Leaves are dark green, leathery and ovate. Some bay trees have less dense foliage than others and slightly elongated leaves. The small, insignificant flowers appear at the base of the leaf stem. These flowers then turn into hard, green berries which will eventually become purple.

CULTIVATION
Bay trees will take full sun, but need shelter in areas where frost occurs. Before planting, prepare the ground well with compost, bone meal and also a handful of superphosphate. For planting in containers, mix a smaller quantity of this nourishment with the soil and compost. Bay trees are adaptable and can be kept well clipped for container culture. They make a good hedge. Propagate from heel cuttings taken in autumn or spring, although these do not take readily. Older trees may sucker. The suckers can be severed from the tree and left in the ground for a few weeks to recover from the shock. Carefully dig them out and plant in bags or pots of good soil until well grown. As this takes time, purchasing a tree from a nursery might be worthwhile.

HARVESTING
Cut branches of the mature leaves and hang them up to dry, otherwise dry the individual leaves on racks.

DISEASES
Bay is subject to both sooty mildew and scale (*see* pages 87–88). On a small tree, the scale can be removed by brushing the leaves with an old toothbrush dipped into a mixture of half water and half methylated spirits. Larger trees will probably have to be treated with an horticultural oil.

CULINARY USES
Bay has a spicy fragrance and flavor. Most fish, meat and chicken dishes are improved with the addition of bay leaves. The leaves are also used to impart flavor to marinades, soups, stews and custards. Bay has rather a strong flavor, so use it with discretion. Bay leaves are one of the ingredients of *bouquet garni* and are also an ingredient of pickling spice. Use bay leaves fresh or dried, but check for and remove scale from the undersides of the leaves. Never use immature, droopy leaf tips, as they shrivel, lack fragrance and have a high hydrocyanic acid content.

BAY

OTHER USES

To prevent silverfish damaging books or clothing, place bay leaves in drawers or bookcases. When storing dried legumes, cereals, pasta or rice, a few leaves in the containers keep weevils away.

Lavandula angustifolia

ENGLISH LAVENDER

Lavandula dentata

FRENCH LAVENDER

Lavandula dentata var. *candicans*

GRAY FRENCH LAVENDER

Lavandula stoechas

SPANISH OR ITALIAN LAVENDER

The above examples of lavender are only a few of the most commonly grown of the many different available varieties of this herb.

ORIGIN

Iran

DESCRIPTION

L. angustifolia
Height about 5 ft (1.5 m). This variety of lavender is a subshrub. The strong, gray stems branch out near ground level. These stems become woody with maturity. The many small branches have narrow, downy, blue-gray, slightly serrated leaves. Stiff, elongated stems bear compact circles of small lavender-colored flowers for about 4 in (10 cm) down from the tip of the stem.

L. dentata var. *candicans*
Height about 32 in (80 cm). The growth of this variety is slightly woody and the leaves are gray and serrated. The stems of about 8 in (20 cm) in length bear fat cones of dense lavender-colored flowers.

L. dentata
Height 28 in (70 cm). This is a compact subshrub with small, green, serrated leaves. Short, slender stems bear cone-shaped clusters of blue-gray flowers.

L. stoechas
It has characteristic squared flower heads topped with "wings." Foliage is small and almost pinnate. A handsome long-stemmed variety with deep purple flowers is *L. stoechas* ssp. *pendunculata*.

CULTIVATION

Grow lavender varieties from seed sown in trays when varieties are not available to take cuttings. Propagating from small heel or tip cuttings is more usual. Lavender needs a sunny, well-drained position with slightly alkaline soil. The addition of a little agricultural linden and bone meal is advisable when planting. Cut back after flowering to neaten and encourage more flowers to form. Clip into low hedges for edging beds. These are useful in formal herb gardens. With the exception of the tall varieties such as *L. angustifolia*, lavender may also be grown in containers of a suitable size. Some tall and dwarf varieties to look for are the tall 'Dutch White,' the dwarf and medium-sized *L. stoechas*, purple 'Hidcote,' gray-leafed wooly lavender, dwarf and average-sized blue 'Folgate' and 'Munstead.' Others bear white, pink, rose and green flowers. The gray and green fern-leafed *L. multifida*, which comes from the Canary Islands and North Africa, is also a very interesting variety.

PESTS AND DISEASES

Cottony cushion scale (*see* page 87) in the southern hemisphere; yellow foliage caused by poor drainage.

CULINARY USES

Lavender has a strong, spicy flavor. When making apple jelly, mix in six flower heads to each 1¾ pints (1 liter) of juice. Remove flowers before bottling. To add flavor to indifferent honey, stir in a few flowers and allow to stand for two weeks. To make an old Elizabethan cake icing, crush enough flowers into the icing sugar for a good color and then stir in a little rosewater and lemon or orange juice for the right consistency. Break up a few flower heads and add to a salad for color and flavor. Cook chicken with a few sprigs of lavender instead of rosemary. Lavender ice cream is also delicious (*see* page 208).

ENGLISH LAVENDER

SIMPLE REMEDIES

A lavender bath is very relaxing, because lavender is such a calming herb. A little lavender vinegar (*see* page 104) or a few drops of lavender oil will relieve a headache when it is applied to the temples. Lavender oil has antiseptic and healing properties when applied to burns and blisters. A lavender tea made with three flower heads is sleep-inducing, as is a lavender pillow.

OTHER USES

After pruning lavender, bunch and hang the foliage to dry. It is used for potpourri and also for its moth-repellant properties. It is an attractive garden plant and a very useful cut flower. Cut flowers on a full length of stem when almost open. To dry flowers, cut them as soon as they begin to open. To make lavender "baskets," *see* page 114.

Levisticum officinale

LOVAGE

ORIGIN

Southern Europe and the Balkans

DESCRIPTION

Average height 3 ft (1 m). A fleshy, carrot-like root produces many straight, brittle, hollow stems. The flat, leathery, serrated leaves are bright green. It has small, sulfur-yellow flowers which appear in the form of umbels. The seeds are ridged and crescent-shaped.

CULTIVATION

Lovage, a perennial which should last about four years, is grown from fresh seed which is sown in trays in spring and autumn. Transplant seedlings into bags or pots when four to six leaves appear. Plant out in well-dug, rich soil in semishade when well grown. When watering, make sure the moisture penetrates well to encourage deep rooting. Plants die back in winter. In areas of frost, protect roots with a heavy mulch.

HARVESTING

Cut the stems and the foliage for drying in autumn. The stems and foliage are somewhat slow to dry, depending on weather conditions. Cut stalks of seed heads and hang them to dry, using the bag or tray method (*see* page 104). Roots should be lifted after three or four years.

PESTS

Aphids, caterpillars, and also slugs and snails (*see* pages 87–88)

CULINARY USES

Lovage has a strong, spicy flavor, almost a cross between celery and parsley. It is known as "maggi" in countries like Italy, Switzerland and Austria. When cutting the foliage, take care not to damage the center growth. Chop the young leaves finely and add them to salads — lovage has a strong flavor, so use it sparingly. Cook the stems as a vegetable, after removing the leaves for drying. Use the dried, powdered root, leaves and crushed seeds to flavor soups and stews. The roots may also be scrubbed, peeled and pickled.

OTHER USES

The foliage of lovage is decorative in fresh flower arrangements.

Linum usitatissimum

FLAX (LINSEED)

ORIGIN

Unknown (Egyptians made linen from the fibers 4,000 years ago)

LOVAGE

DESCRIPTION

Height 24 in (60 cm). Flax has a deep taproot with a slender stem of narrow, sword-shaped leaves which are covered in fine hairs. The undersides are quite heavily veined. There are sparse clusters of pale blue flowers, and an occasional white flower may be seen. The mature flowers produce spherical capsules of shiny, light brown seeds with a high oil content. There are also other decorative varieties of flax which are suitable for use as bedding plants.

CULTIVATION

This is a hardy annual. Sow the seed directly in late spring in rich, well-dug soil and preferably in full sun. Do not overwater. Flax is usually grown as a field crop and it is then harvested for its oil content and linen fiber.

FLAX

HARVESTING

Harvest the seeds of flax (linseed) in autumn as soon as they are ripe. Cut the whole plant off at ground level and hang it up to dry, using the bag method (*see* page 104).

MEDICINAL USES
See page 139

Marrubium vulgare

WHITE HOREHOUND

ORIGIN
Europe

DESCRIPTION
Height 16 in (40 cm). White horehound has an upright growth of square, furry stalks with a pair of crumpled leaves at each joint. These oval leaves are soft and gray-green. The whorls of small white flowers cluster around the joints. The flowers eventually turn into seeds which are contained in prickly husks. The leaves have a pleasant aroma when they are crushed.

N.B. In Australia, white horehound is categorized as a noxious weed.

CULTIVATION
As the seed is rather slow to germinate, root division and cuttings are much better ways of propagation. White horehound is not particularly fussy about soil conditions. It self-sows readily, but I prefer to remove most of the flowers appearing in the second year, before the seed sets. The husks can be quite a nuisance as they stick to clothing. Keep the plant trimmed to prevent it from straggling as it matures.

CULINARY USES
As white horehound has rather a bitter taste, use only very small quantities to season meat dishes.

SIMPLE REMEDIES
Cut sprigs or young flowers and leaves of horehound to make a tea, using 1 tsp (5 ml) finely chopped greenery to 8 oz (250 ml) boiling water. A little honey and lemon improves the flavor. Use horehound to make a herbal sweet which relieves a cough and sore throat:

HOREHOUND COUGH DROPS
a handful of horehound
3 sprigs mint
4 rose pelargonium leaves
8 oz (250 ml) water
1 TBS (15 ml) honey
14 oz (400 g) brown sugar
1 TBS (15 ml) lemon juice
1 oz (25 g) butter

Simmer the herbs in the water for about 10 minutes, then set aside and leave to cool. Strain the liquid.

Pour 4 oz (120 ml) of this liquid into a heavy saucepan, then add all the remaining ingredients and stir over gentle heat until the sugar has dissolved. Boil rapidly for 5 minutes until it reaches the soft ball stage. Drop a small amount of the syrup into a cup of water. It will form a soft ball if it is ready. The thermometer reading should be 239°F (115°C).

Remove the syrup from the heat and beat until thick. Pour it out onto a greased dish and, when it is nearly cool, mark into squares with a sharp knife. When completely cold, break it up and store in an airtight jar.

MEDICINAL USES
See page 139

WHITE HOREHOUND

ALFALFA

Medicago sativa

ALFALFA (LUCERNE)

ORIGIN
Mediterranean area and West Asia

DESCRIPTION
Height 24–36 in (60–90 cm). A deep, matted root system produces many tough, erect stalks from which grow short, slender stems bearing oval gray-green leaflets. The flowers are small, purple and typically legume-like.

CULTIVATION
Alfalfa is a perennial plant which is propagated from seed or by root division. It will self-sow and requires a rich soil and a position in full sun. Alfalfa is most often grown as stock fodder. The roots are plowed back into the ground for their nitrogen content.

HARVESTING
Cut the leaves and the young shoots as they are required.

CULINARY USES
Use the leaves, young shoots and also the sprouts in salads.

MEDICINAL USES
See page 140

Melissa officinalis

LEMON BALM

ORIGIN
The mountainous areas of southern Europe

DESCRIPTION
Height 16 in (40 cm). Lemon balm is a bushy perennial, rather similar in appearance to mint. The stems are square and brittle and they bear pairs of crinkly, toothed, bright green leaves as well as small white flowers. There is also a variety of lemon balm available with golden-streaked foliage.

CULTIVATION
The seed of this herb is rather slow to germinate. It occasionally self-sows. It is usually propagated by root division or by tip cuttings which are put into water to root. Lemon balm is a root spreader, but it is not quite as invasive as mint. After flowering, cut the plant down to where the new growth shows above the ground. It needs a well-composted, moist soil in a sunny or semishaded position. Protect lemon balm from the midday sun in very hot areas and from frost in winter. It is also suitable for growing in a container.

PESTS AND DISEASES
Caterpillars and rust (*see* pages 87–88)

CULINARY USES
This herb, as its name indicates, has a lemon flavor and fragrance. Add a few of the torn young leaves to a salad. The leaves may also be used to flavor milk puddings, custards and quiches. The chopped leaves enhance both chicken and fish dishes — they are best added during the last few minutes of cooking time. The finely chopped leaves may also be sprinkled over a wide variety of cooked vegetables.

MEDICINAL USES
See page 140

OTHER USES
A tea which is made from a few sprigs of lemon balm is an excellent remedy to help ward off the effects of heat stress. Dry the herb for using in potpourri. Apiarists have been known to rub the insides of their new hives with lemon balm in order to settle the bees. You can also make a stronger brew of the tea and use this as a rinse for greasy hair. As a facial steam, lemon balm is said to delay the ageing process.

LEMON BALM

Mentha x piperita

PEPPERMINT

Mentha pulegium

PENNYROYAL

Mentha rotundifolia

CRINKLE-LEAFED SPEARMINT

Mentha spicata

SPEARMINT

Mentha suaveolens

APPLEMINT

These are some of the most useful of the many varieties available.

ORIGIN
Southern Europe, the Middle East and Asia

DESCRIPTION
The height of the different varieties varies. They all have a shallow, fleshy running root system. All varieties of mint have square stems and pairs of leaves with pungent oil ducts on the undersides. The flowers grow in whorls on stems which may vary in length.

M. x piperita
The leaves are dark green on purple-tinged stalks. The flowers are mauve.

M. pulegium
The leaves are small, shiny and slightly rounded. The plant is low growing until the blue-mauve flowers appear.

M. rotundifolia
The leaves are rounded and crinkled and the flowers are blue-mauve.

M. spicata
The leaves are long and lightly veined. The flowers are white.

M. suaveolens
The leaves of this variety are round and rather furry. There is also a variegated kind which has creamy splotches on the leaves. The flowers are white.

CULTIVATION
Mint is a perennial herb. Propagate by root division or by cuttings rooted in water. Rooted runners are invasive, so plants should be grown in containers or be confined by plastic or other material barriers which can be buried in the ground. Plant in a damp, shady position with rich soil. There are varieties which will take full sun. Cut the plant right down after flowering. Some varieties die back in winter. Mulch the plants against damage by frost. Apart from container planting, pennyroyal is also a good addition to a hanging basket.

PESTS AND DISEASES
Caterpillars and rust (*see* pages 87–88)

CULINARY USES
Spearmint and crinkle-leafed spearmint are the best varieties to use for making a classic mint sauce. Cook mint with peas and young potatoes in order to enhance their flavor. A few leaf tips may be chopped and stirred into butters and cottage cheese. Spearmint makes a very attractive addition to drinks or fruit dishes and is also used as a garnish.

PEPPERMINT

PENNYROYAL

It makes a very refreshing tea. Make a tea of applemint, add the leaves to drinks or chop the young leaves to add to a fruit salad. Peppermint makes an excellent flavoring for ice cream, as well as for chocolate desserts and cakes, cookies, drinks and teas.

N.B. Pennyroyal should never be taken internally, as it has toxic properties.

MEDICINAL USES
See page 140

OTHER USES
Rub pennyroyal on the neck, face and hands to help deter insects. First test it on a small patch of skin, as rare cases of irritation have been reported. Pennyroyal can also be rubbed on a dog's coat and sprigs of it can be placed in the kennel or basket as a flea deterrent. Plant it under your roses to retain soil moisture and to keep roses healthier. Grow in walkways for fragrance. Dry any pleasantly fragrant mint, with or without flowers, for potpourri. Mints are good as cut flowers and provide foliage for indoor arrangements.

BERGAMOT

Monarda didyma

BERGAMOT

ORIGIN

North America

DESCRIPTION

Height 24 in (60 cm). Bergamot has strong, slightly hairy, square stems. The heads of narrow, tubular flowers, which appear in the form of whorls on single stems, are usually bright red and appear in midsummer. The flowers can also range in color from pink to mauve. The oval green leaves grow in pairs and are slightly rough to the touch. There is also an annual lemon bergamot with narrow, tender, bright green leaves and whorls of soft lilac flowers.

CULTIVATION

This is a perennial which grows from clumps of rooted runners. Propagate by root division in spring or from cuttings in summer. It is necessary to lift and divide the plants every two to three years. Break up the clumps and discard the old, woody growth. Plant in sun or semishade in a rich, light soil with the addition of bone meal. At the end of summer, cut the plant back to the small, reddish leaves near the ground. It is also suitable for container planting. Sow the seed of lemon bergamot *(M. citriodora)* in trays for transplanting in late spring.

CULINARY USES

Bergamot has a savory, fruity aroma. Use the flowers and chopped young leaves in salads, fruit salads and fruit drinks. Improve any pork dish with the addition of bergamot leaves during cooking. Freeze the chopped leaves with water in ice cube trays, or place single flowers in ice cube compartments, pour water over them slowly and then freeze. Make a tea with five or six large, fresh leaves or 1 tsp (5 ml) crushed, dried leaves to 8 oz (250 ml) boiling water. Dried bergamot leaves are also added to Indian or Ceylon tea.

OTHER USES

Use the leaves to make a facial steam which is suitable for all types of skin. Leaves and flowers may be dried for color and fragrance in potpourri. Cut flowers and foliage on long stems in late summer, tie in bunches and hang up to dry. Fresh or dried flowers are useful for arrangements. Bergamot is a colorful garden plant. Lemon bergamot is a long-lasting cut flower.

Myrtus communis

MYRTLE

ORIGIN

Southern Europe and northeast Asia

DESCRIPTION

Height 13 ft (4 m). An upright, many-branched, shrublike tree. When young, the bark is reddish brown, becoming gray and cracked with age. Woody stems produce a dense growth of ovate leaves. The leaves are dark green, shiny above and paler on the undersides. The flowers are a creamy white with soft clusters of golden stamens. In turn they become blue-black berries. There are variegated varieties of dwarf and tall myrtles with cream and green foliage. The cultivar *M. communis* 'Tarantina' is also a dwarf variety with small, shiny dark green leaves.

CULTIVATION

This evergreen shrub is grown from cuttings taken in late summer, but is easier to propagate by layering. Grow in a sheltered position in good, well-drained soil. Myrtle is frost tender, and should therefore be grown in a container and overwintered indoors in areas where frost occurs.

HARVESTING

Cut leaves, buds and flowers as they are required. Flowers and leaves for drying should be cut in early summer and the berries when they are nearly black.

CULINARY USES

The leaves are used in marinades. Remove the green ends of the buds and toss in salads. Use the flowers for

MYRTLE

WATERCRESS

stems. A few sprigs of watercress taken from a bunch bought commercially will soon produce roots if they are left in water. Transplant to containers to be sunk in a pond or a gently flowing stream. The pond should be aerated once a week by running in fresh water. Watercress will also grow in a very damp corner of the garden.

N.B. Unless watercress is growing right at the source of a stream, it is inadvisable to harvest it from either streams or canals, because of possible contamination by chemicals, animals or humans.

CULINARY USES

Watercress is delicious when used in salads and sandwiches. It may also be used for garnishing. Use the leaves and the stems in soups.

will also take quite easily and catnip will often self-sow. It does very well when it is planted in well-drained and slightly alkaline soil in a sunny position. The plants need a fair amount of water, but they also need very good drainage. Cut back the plants when growth becomes lush. If cats start to make the plants tatty, cover them with wire netting until the growth improves.

USES

Catnip is grown mainly for the pleasure of cats. They eat it when they think that medication is required and they can also often be seen rolling in it for sheer joy. Dried catnip leaves stuffed into cotton bags provide playthings for cats. To dry catnip, tie it in bundles and hang it up until completely dry. When it is dry, crumble it for use.

garnishes and salads. The berries are ground when they are dry and then used as a seasoning in savory dishes.

OTHER USES

For potpourri, dry the flowers face down and hang the leaves in bunches. Myrtle makes an attractive shrub for the garden. There are dwarf varieties which may be grown in large containers.

Nasturtium officinale

WATERCRESS

ORIGIN

Western and Central Europe

DESCRIPTION

This herb is a water-loving plant. It has a trailing growth and it sends down white roots from the stems. The shiny, dark green, round to pinnate leaves grow in sprigs from the stems. The small flowers are white.

CULTIVATION

Propagate watercress by sowing the seed in trays or, easier still, from rooting

Nepeta cataria

CATNIP

ORIGIN

Mediterranean area

DESCRIPTION

Height about 20 in (50 cm) when in flower. Catnip is a perennial. This herb has typical square stems which have toothed, heart-shaped leaves growing in pairs. The leaves are soft green with graying undersides. The stems branch and the whorls of white flowers have tiny, distinct red spots on the lip of each floret. *N. cataria* 'Citriodora' is a variety of catnip which has lemon-scented foliage.

CULTIVATION

Catnip is usually propagated by root division in the autumn. Cuttings

CATNIP

CATMINT

Nepeta x *faassenii*
(= Nepeta mussinii)

CATMINT

ORIGIN
Mediterranean area

DESCRIPTION
Height in flower about 8 in (20 cm). It has a trailing habit which spreads from the clumps of roots. The typical stems are square with pairs of toothed, gray leaves. Catmint is low growing until the stems produce whorls of soft blue-mauve flowers in midsummer. When obtainable, there is also a tall variety, 'Six Hill Giant,' which is beautiful when it is planted among roses. There is also a smaller-leafed variety of catmint which is very compact.

CULTIVATION
Catmint is a perennial herb which can be grown from seed sown in trays. It is usually propagated by root division in the cool season or from cuttings. It prefers a sunny position with well-drained, slightly alkaline soil. After

flowering, cut the plant back to the basal clump where there is usually a good growth of new leaves.

USES
It makes an attractive border to an herb garden. It is also a good ground cover and is especially beneficial to roses and lavender. It is ideal for a hanging basket and can be used to soften the edges of containers. It cuts well for fresh flower arrangements. The leaves can be dried for adding to potpourri. This herb appeals greatly to some cats who partake of it as a medicine (*see also* Catnip).

Ocimum basilicum

SWEET BASIL

Ocimum basilicum 'Crispum'

LETTUCE-LEAFED BASIL

Ocimum basilicum 'Minimum'

DWARF BUSH BASIL

Ocimum basilicum 'Purpureum'

DARK OPAL BASIL

Of the many varieties of basil which are available, the above examples are some of the most widely used.

ORIGIN
India and Egypt (many forms are also found in different climates)

DESCRIPTION
O. basilicum grows to a height of 18 in (45 cm). The plant is bushy and has stiff, branching stems. The glossy, bright green, ovate leaves have short stalks. Spikes of small white flowers grow in circles above the foliage.

O. basilicum 'Crispum' grows to a height of about 20 in (50 cm). Lettuce-leafed basil is a tall, vigorous variety of basil with large, serrated, crinkled, bright green leaves which have the habit of curling back on themselves.

O. basilicum 'Minimum' grows to a height of 18 in (45 cm). This variety is similar to *O. basilicum*, but its smaller leaves are denser on the stalk. There is a dwarf variety, round in shape, with very dense foliage and tiny white flowers. Height 6–8 in (15–20 cm).

O. basilicum 'Purpureum' grows to 12 in (30 cm). This variety of basil is a very attractive plant with shiny, ovate, purple leaves, almost black at times and at other times blotched with green. The spikes of flowers are pinky mauve.

CULTIVATION
Basil is an annual which requires a good, well-drained soil and a warm position. It is a good container plant, and is also suitable for a windowsill. In very hot climates, all the varieties of basil tend to droop and should therefore be gently hosed down in hot weather. Seed may be sown continuously from spring right through to late summer, either directly or in trays. Germination is rapid. Transplant seedlings when four leaves appear. When they have settled

SWEET BASIL

in, nip out the center stem to promote bushing. Continuous picking prolongs the life of the herb. Seed collected from your garden will not always germinate true to form, as hybridization takes place readily. Over the past few years some interesting varieties such as cinnamon, camphor, crinkle-leafed purple and green, and lemon-scented basils have been grown.

PESTS
Slugs and snails (*see* page 88)

CULINARY USES
Basil has a warm, resinous, clove-like flavor and fragrance. The flowers and leaves are best used fresh and added only during the last few minutes of cooking. For any dish with tomato, such as salads, soups, pizzas and pastas, it is a must. Finely chopped basil stirred into mayonnaise makes a good sauce for fish. Use as a garnish for vegetables, chicken and egg dishes. Large leaves of lettuce-leafed basil are used to envelop various foods, as one would use vine leaves. Tear rather than chop leaves for salads.

DARK OPAL BASIL

Oils and vinegars are good mediums for flavoring food (*see* page 104). At the height of the growing season, make pesto as well as pistou (*see* page 181) and freeze in small containers for use in winter. Basil does not dry well for cooking, but leaves may be layered with salt and kept in a crock in a cool place for use in winter. (Take care to rinse off all the salt before using the leaves.) The leaves can be frozen by brushing them with oil and wrapping them in freezer paper. Try a perennial basil such as *O. kilimandscharicum*, which is acceptable for culinary use.

SIMPLE REMEDIES
To relieve sore gums, swish out the mouth often with a solution made from about eight basil leaves added to a cup of boiling water. A basil leaf tucked into the mouth over an ulcer and kept there for as long as possible will ease the pain.

OTHER USES
Basil in the bath is refreshing. Dry the leaves and flowers for potpourri and the seed for germinating. Cut flower heads as they mature, then dry until crisp. Burn sprigs of basil on barbecue fires to deter mosquitoes. A bunch of basil hung in the kitchen or a pot of basil on the windowsill will help to deter flies.

Oenothera biennis

EVENING PRIMROSE

ORIGIN
Eastern North America

DESCRIPTION
Height 3 ft (1 m). A fleshy rootstock produces a rosette of dull green, oblong, lanceolate leaves. The leaves on the strong, erect, hairy, reddish stems are ovate and smaller. The branching stems bear large, long-tubed, fragrant, four-petaled flowers which open at sunset (one can actually stand and watch them opening). They close again just after

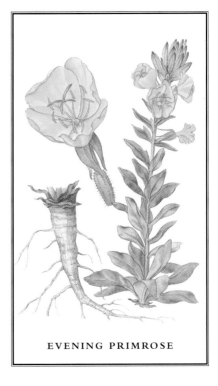

EVENING PRIMROSE

sunrise. Flowering continues up the stem as long seed pods develop below.

CULTIVATION
This biennial is usually propagated from seed sown in a sheltered position in late spring. It self-sows freely and transplants very successfully. It is not fussy about soil conditions, provided it is in the sun and well drained. There are many other species of evening primrose available with different growth habits and with flowers varying in color from white or pink to deep rose. It is a good plant for a night garden. There are also creeping varieties which make attractive subjects for containers or hanging baskets.

HARVESTING
O. biennis and many of the hybridized varieties are grown as crops for the highly regarded content of the seed oil.

MEDICINAL USES
See page 141

CULINARY USES
Use the edible flowers for garnishing.

COSMETIC USES
Grind flower tops for a face mask.

OLIVE

Olea europaea

OLIVE

Purchase from a reputable source.

ORIGIN
Middle East

CULINARY USES
The fruit of the olive tree is used as a garnish in salads, snacks and drinks.

MEDICINAL USES
See page 141

Origanum majorana

SWEET OR KNOTTED MARJORAM

Origanum onites

POT MARJORAM

Origanum vulgare

COMMON MARJORAM

The above are some of the most common varieties of marjoram available.

ORIGIN
Southeastern Europe and Asia Minor

DESCRIPTION

O. majorana

Height 12–24 in (30–60 cm). Sweet (or knotted) marjoram has a compact, bushy growth. This variety has thin stalks which bear a number of soft, veined, gray-green, oblong leaves. The slender stems bear knot-like buds. The sweetly scented flowers are pinkish white.

O. onites

This variety is low growing until the flowers appear. The heart-shaped, dark green leaves are borne on the purple-tinged, hairy stems. The flowers are mauve. *O. onites* 'Aureum' makes a very pretty golden ground cover.

O. vulgare

Height 36 in (90 cm) when in flower. This variety has coarse, wiry stalks with slightly longer, greener leaves than those of *O. majorana*. The buds are a little looser and the flowers are usually white. The flowers can also range in color from rose and purple to the palest pink and white. An attractive cultivar of this herb is 'Golden Tip' which has light green foliage with golden tips.

CULTIVATION
Marjoram is a perennial herb. The seed may be sown in trays in spring or cuttings may be taken, but root division is generally the quickest way of propagating this plant. *O. majorana* is frost sensitive and may therefore need to be overwintered in colder climates. To keep the plants neat, cut out all dead wood and remove the dead flowers and stalks, making sure that there is still plenty of foliage left on the bushes. *O. onites* should be cut down to new growth near the ground.

PESTS AND DISEASES
Cottony cushion scale in the southern hemisphere and also downy mildew (*see* page 87)

CULINARY USES

O. majorana

Because of its mild, sweetish flavor, this variety enhances fish, eggs, salads, salad dressings, chicken, soups, stews, herb

SWEET MARJORAM

COMMON MARJORAM

butters and cottage cheese. Add a sprig to mixed herb tea. For flavoring cooked dishes, discard the stems, chop the leaves and stir them in during the last few minutes of cooking.

O. onites and *O. vulgare*

These have a more robust flavor and a spicier fragrance than *O. majorana* and are best used in pizza and with pasta.

OTHER USES

Marjoram is attractive in flower arrangements and, when dried, adds fragrance to potpourri. It is a fragrant bath herb.

Panax ginseng

GINSENG

Purchase root for your requirements.

ORIGIN

North America

MEDICINAL USES

See page 141

Pelargonium capitatum

ROSE-SCENTED PELARGONIUM

Pelargonium citriodorum

LEMON-SCENTED PELARGONIUM

Pelargonium crispum 'Minor'

LEMON-SCENTED PELARGONIUM

Pelargonium graveolens

ROSE-SCENTED PELARGONIUM

Pelargonium tomentosum

PEPPERMINT PELARGONIUM

There are many scented pelargoniums, so look for varieties at nurseries and in the gardens of fellow herb-growers.

GINSENG

These herbs are also known as scented geraniums, but are here referred to as pelargoniums to avoid confusing them with the *Geranium* genus.

ORIGIN

Southern Africa

DESCRIPTION

P. capitatum

Height 32 in (80 cm). This herb is a woody subshrub which has a compact growth. *P. capitatum* has rather shallow indentations on rounded leaves with wavy edges, and it has clusters of small pink flowers. (*P. graveolens* has deeply indented, firm, light green leaves.) The rose fragrance of these varieties varies with the growing conditions.

P. citriodorum

Height over 3 ft (1 m). This variety has stiff, upright, woody growth. Leaves are firm, light green and deeply toothed. The small flowers are dark pink and the plant has a strong lemon fragrance. *P. crispum* 'Minor,' also known as 'Fingerbowl' in certain countries, is another lemon-scented herb. This variety has miniature leaves, no bigger than the nails of a baby's fingers.

P. tomentosum

This herb has a sprawling, loose growth. The leaves are rounded and slightly indented with a soft, velvety texture. These deep green leaves grow on longer stems than the other varieties. There are loose clusters of small white flowers with red lines on the upper petals. It has a strong peppermint fragrance.

CULTIVATION

Propagate scented pelargoniums from cuttings, or if mature plants have sent out rooted suckers, carefully remove from the mother plant and grow in bags or pots of average soil until established. Cuttings may be left to dry for about 24 hours before placing them in a sand box. Pelargoniums can be grown from seed sown in trays. Plant seedlings in full sun in well-drained, average soil and take care to water them well during hot weather. Peppermint pelargonium does better when planted in the shade of a tree or shrub and allowed to grow right

ROSE PELARGONIUM

PEPPERMINT PELARGONIUM

herb tea. Flowers may be used as a garnish.

P. tomentosum

For a chocolate cake, line bottom of pan with leaves. Flavor stewed pears with leaves. Use the small flowers as a garnish, particularly for chocolate desserts.

OTHER USES

Use pelargoniums in the bath. Dry for potpourri by spreading leaves on a rack. (Peppermint pelargonium dries slowly, so remove stems to speed up the process.) Add the leaves to a posy or small arrangement. The commercial oil for which the Indian-ocean island of Reunion is famous is extracted from *P. graveolens* and *P. capitatum*.

foliage is smooth and the flat leaves are deeply serrated, similar to those of celery.

CULTIVATION

Parsley is a biennial. To ensure a constant supply, sow small quantities of seed throughout the year in trays. To speed up the slow germination (three weeks), steep seed in lukewarm water overnight or place in the freezer for 24 hours. Warm the soil by pouring hot water over the soil *before* sowing the seed. Do not allow trays to dry out.

Transplant the seedlings while young (four- to six-leaf stage), as moving the more mature plants causes early bolting.

Parsley requires a rich, moist soil in sun or semishade. Flat-leafed parsley may grow for up to four years before bolting, especially if the middle of the plant is snipped regularly. If parsley is left in the bed until the seeds are completely dry, it will self-sow readily. Curly parsley is suitable for planting in containers and hanging baskets.

PESTS

Caterpillars (*see* page 87)

up into the branches. This also has the advantage of keeping soil off the leaves. Both the rose and lemon varieties are suitable for a large container.

CULINARY USES

P. capitatum and *P. graveolens*

Flavor stewed apples and pears as well as apple jelly with whole leaves. For cakes and fruit pies, line the pans with leaves. To make them lie flat, dip in hot water and shake dry. For custards or milk puddings, steep leaves in hot milk for 10 minutes, then remove. Chop finely before mixing into biscuit or scone dough. A leaf improves a herb tea. Flowers may be used as a garnish.

P. citriodorum

As you would with the rose-scented pelargonium, flavor custards and milk puddings by steeping leaves in the hot milk for 10 minutes. Add leaves to a

Petroselinum crispum

CURLY PARSLEY

Petroselinum crispum
var. *neapolitanum*

FLAT-LEAFED (ITALIAN) PARSLEY

ORIGIN

Sardinia, Turkey, Algeria

DESCRIPTION

P. crispum

Height 10 in (25 cm). A taproot produces ridged stalks. Dark green foliage branching from upper stalk is curled and crisp. The pretty, small, greenish-yellow flowers appear in the form of umbels.

P. crispum var. *neapolitanum*

Height 18 in (45 cm). It has a deep taproot from which a number of ridged stalks fan out. The dark green, tender

CURLY PARSLEY

ANISEED

CULINARY USES
Use in herb butters and cheeses, soups and omelettes. It is a decorative garnish.

HEALTH AND COSMETIC USES
A parsley solution is a good skin tonic. Store in the refrigerator until needed.

OTHER USES
Chew parsley to sweeten the breath. Curly parsley makes a decorative border plant. Roses also benefit from an under-planting of this herb. In China it is known as "kill flea" — maybe!

Pimpinella anisum

ANISEED

ORIGIN
Egypt and other Middle Eastern areas

DESCRIPTION
Height 8–18 in (20–45 cm). The tiny, strap-like primary leaves develop into a cluster of toothed, round-lobed green leaves. A ridged, round stem rises from this cluster of leaves and bears finely divided, feathery upper leaves. The stem also bears a loose cluster of small white or pink star-like flowers. The mature flowers produce capsules, each containing two aromatic, ridged, hairy seeds.

CULTIVATION
Aniseed is an annual. Sow seed directly (it does not transplant well) in early spring from the previous year's harvest, as it does not remain viable for long. Sow thickly in clumps in a sunny, sheltered situation. Thin out lightly if necessary, but remember that the plants need to be quite close together in order to support each other. The soil should be light, composted, alkaline and well drained.

HARVESTING
Use the leaves as the plant grows. It takes four months of hot weather for seeds to mature. When seed begins to turn grayish green, cut the whole plant close to the ground and then dry using the bag method (*see* page 104).

CULINARY USES
The seed can be added to the dough for bread and cookies, and may also be used in cakes and desserts as well as in confectionary.

OTHER USES
The seed can be used in potpourri.

rosette. The leaves each have three to five deep ribs running their length. The softly haired, loose stems bear dense, thimble-like flower heads. The sepals have attractive white stamens. *P. major* 'Rubrifolia' is a very attractive broad-leafed variety with its purple foliage providing color in the garden.

CULTIVATION
This perennial self-sows in average soil. It is usually found on wasteland and in hedgerows. It can become a nuisance in the garden if not controlled.

HARVESTING
Cut the leaves as required.

MEDICINAL USES
See page 141

SIMPLE REMEDY
Crushed ribwort leaves help to relieve bee-stings and insect bites.

RIBWORT

Plantago lanceolata

RIBWORT (PLANTAIN)

ORIGIN
Europe, North and Central Asia

DESCRIPTION
Height 20 in (50 cm) when it is in flower. Growing close to the ground, the slender dark green leaves form a

LUNGWORT

Pulmonaria officinalis

LUNGWORT

ORIGIN
Central Europe

DESCRIPTION
Height 9 in (23 cm). This herb has quite a fleshy rhizome which produces an erect, slender, rather hairy stem. This stem grows from a rosette of bristly, tongue-shaped, white-spotted green leaves. The leaf growth improves as the flowers start to fade. The pretty tubular, drooping flowers are pink when they first open but later change to shades of blue and purple.

CULTIVATION
Lungwort is a perennial herb which is propagated by root division in autumn. It may also be grown from seed which is sown directly in spring. This plant requires a shady and reasonably moist position with an average soil. Make sure that you always give it sufficient water during very hot conditions. Cut back the flowering stems in early winter and mulch the plants well.

HARVESTING
Harvest the whole plant during the middle of summer.

MEDICINAL USES
See page 142

OTHER USES
A decorative ground cover, lungwort is also used as an ingredient of vermouth.

Rheum officinale

MEDICINAL RHUBARB

Rheum rhaponticum

GARDEN RHUBARB

ORIGIN
Central Asia

DESCRIPTION
R. officinale
Height 6½ ft (2 m). Thick rhizomes form crowns from which grow thick green stems, bearing large, deeply indented leaves with heavy veining. A thick fibrous stem bears a cluster of quite closely packed, small greenish-yellow flowers.
R. rhaponticum
Height 3 ft (1 m). It has a thick fibrous rhizome with a reddish tinge. The thick stems, flat on one side and rounded on the other side, are also tinged with red. The dark green leaves, which each have five lobes, are rounded. The leaves are also quite heavily veined. A thick rounded stem bears a dense cluster of tiny creamy flowers.

CULTIVATION
R. officinale and *R. rhaponticum*
This perennial may be grown from seed, but usually mature plants are lifted and divided so that each piece of rhizome has a crown. Plant both these varieties in rich, well-composted soil in a sunny position, except in hot climates where dappled shade would be preferred.

HARVESTING
R. officinale
Harvest the roots of medicinal rhubarb in the fourth or fifth year.
R. rhaponticum
Pull up the stems of garden rhubarb after the first year when required.

COSMETIC USES
Use the root of *R. officinale* to make a hair dye (*see* page 171). (*R. rhaponticum* is not as potent as *R. officinale*.)

GARDEN RHUBARB

CULINARY USES

Use the stalks of garden rhubarb stewed for dessert (*see* page 210), in pies and for jams and chutneys.

OTHER USES

Boil the leaves in kettles to dislodge scale. Rinse thoroughly.

N.B. Owing to a high concentration of oxalic acid, the leaves of rhubarb are highly toxic and should therefore not be used for culinary purposes. Use the stalks only.

Rosa

ROSES

ORIGIN

Iran, the Middle and Far East, Europe and Britain

DESCRIPTION

The flowers and foliage of the old rose species and the newer, highly fragrant varieties are much too numerous and well listed to warrant description here. Many original roses have now been hybridized. While keeping both their fragrance and their form, they now produce two flowerings a year. Ask for Heritage roses (hybrids) at your local nursery or garden center.

CULTIVATION

Before planting a rose, prepare a hole of approximately 20 in (50 cm) square. The soil for roses should be slightly acid. If necessary, add a handful of sulfur dust. A handful of bone meal should also be mixed in with compost and well-rotted manure. When planting out, make sure that the soil level in the hole is the same as it was in the bag or container in which the plant was purchased. Slip the rose into the hole while it is still in the bag in order to check the levels. Remove the bag before you actually plant the rose. Bare-root roses should be planted to the same depth as their original soil level. Roses will grow equally well in sun or semi-shade, but in very hot areas Heritage roses need some protection from the harsh sun. Old-fashioned roses are propagated either from cuttings or from rose hips. Roses grown from hips are usually quite interesting, but are not always true to form. Keep on deadheading, unless hips are required. Prune lightly as soon as pruning time comes around. Roses can make good container plants, provided the size of the pot is appropriate.

PESTS AND DISEASES

The advantage of old-fashioned roses is that, though they may sometimes become slightly diseased, they do not generally succumb to most of the usual rose ailments. Do, however, watch out for beetles and aphids (*see* page 87).

CULINARY USES

N.B. For culinary purposes, do not use roses which have been sprayed with chemicals.

The pale heel at the base of a rose petal is bitter, so it should be removed before use. Cut the flowers when they are nearly open and, using the most fragrant petals, chop and mash them into butter and use for sandwiches or for making cakes. Rose petals make a pretty and tasty sandwich filling and they can also be scattered in a salad. Crystallize rose petals (*see* page 104) and use them for decorating cakes, desserts and so on. If you can collect enough deep red petals, make a few jars of rose petal jam. Crush bright red, slightly soft rosehips and add boiling water to make rosehip tea. The coarse bud end of the rosehip must first be removed. Rosehips make an excellent jam. When cooked, puréed and sieved, they also make a good base for various sauces, which are especially good with venison. Rosewater, which can be purchased from a drugstore, can also be used as a flavoring agent in cooking.

HEALTH AND COSMETIC USES

Rosewater is a refreshing face tonic. Rose petals are an exotic, fragrant addition to your bath.

OTHER USES

Dry rose petals to use in potpourri. Always include some of the green leaves for color as they become a lovely soft green when dried. Use roses for hedges, arches and screens in the garden, as they are both beautiful and practical.

APOTHECARY'S ROSE

Rosmarinus officinalis

ROSEMARY

Rosmarinus officinalis
'McConnell's Blue'

McCONNELL'S BLUE
ROSEMARY

Rosmarinus officinalis
'Prostratus'

TRAILING
ROSEMARY

ORIGIN
Mediterranean region and Asia Minor

DESCRIPTION
R. officinalis
Heigh 3–5 ft (1–1.5 m). It has a sturdy, bushy growth which becomes woody with maturity. The branches carry long, narrow, leathery leaves which are dark green with graying undersides. The leaf edges tend to curl under upon themselves. Pale blue flowers appear from midsummer onwards, clustered among the leaves towards the top of slender branches. There is also a rare yellow-leafed form, *R. officinalis* 'Aureus.'
R. officinalis 'McConnell's Blue'
Height 3 ft (1 m). This variety (where available) tends to grow into its own attractive shape, both upwards and sideways. Narrow dark green leaves grow more densely than those of *R. officinalis*. The flowers are a deep, true blue. 'Miss Jessop's Upright' is another blue variety.
R. officinalis 'Prostratus'
This variety has a low-growing, trailing habit. Firm, slender stems bear dense, narrow dark green leaves. The flowers are a pale shade of blue.

CULTIVATION
Propagate by sowing seed in a tray, or better still, by taking heel cuttings or by layering. Prepare the soil well before planting, as rosemary will grow in one position for up to 30 years. Dig a hole measuring 16 x 16 in (40 x 40 cm).

Work in compost, well-rotted manure, a handful of bone meal and another of hoof-and-horn meal. A sunny, well-drained position is required. Rosemary does not like wet roots. As its botanical name (Dew of the Sea) implies, it is ideal to grow in seaside gardens. Hose down the foliage lightly in hot weather. Give the plant a good annual mulch of well-rotted manure. Rosemary will form a lovely hedge if kept pruned, otherwise just keep it in shape and remove deadwood. 'McConnell's Blue' and trailing rosemary are best left unpruned, provided that the deadwood is removed regularly. *R. prostrata* is a good container plant and makes a magnificent show when trailed in a mass over walls and banks. Another form of low-growing rosemary is 'Highbury.' There are other varieties with flowers ranging in color from white and pink to light and deep blue.

PESTS
Cottony cushion scale in the southern hemisphere (*see* page 87).

CULINARY USES
It is strongly aromatic, with a resinous flavor. Chop leaves, otherwise they fall off the stems during cooking and are unpleasant to chew. Use chopped leaves in cookies, breads and scones. Cook rosemary in stews and soups and scatter over vegetables. Use it sparingly, except when roasting poultry or meat, when whole sprigs are used and then removed before serving. Rosemary is very good for flavoring both oils and vinegars (*see* page 104). The flowers are pretty

and tasty in salads, butters and cottage cheese. They make an attractive garnish.

MEDICINAL USES
See page 142

SIMPLE REMEDY
An old herbalist wrote that eating exactly thirteen rosemary flowers would help to cure a sore throat. For a quick pick-me-up, make a tea with a thumb-length sprig of this herb and flavor with honey and lemon.

HEALTH AND COSMETIC USES
A rosemary bath revitalizes. For a hair rinse, pour 8 oz (250 ml) hot water over 2 TBS (30 ml) crushed leaves, steep for 30 minutes and strain. Use as is, or mix in equal parts with shampoo and keep in the refrigerator until required.

OTHER USES
Dry by bunching and hanging. Add it to potpourri, or use as a moth deterrent.

ROSEMARY

Rubus idaeus

RASPBERRY

ORIGIN
China, North America and Europe

DESCRIPTION
Height 3 ft (1 m). A creeping root system produces prickly stems (canes) and suckers. The leaves are composed of five or seven leaflets. They are deeply veined, dull green, serrated, hairy and downy white on the undersides. Clusters of simple white flowers become bright red, rounded, dimpled berries.

CULTIVATION
This is a perennial plant. It is advisable to replace old plants every four years. Propagate from suckers or by layering or root division. It requires well-drained soil and a sunny position. Soil should also be well composted and alkaline. To ensure good fruiting, allow a lot of space — set plants 24 in (60 cm) apart in rows. In late autumn, cut down all the older canes that have borne fruit. Trim new canes back to 24 in (60 cm).

The berries of some of the new Scottish hybrids are good for freezing, as they do not stick together in the process.

HARVESTING
Cut leaves as required and flowers just before fully open. Pick berries from midsummer when ripe.

CULINARY USES
Use the berries for pies, jams, jellies, cordials, vinegars, wine, etc.

MEDICINAL USES
See page 142

Rumex acetosa

GARDEN SORREL

Rumex scutatus

FRENCH (BUCKLER) SORREL

ORIGIN
Europe and North Africa

DESCRIPTION
R. acetosa
Height 16 in (40 cm). It grows in thick clumps. Crisp, bright green, broad oval leaves form an inverted "V" to make them arrow-shaped at the base where they join smooth brittle stems.

R. scutatus
It has a low-growing, spreading habit. The shield-shaped light green leaves are blotched with silver. There is a gray-green variety which is also blotched.

CULTIVATION
Propagate this perennial by sowing seed in trays or by dividing clumps. Propagate *R. scutatus* by layering or dividing clumps. (Do not disturb plants often.) *R. acetosa* should be lifted, divided and replanted every two or three years. For *R. acetosa*, dig ground to a spade's depth, compost well and mix in a handful each of bone meal and hoof-and-horn meal. The roots of *R. scutatus* do not go down very deep. Grow this variety in semishade to protect the leaves from sunburn. Apply

GARDEN SORREL

an occasional dressing of well-rotted manure, as the plants are greedy feeders. Water well in hot weather, as the leaves tend to droop. Remove flowering stems as they appear, unless seed is required. *R. acetosa* will grow in a deep container and *R. scutatus* in a fairly shallow one.

PESTS
Slugs and snails (*see* page 88)

CULINARY USES
Sorrel has a sharp, acid, lemon flavor. The leaves of French sorrel are tender. Cut leaves with stems, wash, shake dry and roll in a tea towel. Keep them in the refrigerator until required. Shred leaves to use in sandwiches with vegetable or meat extract, cottage cheese, or any other filling. Tear the leaves for salad. Make an interesting cream soup from leaves and stalks. Use sorrel to enhance a white sauce or add it to butter sauce for fish. Cook it gently, as for spinach. *N.B. People who suffer from inflammatory complaints of the joints and the muscles should eat sorrel with discretion, because of its high oxalate content.*

RASPBERRY

FRENCH SORREL

Ruta graveolens

RUE

ORIGIN
Southern Europe and Middle East

DESCRIPTION
Height 20 in (50 cm). This herb is a subshrub which branches close to the ground. The mature, slightly woody branches produce firm gray-green stems of blue-gray leaves, giving the plant a lacy effect. The clusters of simple greenish-yellow flowers in turn become attractive, green-lobed capsules of black seed. One variety of rue, 'Jackman's Blue,' is a much more compact, lower-growing plant which has considerably smaller, almost blue leaves. There is another variety available which has attractive cream-splotched foliage.

CULTIVATION
This herb is a perennial which is propagated by sowing seed in trays, by taking cuttings, by root division or by layering in spring. It self-sows freely. Transplant the seedlings when they

are about 4 in (10 cm) high. Rue is not really very fussy about position, but grows best in sun with average soil. Keep it neat by cutting out the old woody and seeded stems. Rue is frost sensitive. If it is used as a hedge, keep well clipped. 'Jackman's Blue' is most suitable for growing in a container.

PESTS
Caterpillars and snails (*see* pages 87–88)

CULINARY USES
This bitter, pungent and aromatic herb is not commonly used in food. Some people add small amounts to certain dishes and cordials. It is an ingredient of the Italian spirit, grappa. Ethiopian coffee drinkers often add a leaf to the cup.

MEDICINAL USES
See page 142

Salvia elegans

PINEAPPLE SAGE

ORIGIN
Mexico

DESCRIPTION
Height 3 ft (1 m). Pineapple sage has firm, upright, reddish stems and soft green leaves, the edges of which are tinged with red as they mature. From late in the summer right into winter, the plant bears spikes of long, delicate scarlet flowers.

CULTIVATION
Pineapple sage is a perennial which usually spreads by means of suckers, but is not so invasive as to become a serious problem. Propagate this herb by lifting and separating the clumps or by taking semihardwood cuttings in spring. Grow pineapple sage in the sun or semishade in well-composted, light soil. Cut back to the base after flowering. Pineapple sage is frost sensitive and may need to be overwintered indoors.

CULINARY USES
The leaves and flowers have the taste and fragrance of pineapple. The whole flowers and snipped young leaves are used in fresh vegetable and fruit salads. Add the mature leaves to an herbal tea.

RUE

PINEAPPLE SAGE

Chopped leaves are added to chicken and pork dishes at the end of cooking time, or to any other food which is enhanced by a pineapple flavor.

OTHER USES

Pineapple sage is a decorative garden plant in winter. The flower spikes last well in water when cut.

Salvia officinalis
SAGE

ORIGIN

Spain and Mediterranean region

DESCRIPTION

Height 14–24 in (35–60 cm). This herb is a subshrub which has flexible stems. The leaves, when they are young, are oval and pale green, and they later mature to gray with a wrinkled, pebbled surface. The spikes of flowers are usually either blueish-mauve or pink. There are also varieties with white and deep blue flowers.

The following are some of the most common cultivars of sage which are readily available:

S. officinalis 'Purpurascens'

This variety has reddish-purple leaves and it seldom flowers.

S. officinalis 'Variegata'

The green leaves are streaked with cream. It has blue flowers.

S. officinalis 'Tricolor'

The leaves are streaked with purple, green and cream.

S. officinalis 'Aurea'

The leaves are streaked with gold.

CULTIVATION

Sage is a perennial with an average life span of four years. Sometimes, for no reason, a sage plant will curl up and die, so it is advisable to keep extra plants growing in bags or pots. Grow from seed sown in trays or by layering, cuttings or root division done in spring and autumn. Sage needs well-drained, light and slightly alkaline soil and full sun. It does not like to have wet roots. Cut plants back after flowering and remove all the deadwood. Protect plants from cold, wind and frost. Sage is also suitable for growing in a container.

PESTS AND DISEASES

Cottony cushion scale (*see* page 87), grasshoppers and stem or root rot caused by poor soil drainage

CULINARY USES

It has a strong, warm, pungent flavor. For the best flavor, pick the younger leaves rather than the mature ones. Sage aids the digestion of rich foods, therefore it is excellent cooked with oily fish and fatty meats and poultry. It is an important ingredient in certain pork sausages and it is a good herb to add to both culinary oils and vinegars. The fresh, finely chopped leaves will add flavor to bread and scone doughs, or to cottage cheese. Use these sparingly for the best results. Sprinkle the chopped leaves over any cooked vegetables. Chop and cook sage in olive oil or butter and then pour the cooked sage over any simple pasta dish. The flowers are a decorative and tasty garnish. Cheese with sage is produced commercially. To freeze sage, chop the leaves and mix with a little water, then freeze in ice cubes.

HEALTH AND COSMETIC USES

Sage acts as a general tonic and is said to extend the life span. For a hair rinse, simmer 10 leaves with 17 oz (500 ml) water for 10 minutes, cool and store for

SAGE

future use. To darken graying hair, add 4 tsp (20 ml) of used tea leaves to the mixture. Strain before use. As sage is a natural deodorant, it is a good bath herb.

MEDICINAL USES

See page 143

OTHER USES

Dried sage is added to potpourri for its moth-repellant properties. Cut long stems before flowering to bunch, hang and dry. Sage is an attractive cut flower.

Salvia sclarea
CLARY SAGE

ORIGIN

Syria and Southern Europe

DESCRIPTION

Height 30 in (75 cm). Width 20 in (50 cm) . Clary sage is a very handsome

CLARY SAGE

plant. The strong, hollow, central stem, which is covered in fine hairs, bears pairs of stemmed leaves. These gray-green, pebbled leaves are heart-shaped and have slightly toothed margins. The upper surface of the leaves is downy. Branched flowering spikes bear whorls of pretty pale blue flowers which are surrounded by creamy white or rose-colored bracts. They look somewhat like small orchids. When the flowers drop from the plant, four large black seeds will have set in the bracts.

CULTIVATION

This herb is a biennial. Sow the seed annually for a continuous supply of flowering plants. It will also self-sow. Seedlings will transplant easily. Clary sage should be planted in a good, well-drained, alkaline soil in full sun. *S. horminum*, painted sage, is a very pretty

annual variety which makes a very attractive cut flower. This variety needs a rich soil and regular watering.

HARVESTING

Collect seed as it ripens, or cut the stems for bag hanging just before seeds drop (*see* page 104).

USES

Use the seeds in pot-pourri for their fruity aroma. Clary sage is a decorative plant to use in a large garden.

Sambucus nigra

ELDER

ORIGIN

Europe, North America and parts of Asia

DESCRIPTION

Height 13 ft (4 m). The elder is a deciduous bushy shrub or small tree. Elder has woody stems with loose, serrated, matt green oval leaves and masses of flat-topped umbels of star-shaped, fragrant creamy white flowers. After flowering, the branches tend to droop with the weight of the small purple-black berries. A cold spell in autumn produces an even bigger crop of berries than usual. Other available cultivars are *Sambucus nigra* 'Argentea' (cream and green elder or variegated elder), which has variegated cream and green foliage, and *Sambucus nigra* 'Aurea' (gold elder), which has lovely golden foliage.

CULTIVATION

Propagate elder from 10 in (25 cm) hardwood cuttings in autumn. Mature trees usually produce suckers which can be removed from the tree and transplanted. Self-sown saplings may also be

found growing in the near vicinity. The elder is not particularly fussy about its growing conditions. Elder may also be pruned to any required shape, such as a tall hedge.

CULINARY USES

The flowers have a mild, sweet taste, and the berries are slightly sour. For a simple dessert, dip flower heads in a light batter, deep-fry until just golden, drain on paper, remove main stem and dredge with powdered sugar.

To flavor rolls, scones and breads, place flower heads in a plastic bag and leave in the sun for an hour to sweat. The florets are then easily removed from the stems, ready to add to dough mixtures. Cut sprays of berries when they turn purple — they are a good addition to apple in a pie or tart. Stew with any other available fruit. Elder-berries make a palatable jelly. They are also used to make wine and cordials, as well as sambuca, an interesting liqueur.

MEDICINAL USES

See page 143

ELDER

SALAD BURNET

Sanguisorba minor ssp. *muricata*
(= Poterium sanguisorba)

SALAD BURNET

ORIGIN
Mediterranean region and some parts of Asia Minor

DESCRIPTION
Height 18 in (45 cm) when the plant is in flower. It grows in the form of a rosette with the stems falling outward. The slender stems bear many pairs of small, round, serrated, soft green leaves to give the plant a fern-like effect. Long firm stems bear green, thimble-like heads of flowers from which the reddish, thread-like sacs of pollen hang.

CULTIVATION
Salad burnet is a perennial plant. If seed is not available commercially, obtain a plant from a friend or neighbor and propagate it by root division. Salad burnet self-sows readily. Do not allow too many of the flower heads to mature, as there will then be a surfeit of seedlings. Grow these plants as a group or as a border. They do best in their own company. Salad burnet requires a sunny position with average soil. Always keep the plants well watered during spells of very hot weather. Remove the dead leaves from the outer edge of the plant and also remove the unwanted flower stems as they appear. The herb is frost sensitive and is suitable for container growing.

CULINARY USES
Salad burnet has a flavor similar to that of cucumber. The fresh leaves (except those forming the center crown of the plant) are stripped from the stems and used whole in salads and sandwiches. Shred the leaves for herb butters or cottage cheese. Leafy stems are both attractive and tasty as a garnish. Cook the stems and leaves of salad burnet in delicately flavored cream soups, such as mushroom or chicken, to enhance the flavor.

HEALTH AND COSMETIC USES
Steep the fresh leaves of salad burnet in hot water to make a skin tonic. A good handful of the foliage can be used to make a refreshing bath.

OTHER USES
The flower heads are decorative whether they are used fresh or dried. Salad burnet has very attractive foliage and looks lovely in the garden.

Santolina chamaecyparissus

LAVENDER COTTON (SANTOLINA)

Santolina neapolitana

LAVENDER COTTON (SANTOLINA)

ORIGIN
Mediterranean coastal region

DESCRIPTION
S. chamaecyparissus
Height 18 in (45 cm). This variety is a subshrub with firm stems of close-growing, narrow, toothed gray leaves — it actually looks a bit like coral. Flowers of *S. chamaecyparissus* are exactly the same as those of *S. neapolitana*.
S. neapolitana
Height 24 in (60 cm). It is a subshrub tending to grow outwards. Loose stems of soft, gray leaves give the plant a feathery overall appearance. The long slender stems bear golden yellow, button-like flowers with fluffy edgings.

LAVENDER COTTON

SOAPWORT

Other available varieties are a dwarf *S. chamaecyparissus* 'Nana,' which has rather compact gray foliage, and also *S. rosmarinifolia (= S. viridis),* which has small, narrow green leaves.

CULTIVATION
Santolina is a perennial which is propagated from heel cuttings and by layering in spring and autumn. A sunny position with an average, well-drained soil is required. Give it an annual mulch of well-rotted manure and compost. Prune back after flowering to prevent the plants becoming too floppy or untidy. Santolina does very well in coastal gardens, but it is frost sensitive. *S. neapolitana* may also be grown in a suitably large container.

PESTS
Cottony cushion scale occurs sometimes (*see* page 87).

USES
S. neapolitana has a sweetly pungent aroma. *S. chamaecyparissus* is sharply aromatic. Dried santolina is used in cupboards, drawers and bookcases to get rid of moths and silverfish. It is very

effective for this purpose. Scattered freshly in kennels and dog and cat baskets, it also discourages fleas. It gives a decorative gray accent in a garden. *S. chamaecyparissus* lends itself to being clipped into a low neat hedge, suitable for a formal herb garden. The flowers last very well in fresh arrangements and may be cut at any time from the first show of color to maturity. They tend to keep their color when dried. Use the foliage to soften the appearance of a tussie mussie (*see* page 108). Dry foliage and flowers to add to potpourri. Wait until the flowers are fully open before cutting them for drying purposes, then bunch and hang to dry.

Saponaria officinalis

SOAPWORT

ORIGIN
Europe and western Asia

DESCRIPTION
Height 12–36 in (30–90 cm). It has a sturdy, small, narrow rhizome which branches freely and can become invasive. It has an erect stem which bears several pairs of smooth, light green oval leaves with distinct longitudinal veining. The loose clusters of simple five-petaled pink or creamy white flowers have a fruity fragrance. *S. officinalis* 'Rosea Plena' has soft pink double flowers.

CULTIVATION
This plant is a perennial propagated from seed, cuttings or root division and needs rich, moist soil in sun or semi-shade. Deadhead regularly in order to prolong flowering. In some areas it tends to die back in winter, shooting up again in spring. Do not grow near a fish pond, as the roots will poison the fish.

HARVESTING
Cut the leaves as required. Lift the roots in autumn. The roots may be used fresh or they may be dried for future use.

MEDICINAL USES
See page 143

HEALTH AND COSMETIC USES
Use the roots and foliage of soapwort for skin rinses and shampoos.

OTHER USES
As soapwort contains saponin, a substance which forms a lather, it makes an excellent solution for washing fine old fabrics and laces and can also be used for sponging tapestries. Simmer two to three handfuls of the foliage in 1¾ pints (1 liter) of water for approximately 15 minutes, strain and then use. A little of the root simmered in water will serve the same purpose.

Satureja montana

WINTER SAVORY

Satureja hortensis

SUMMER SAVORY

ORIGIN
Mediterranean and Middle East

SUMMER SAVORY

WINTER SAVORY

DESCRIPTION

S. montana

Height 10 in (25 cm). Winter savory is a low-growing, compact plant which is woody close to the ground. It has tender stems of leathery dark green leaves. These leaves are quite similar in appearance to those of rosemary. In late summer there are sprigs of small pure white flowers. There is also a creeping variety, *S. spicigera*.

S. hortensis

Height 14 in (35 cm). It has slender, erect stems which bear sparsely placed, pointed bronze leaves. It has a softer growth than that of *S. montana*. The flowers are pale pink in color.

CULTIVATION

S. montana is a perennial, propagated by tip and heel cuttings or layering. It requires well-drained, average soil and prefers a sunny position. Cut it back after flowering. It is frost sensitive and is suitable for a container.

S. hortensis is an annual herb. Sow the seed in trays or directly throughout the spring and summer. Germination is rapid, in approximately ten days. Grow the plants fairly close together so that they support each other. Summer savory requires a rich soil and also prefers a sunny position.

PESTS

Summer savory: slugs and snails (*see* page 88).

CULINARY USES

Savory has quite a strong, peppery flavor. The flavor of summer savory is the stronger of the two kinds. Cut the stems and then strip the leaves as required. Chop the leaves finely and add to soups and stews near the end of the cooking time. Rub savory into meat and poultry before roasting or grilling it. Scatter a small amount of chopped savory over a salad. Cook it with all types of beans, dried or green, and with other legumes. Savory makes a flavorsome oil and vinegar. To freeze, chop and mix with a little water, then pour it into ice cube compartments.

OTHER USES

Use the flowers and the foliage in arrangements. To dry, bunch together the stems and the foliage and hang upside down.

Scuttelaria lateriflora

SKULLCAP

ORIGIN

Eastern North America

DESCRIPTION

Height 6–30 in (10–75 cm). The creeping, fibrous, yellow root system produces square, slender, branching stems with oblong, tapering deep green leaves which grow in pairs. These leaves are coarsely serrated. Pairs of blue flowers come from the upper leaf axils, growing only on one side of the stem.

CULTIVATION

Skullcap is a perennial plant. Sow the seed directly in early spring. Divide the roots in spring, but only when matting makes it necessary to do so.

HARVESTING

The whole plant may be lifted and dried in autumn.

MEDICINAL USES

See page 143

Silybum marianum

MILK THISTLE

ORIGIN

Southwest Europe

SKULLCAP

MILK THISTLE

GOLDENROD

DESCRIPTION

Height 1.5 m (5 ft). Milk thistle has deeply cut, spiny-edged dark green leaves. These leaves are very strongly veined in white and they grow in the form of a dense rosette. The plant has an erect stem which is rather prickly and which produces a typical thistle-shaped pink or white flower.

CULTIVATION

Milk thistle is a biennial plant which is usually propagated by sowing seed. As the plants flower and die in the second year, it is a good idea to sow the seed annually so as to keep a stock of mature plants handy. This plant is not really fussy about habitat and can be found growing in open land, cultivated fields and along roadsides.

HARVESTING

Lift the roots of milk thistle during autumn. Cut the leaves as they are required and harvest the seed when it is completely ripe.

MEDICINAL USES

See page 144

Solidago virgaurea

GOLDENROD

ORIGIN

Southern Europe

DESCRIPTION

Height approximately 75 cm (30 in). This plant has a many-rooted rhizome with a creeping, somewhat invasive habit. The leaves at the base of the plant are a bright green colour and they are also pointed, oval and serrated. The leaves on the firm, erect flower stems are smoother and somewhat smaller. These flower stems produce spikes of simple golden yellow flowers which have clusters of stamens.

CULTIVATION

Goldenrod is a perennial plant which may be propagated either by root division or by sowing seed. As it is rather a greedy plant, the soil in which it is planted should be rich and light. It requires a position in full sun. Goldenrod should be lifted and then replanted every second year, as it can

---

easily mat or spread into other plants. *S. canadensis* is an ornamental variety, suitable for herbaceous borders.

HARVESTING

Cut the leaves as they are required. Cut the plant at ground level and hang the leaves and flowers to dry.

MEDICINAL USES

See page 144

Stellaria media

CHICKWEED

ORIGIN

Unknown

DESCRIPTION

This herb is a 'weed' with a low, trailing habit. It has delicate, heart-shaped light green leaves growing from branched, slender, brittle stems. It has sparse, white, star-like flowers.

CULTIVATION

Chickweed is an annual which can be found growing in gardens that are not too well weeded. If there is none in

CHICKWEED

your garden, dig up a clump from a friend's garden and allow it to self-sow. It requires a position in full sun or semi-shade and an average soil which should not be allowed to dry out in summer. Chickweed will survive a mild frost.

CULINARY USES

Strip leaves and sprinkle on salads. For extra nourishment, lightly chop leaves and stems to add to soups and stews in the last few minutes of cooking.

MEDICINAL USES

See page 144

OTHER USES

Caged birds enjoy chickweed.

Symphytum officinale
COMFREY

ORIGIN

Europe and Asia

DESCRIPTION

Height 28 in (70 cm). There is lush growth from a strong taproot. The dark green leaves of this plant are ovate at the base, becoming pointed. The leaves, which are approximately 10 in (25 cm) long, grow in fountain-shaped clumps. These leaves, with their deep veining, are covered with rough bristles which are thicker on the undersides. The flowering stems have smoother, small leaves. The clusters of bell-shaped mauve flowers droop from one side of each stem. The flowers could also be blue, pink or white.

CULTIVATION

Comfrey is a perennial. Propagate it by root or crown division. Root cuttings may also be struck in the spring or autumn. Grow in full sun or semishade and a little distance away from other plants, as comfrey spreads easily and it can be difficult to remove without damaging its neighbors. The soil should be well manured and slightly acid. Cut down as the flowers begin to form — plants will then rapidly produce new growth. Comfrey tends to die back in winter. Lift and divide the plants every two or three years.

CULINARY USES

Although comfrey is a nutritious herb, it should always be used sparingly, as excessive use could affect the liver and kidneys. Cook the young leaves, which have a cucumber-like flavor, gently. Serve as a vegetable. Leaves are added fresh to a salad or dipped in batter and fried as fritters. Finely cut leaves are added to stews and soups before serving.

MEDICINAL USES

See page 144

OTHER USES

Feed comfrey to poultry to increase egg production. Bird fanciers feed small quantities to canaries and other caged birds. A small quantity added to dog food improves the skin and coat. The high potash content makes comfrey a good liquid fertilizer (*see* page 89). Add it to compost heaps as an activator and use surplus foliage as a mulch.

COMFREY

Tagetes erecta
AFRICAN MARIGOLD

Tagetes minuta
INCA MARIGOLD, KHAKI WEED

Tagetes patula
FRENCH MARIGOLD

ORIGIN

Mexico

DESCRIPTION

Height differs with each variety, from 4 in (10 cm) to 6½ ft (2 m) in the case of Inca marigold. Brittle stems branch from an erect, hollow main stalk. The foliage is fairly dense and made up of finely divided leaves, feathery in some instances. The dark green leaves are a foil for the bright single or double yellow and orange flowers. There are also some bicolored varieties. Inca marigold (where available) stands erect and has sparse branches of fine, deeply indented, dull green leaves and spikes of

AFRICAN MARIGOLD

FEVERFEW

small creamy yellow flowers. Seeds are ½ in (2 cm), black at one end and white at the other. New hybrids of *T. erecta* are now available, such as 'Vanilla' and 'Snowbird' which are of medium height with creamy white flowers.

CULTIVATION
Marigold is generally regarded as a summer-flowering annual. Sow seed directly or in trays. It often self-sows and requires average soil and a sunny position. It may be successfully thinned and also transplanted. Inca marigold (khaki weed) tends to droop when moved, so water the foliage well. Nip out centers of young plants to encourage them to bush. Remove the dead heads often to prolong flowering. Marigolds are suitable for container planting, with the exception of khaki weed and other tall varieties. Be careful when collecting the seed of

khaki weed, as it sticks to clothing and is difficult to remove.

USES
Marigold has rather a pungent aroma. It is a plant which is essential for keeping soil healthy, especially *T. minuta*. The Incas and other South American Indians planted this herb for well over a thousand years in order to keep their somewhat limited (and usually terraced) growing areas healthy. Marigolds, where they grow in the garden, repel eelworm (nematode), which very often attacks the root system of plants such as proteas, potatoes and dahlias. A brew of marigold leaves and soapy water makes an excellent spray to counteract thrips. For potpourri, use dried flowers and foliage stripped from the stems. The seed of Inca marigold helps to retain the fragrant oils in potpourri. All three varieties have moth-repellent properties when dried. Both *T. patula* and *T. erecta* brighten a garden and make excellent cut flowers.

Tanacetum parthenium
FEVERFEW

ORIGIN
Southeast Europe
DESCRIPTION
Height 24 in (60 cm) when it is in flower. It forms a low, compact clump of erect, furrowed, branching stems of finely divided, dull green ovate leaflets which have deeply indented edges. The

firm slender stems bear loose clusters of white daisy-like flowers. These flowers have flat yellow centers.
N.B. This variety has the highest medicinal properties of the many varieties of feverfew.

CULTIVATION
This perennial is propagated by cuttings taken in early summer or else by root division in autumn. It can also be grown from seed, but germination is not always successful. Other varieties may self-sow freely. Grow feverfew in a sunny position in average soil, as it is liable to mildew when it is grown in the shade. This form of feverfew may take up to eighteen months to flower.

HARVESTING
Cut the leaves and the flowers as they are required. The flowers may be dried face down on a flat surface and then used for potpourri.

MEDICINAL USES
See page 145

OTHER USES
Grow feverfew in rose gardens to attract aphids away from the rose bushes. Both the leaves and the flowers act as a good moth deterrent and can also be used in potpourri. Feverfew is very decorative as a cut flower.

Tanacetum vulgare
COMMON TANSY

Tanacetum vulgare var. *crispum*
CURLY TANSY

ORIGIN
Europe
DESCRIPTION
T. vulgare
Height 3 ft (1 m) when in flower. This variety is low growing with loose, deeply indented green leaves on red-tinged stems. The firm upright stems bear several clusters of small, yellow, button-like flowers.

COMMON TANSY

DANDELION

T. vulgare var. *crispum*

Height 60 cm (24 in) when in flower. The foliage of this variety is compact, crisp, fern-like and a bright lime green. When the flowers do appear, they are clusters of small yellow buttons.

CULTIVATION

This is a perennial herb. Propagate it by root division in spring and autumn. It has a spreading root habit which can be invasive in a good locality. It needs full sun or semishade, as well as an average, slightly alkaline soil. Tansy may die back in winter. Cut off all dead leaves, as slugs and snails tend to lurk around the plants. Tansy is frost sensitive.

HARVESTING

Cut flowers when fully mature, bunch them and hang to dry. Foliage cut and stripped from the stems is spread to dry, or stems are bunched and hung to dry.

USES

Tansy has an acrid, spicy fragrance. It is no longer used as a culinary herb, as it has been found to have toxic properties. Hang bunches of fresh tansy in the kitchen to deter flies, and spread the crushed leaves on shelves to stop ants. It is a decorative plant, especially the curly variety, although this seldom flowers. Dried tansy is a pleasant moth-repellant and is also added to potpourri. Tansy is also an important compost activator.

Taraxacum officinale

DANDELION

ORIGIN

Northern Europe

DESCRIPTION

Height in flower 10–20 cm (4–8 in). A rosette of foliage grows from a deep, fleshy root, which is white inside and brown on the outside. The leaves are light green, lanceolate and deeply in-dented. The hollow upright stem bears a flat, bright yellow daisy-like flower with downward-turning green bracts. This flower in turn becomes a fluffy seed head (clock).

CULTIVATION

Dandelion is a perennial herb which self-sows readily. These self-sowings are quite easily transplanted. To control seeding, remove the mature flowers. A rich, well-composted soil in a sunny position will produce lush growth. Always keep dandelion well watered, especially during hot weather.

CULINARY USES

As this herb has a high vitamin and mineral content, the young leaves nipped from the centre of the plant are good to use in salads. Since the more mature leaves have a slightly bitter taste, soak them in salt water for 30 minutes, rinse well and then cook like spinach. For a 2-egg omelette, collect 60 ml (4 tbsp) dandelion buds, fry gently in butter and fold into the omelette, or stir them into scrambled eggs. Mature roots are lifted, scrubbed, minced, dried and roasted to be used in the same way as chicory or as a coffee substitute.

MEDICINAL USES

See page 145

SIMPLE REMEDY

Apply the white sap of the plant to warts as often as possible.

OTHER USES

Chop up any surplus plants and add them to the compost heap.

Thymus vulgaris

COMMON THYME

Thymus x *citriodorus*

LEMON THYME

ORIGIN

Mediterranean region

DESCRIPTION

T. vulgaris

Height 30 cm (12 in). Common thyme is a subshrub which has rather tough, woody branches. From these branches grow the more tender stems of small, stalkless, thin, dark grey-green leaves. In summer, the tips of the stems bear whorls of pale pink flowers.

COMMON THYME

T. x *citriodorus*
Height 15 cm (6 in). Lemon thyme is a low-growing herb with soft, round, lemon-flavoured leaves. The flowers are a pinky mauve colour. A variegated form is also available, which makes an even prettier border plant.

CULTIVATION
Thyme is a perennial. *T. vulgaris* may be propagated from seed sown in a tray in spring, and also by dividing the mature plants, by layering or by cuttings made in the spring and autumn. To propagate *T.* x *citriodorus*, carefully remove rooted sections from the side of the plant or sow seed. It requires full sun and a well-drained, slightly alkaline soil. Cut out all the old wood from *T. vulgaris*, remove the dead flower heads and generally neaten the plant. Cut back the dead flower heads from *T.* x *citriodorus*. Thyme is suitable for container planting. It is sensitive to frost.

There are many varieties available, all varying in height, foliage and colouring, and with flowers varying in colour from pure white to the deepest purple.

PESTS
Cottony cushion scale (*see* page 87), and also root rot

CULINARY USES
Thyme has a strong piquant or lemony flavour. For fresh use, cut throughout the year, though the flavour is best just before flowering. Strip the small leaves from stems and use to enhance savoury dishes. Thyme complements meat, fish and poultry dishes. Chop it and mix into dumplings, scones and breads. Blend a little into herb butter and cottage cheese. Add it to herb vinegars and oils. It is also a *bouquet garni* herb.

SIMPLE REMEDIES
To make tea to soothe a nagging cough, steep a 10 cm (4 in) sprig of thyme and 3 sage leaves in 250 ml (8 fl oz) boiling water for 5 minutes. Make a stronger brew for a healing mouthwash and use for treating sore gums. This is also a good antiseptic wash for wounds.

MEDICINAL USES
See page 145

OTHER USES
T. x *citriodorus* makes an excellent ground cover or border, as do many of the other low-growing varieties. Dry thyme for use in potpourri. Use the bag method, as the small leaves tend to drop (*see* page 104).

Tilia cordata
LIME

ORIGIN
Britain and north-west Europe

DESCRIPTION
Height may reach 10 m (33 ft) or even more, depending on where it is grown. Lime has an upright growth and dense foliage. The leaves are dark green with blue-green undersides, and are heart-shaped with serrated edges. Sprays of delicately perfumed, long-stemmed, fluffy yellow blossoms with bracts flower in midsummer.

CULTIVATION
Lime is a deciduous tree which grows fast once it is established. From sowing the seed to when the tree is planted out takes at least four years. It is therefore sensible to purchase one from a garden centre or arboretum. Lime is primarily a tree of northern European climates.

HARVESTING
Pick the flowers complete with the bracts in midsummer. Pick and dry carefully so as not to bruise them. Do not pick old flowers, because they might be slightly toxic.

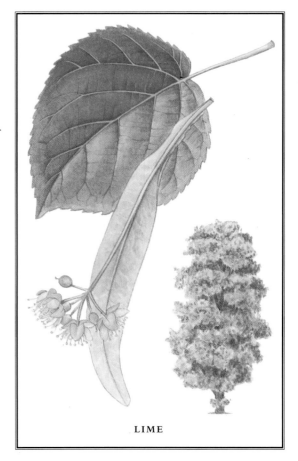

LIME

RED CLOVER

FENUGREEK

alkaline soil. Grow the plants in fairly compact rows in order to enable them to support each other.

HARVESTING
Cut salad leaves as they are required. Cut the whole plant off at ground level and hang it up to dry, using the bag method (*see* page 104).

CULINARY USES
Use the young leaves of fenugreek to add flavor to salads and use the seeds for sprouting. The seeds may also be ground and use as a seasoning.

MEDICINAL USES
See page 146

Tropaeolum majus

NASTURTIUM

ORIGIN
South America and Mexico

DESCRIPTION
Nasturtium is a brittle-stemmed plant of sprawling or climbing habit. The stiff, upright stems bear shield-shaped leaves which tend to face upward. Single or

COSMETIC USES
Adding the flowers of *Tilia cordata* to your bath water is an excellent way to soothe the skin.

Trifolium pratense

RED CLOVER

ORIGIN
This plant is found in most temperate to cold areas of the world

DESCRIPTION
Height 10 in (25 cm). The simple root system of this plant produces slightly hairy stems of typical trifoil leaves. The thin, firm stems bear dense, oval, reddish-purple flower heads rising from purple-tinged bracts. There is a profusion of these aromatic and pleasantly flavored flowers.

CULTIVATION
Red clover is a short-lived perennial. Sow the seed in drills in a light, sandy soil. This plant prefers a position with full sun. It is usually grown in meadows, as it is used as cattle feed.

HARVESTING
Pick the flowers when they are fully grown. Dry them rapidly to retain the medicinal properties.

MEDICINAL USES
See page 145

Trigonella foenum-graecum

FENUGREEK

ORIGIN
Mediterranean area

DESCRIPTION
Height 12–24 in (30–60 cm). It has a taproot which produces an erect, round, light green stem. Leaves are divided into three slightly serrated ovals with downy surfaces. Pea-like, creamy white flowers mature into long, narrow, curved pods, each containing about 16 seeds. Fenugreek seeds are light brown, with a furrow causing an uneven division.

CULTIVATION
Fenugreek is an annual herb which is grown from seed sown in a sheltered, warm position in good, well-drained,

NASTURTIUM

double trumpet-shaped flowers range from creamy yellow and orange to deep red. The flowers have a single nectar-bearing spur at the back. The seeds are large and are formed in three grooved sections. There are also the compact dwarf varieties, as well as the 'Whirlybird' hybrids (where available), which have spurless flowers facing upward and a more restrained growth habit. Another fairly compact variety is the perennial 'Alaska,' with leaves which are heavily marbled with cream and with some of the leaves being pre-dominantly cream.

CULTIVATION

Nasturtiums are usually annual, though some perennial varieties are available. The perennials are usually propagated from cuttings or from seed. The annuals are usually grown from seed sown directly or in containers. The dwarf varieties are by far the most suitable for containers. The seed is sown in winter, but once nasturtiums have grown in a garden, they will self-sow readily. Full sun and average soil are the best conditions in which to grow them. If, however, the soil is too rich, there will be more leaves than flowers. Nasturtiums are frost sensitive.

PESTS

Slugs and snails (*see* page 88)

CULINARY USES

This plant has a strong, pepper-mustard flavor. The leaves make an interesting cream soup (see page 178), especially when garnished with flower petals. Tear the leaves and flowers for sandwiches. In a salad, tear the leaves, but leave the flowers whole. A smallish quantity of finely shredded leaves may also be added to a herb butter or cheese dip. Use the dip or butter immediately, as the flavor

COLTSFOOT

tends to become bitter when it is stored. A few of the pulverized green seeds of nasturtium add piquancy to mayonnaise or salad dressings. Young green seeds and buds can be pickled for use as a caper substitute (*see* page 192). Flowers served with a dollop of cottage cheese in the center make a quick, colorful party snack. The stems, leaves, flowers and seeds are used to make nasturtium vinegar (*see* page 104).

MEDICINAL USES

See page 146

SIMPLE REMEDY

As nasturtium leaves are a natural anti-biotic, they may be used to cure a sore throat. Chew three or four leaves, then another two or three an hour later and repeat if necessary. Do not overdo this treatment. Small children will find the taste of the leaves too strong to chew on

their own, so offer them leaves on a cracker or thin slice of bread and butter instead. This is, however, not quite as effective.

OTHER USES

Allow nasturtiums to grow around fruit trees, as they will help to keep the fruit trees healthy. Dry the flowers face downward and use them for color in potpourri. A bowl of cut flowers will brighten any room. To keep the arrangement simple, arrange the nasturtium flowers with a few sprigs of their own foliage.

Tussilago farfara

COLTSFOOT

ORIGIN

Europe, northern and western Asia and North Africa

DESCRIPTION

Height 6–12 in (15–30 cm). A pale, spreading root produces many stems covered with white hairs and reddish bracts terminating in com-pact, yellow, daisy-like flowers. When flower stems have died back, a rosette of leaves will appear. These leaves are heavily veined, hoof-shaped, toothed and dark green with gray undersides.

CULTIVATION

Coltsfoot is a perennial propagated by taking root cuttings in spring and autumn or by root division in autumn. Seed may be sown in spring. Coltsfoot will grow in any good garden soil and it requires a sunny position.

HARVESTING

Cut the mature leaves as required for drying and cut the flowers when they are fully open. Lift the roots of the mature plants in autumn.

MEDICINAL USES

See page 146

SLIPPERY ELM

Ulmus rubra (= Ulmus fulva)

SLIPPERY ELM

ORIGIN
North America

HARVESTING
As this tree has been known to suffer from 'Dutch Elm' disease, it would be best to locate a reputable source from which to purchase your requirements.

MEDICINAL USES
It is an excellent remedy for the gastro-intestinal tract. It also soothes the mucous membranes. It is nourishing for convalescents. Externally it may be used as a poultice for burns, ulcers and boils.

Urtica dioica

STINGING NETTLE

ORIGIN
Europe and Great Britain

DESCRIPTION
Height 1 m (3 ft). A matted network of spreading roots produces stiff, upright stems. The heart-shaped dark green leaves are toothed and tapered to a point. The flowers on the female plant are in the form of green catkins that appear from early summer to autumn. The downy leaves and stems of the plant are covered with tiny sacs of acid which will cause blistering of the skin. To soothe the irritated skin, dab the affected area with nettle juice, dock leaves (sorrel) or bulbine.

CULTIVATION
Stinging nettle is a perennial which is propagated by root division in spring or by cuttings which can be rooted in water. It prefers dampish soil in semi-shade. Cut the flowering heads and mature stalks down to ground level growth. Lift plants every three years, plant out the most robust growth, and use the rest in compost. Gloves and long sleeves are needed when working with stinging nettles. The less robust annual variety, *U. urens*, which makes its appearance in many gardens, may be used in the same way as the perennial variety.

PESTS
While I was working in my garden recently, I noticed the caterpillar of the citrus butterfly feeding on the nettle. As there is no shortage of this herb, I left the caterpillar there, because the butterflies are beautiful and they have their place in the natural cycle.

CULINARY USES
Cut the young tips of stinging nettle before the flower tassels appear and the texture of the leaves becomes gritty. Nettle may be cooked gently and eaten as a vegetable. It may also be made into a delicious creamy nettle soup or cooked in the same way as spinach and served topped with a poached egg. The heat of cooking renders the stinging acid in leaves and stems harmless.

MEDICINAL USES
See page 146

SIMPLE REMEDY
If drying nettle for tea, cut mature stems before the flowers appear. Drink one cup of nettle tea twice a day to alleviate the misery of pollen- or dust-induced hay fever. To make the tea, pour 250 ml (8 fl oz) boiling water over 5 ml (1 tsp) crushed, dried nettle leaves or six large fresh leaves. Allow the tea to stand for approximately 5 minutes. Strain the tea and add a little honey and lemon if desired. Dried nettle tea is available at some chemists and health shops.

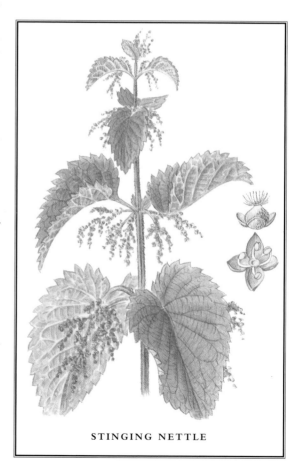

STINGING NETTLE

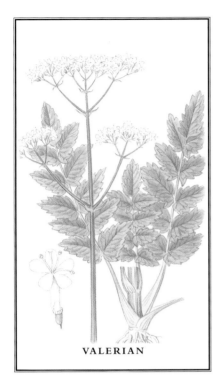

VALERIAN

HEALTH AND COSMETIC USES

Use young leaves to make an astringent facial steam. As a hair rinse, pour 2 parts of boiling water over 1 part of chopped nettle. Allow to cool, strain and keep in the refrigerator until required.

OTHER USES

It is the best herbal compost activator.

Valeriana officinalis

VALERIAN

ORIGIN

Europe and North Asia

DESCRIPTION

Height 60 cm – 1.5 m (2–5 ft) when the plant is in flower. Valerian has a rhizome with many fibrous roots. This rhizome produces several shoots. The toothed, lanceolate leaves grow in pairs, and these leaves become smaller as the flowering stems grow. These round, deeply grooved stems are topped with clusters of pale pink flowers.
NB This plant (Valeriana officinalis) *is*

not to be confused with red valerian or false valerian (Centranthus ruber), *which is a totally different plant.*

CULTIVATION

Valerian is a perennial plant. Because the germination of the seed may be erratic, it is best propagated by root division in spring. Plants tend to die back in winter. Valerian prefers a rich, moist, well-composted soil, either in full sun or else in dappled shade in regions with a hot climate. Keep the roots cool with a good mulch.

HARVESTING

Cut the flowers in spring and summer to improve root development. Lift roots from the end of the second year.

MEDICINAL USES

See page 147

HEALTH AND COSMETIC USES

Add the root of valerian to your bath water for a calming, soothing bath.

OTHER USES

It makes a decorative cut flower. The root of valerian may also be used as rat bait.

Verbascum thapsus

MULLEIN

ORIGIN

Europe, eastern Asia and western China

DESCRIPTION

Height 2 m (6½ ft). The large, grey-white, pointed, soft, ovate, woolly leaves grow in the form of a rosette. After about a year, a pithy, downy, upright stalk will grow rapidly from this nest of foliage. This stem has alternate leaves which are slightly

woolly-stemmed. These leaves grow progressively smaller. In turn, the stem then grows into a long spike of closely packed, simple, five-petalled, cup-shaped, bright yellow flowers. The secondary flower spikes will then make their appearance from the lower part of the plant's main stem.

CULTIVATION

Mullein is a biennial plant which requires space in a very well-drained, sheltered, sunny position. It grows very well in indifferent soil. It is a good idea to stake the plants if this seems to be necessary, before the growth becomes too dense. Mullein is usually propagated by sowing the fine seed either in trays or *in situ*. It usually self-sows freely and it will germinate easily if the soil is fairly loose. Cut back the stems as soon as they finish flowering.

MULLEIN

VERVAIN

HARVESTING

Pick the flowers as required. In some climates, flowers close during the heat of the day. When drying, take care not to bruise petals. Place face down on paper or racks and dry away from light to preserve color and medicinal properties.

CULINARY USES

Flowers are suitable for use as a garnish.

MEDICINAL USES

See page 147

SIMPLE REMEDY

For a sore throat or phlegmy cough, make a tea with a few flowers, sufficient to make a good yellow liquid. Strain through muslin to remove fine hairs that might adhere to the flowers. The tea may also be used as a gargle.

OTHER USES

This tea also makes a very good rinse for fair hair. Use mullein in potpourri for color and perfume. Slip leaves into shoes or slippers to keep the feet warm and also to help ward off chilblains.

N.B. Although the leaves of mullein are also sometimes used in medicinal teas, they should not be taken in excess, as they are mildly toxic to humans.

Verbena officinalis

VERVAIN

ORIGIN

Britain, Europe, North Africa and Asia

DESCRIPTION

Height 24 in (60 cm). A woody root with a mass of smaller rootlets produces several tough, square stems, branching into pairs of deeply indented, spear-shaped, slightly hairy bright green leaves. The dainty, five-lobed mauve flowers appear on the slender spikes.

CULTIVATION

Vervain is a perennial plant which may be grown from seed, but germination is usually somewhat erratic. It does sometimes self-sow. It is, however, much easier to grow from cuttings or by root division in spring. It is not at all fussy about soil conditions, but it does seem to grow better in rich, well-drained soil in a sunny position. This herb will also take partial shade.

HARVESTING

Cut the leaves as they are required. For drying, cut the whole plant when in flower and hang to dry.

MEDICINAL USES

Use small quantities of flowers and leaves to make a calmative tea.

Viola odorata

SWEET VIOLET

ORIGIN

Europe and Britain

DESCRIPTION

Height 4–6 in (10–15 cm). Rhizomes with tough, hairy roots produce rooting runners. The slender, firm stalks bear glossy, dark green heart-shaped leaves. The stems are curved at the flowering heads. The five-petaled flowers have short, fleshy spurs. There are also double varieties available. The flowers are usually a deep purple color. Other colors can range from white to pink and a very soft blue.

CULTIVATION

Violet is a perennial. Propagate it with leafy root crowns taken from runners. Plant these firmly in the soil, leaving a portion of the crown above the ground. Lift and divide every second year after flowering. Violets require a rich, moist, slightly acid soil and will grow in semi-shade as well as full sun. Shelter them

SWEET VIOLET

from the midday sun in very hot areas. If they are growing in the shade, remove some of the foliage in order to increase flowering. Violets are suitable plants for growing in containers.

CULINARY USES

Crystallize the fragrant violet flowers (*see* page 104), or else use them fresh to decorate cakes and desserts. Scatter a few violet flowers in summer beverages as well as in salads. To make very bland, pale soups look more interesting as well as colorful, stir in a few violet flowers just before serving.

SIMPLE REMEDY

For a calmative, a mild laxative or a remedy to relieve a tension headache, pick about five leaves and four violet flowers and cover them with about 8 oz (250 ml) of boiling water to make a tea. Leave the tea to infuse for approximately 5 minutes.

OTHER USES

It makes a very pretty ground cover or edging plant. For potpourri, dry the flowers face down on a rack.

CHASTE TREE

Vitex agnus-castus

CHASTE TREE

ORIGIN

Mediterranean coastal area and Western Asia

DESCRIPTION

Height can reach 20 ft (6 m). The chaste tree is a shrublike tree which bears many spreading branches. The younger shoots of these branches are covered in quite a thick down. The foliage of the chaste tree takes the form of stalked leaflets. These leaflets are long, lanceolate and dark green and they have serrated edges. They are smooth on the top and rather downy on the undersides. The slender, erect racemes carry whorls of scented pink or lilac flowers. When these flowers die, they leave small, aromatic, black or dark purple berries which are encased in green calyxes.

CULTIVATION

This plant is a deciduous tree. It may be propagated by layering in autumn or from cuttings which are taken in spring. The seed may also be sown in spring. It requires a sheltered position in full sun and a well-drained, acid soil. The natural habitat of the chaste tree is a dry, hot, coastal area.

HARVESTING

Harvest the berries of this plant when they are completely mature.

MEDICINAL USES

See page 147

Zingiber officinale

GINGER

ORIGIN

Southeast India and China

DESCRIPTION

Height 3 ft (1 m). The pale, knobbly, pungent rhizomes of ginger grow in clusters. The plant itself has tall,

GINGER

leafy, reed-like stems. The stems bear leaves which are lanceolate in shape and a bright green in color. The slender flower stems, which are approximately 10 in (25 cm) in length, bear a number of perfumed, cream-colored, orchid-like blossoms.

CULTIVATION

Ginger is a perennial plant which may be propagated from cuttings of shooting rootstock. Grow ginger in a very light, moist soil and also in a hot, sheltered position, remembering that this plant is really best suited to the more tropical and subtropical climates.

HARVESTING

The rhizomes are lifted about six to twelve months after planting. When ginger is grown commercially, the crop is usually plowed up.

CULINARY USES

The root can be used either fresh or dried and powdered. It is used in both sweet and savory dishes.

MEDICINAL USES

See page 147

III

CREATING A
HERB GARDEN

"You haven't lived if you have not lain flat

on your middle on a thyme lawn."

CREATING AN
HERB GARDEN

GROWING HERBS CAN GIVE ENDLESS PLEASURE AND MAKE FOR A BETTER WAY OF LIFE, WHETHER YOU HAVE A LARGE GARDEN, LIVE IN A TOWNHOUSE OR HAVE AN APARTMENT WITH ONLY A WINDOWSILL OR BALCONY. THE ADAPTABILITY OF HERBS ENABLES THEM TO BE GROWN IN AN INFORMAL OR FORMAL GARDEN, A VEGETABLE PLOT, IN CONTAINERS OR AMONG OTHER PLANTS IN A BED OR SHRUBBERY.

SITE CHOICE AND SOIL PREPARATION

Many factors have an influence on the choice of position for growing herbs. Most herbs prefer a sunny, well-drained place, whereas there are a few that need more selective growing conditions (*see* individual cultivation notes in Chapter 2). For plants that cannot take hot sun, take note of the sun's movement and grow them where they will be shaded by taller plants. Protection from prevailing winds is important. A high, solid wall is not advisable, as the wind can swoop over and down the wall, damaging other parts of the garden. Gaps in the brickwork can, however, overcome this problem. Shrubby herbs such as rosemary, myrtles, tall lavenders, pelargoniums and bay make good windbreaks. In areas where frost occurs, herbs should be planted in a sheltered corner of the garden, where they are less likely to be exposed to frost.

As sandy soil is often leeched of goodness, work in plenty of well-rotted manure and compost for nourishment and water retention. To make clay friable, work in sand, compost and well-rotted manure. Alkaline soil will also benefit from the addition of compost and well-rotted manure.

If the only site available tends to become waterlogged, it would be advisable to make a drainage area at the lowest point of the bed. Dig a trench 3 ft (1 m) long and 12 in (30 cm) wide. Toss in stones and/or broken bricks to half the depth, then fill in with soil. Alternatively, you could make a raised bed (*see* page 94).

To prepare the planting area, dig down one spade's depth, removing old roots, fibrous matter and weeds. Avoid chemical fertilisers — they promote lush growth, but usually at the expense of fragrance and flavor. Instead, fork in compost, well-rotted manure, hoof-and-horn meal, bone meal (note that bone meal and hoof-and-horn are made of different elements) and milled seaweed. In coastal areas where harvesting of seaweed is not restricted, collect it, chop and add to the compost heap — it is a good source of trace elements. When planting roses, dig holes 20 in square x 20 in deep (50 cm square x 50 cm deep). Trees need bigger holes: 30 in square x 30 in deep (75 cm square x 75 cm) deep. Work in compost, well-rotted manure and two handfuls each of hoof-and-horn meal, bone meal and superphosphate (superphosphate is an inorganic fertilizer). Water the hole well before planting.

As most herbs prefer an alkaline soil, the addition of agricultural lime (dolomite) may be needed. For the few herbs requiring an acid soil, work in a handful of sulfur dust (vine dusting powder) for each plant. Pine needles and oak leaves also increase soil acidity. If you are not sure of the pH of the soil, soil testing kits are obtainable at garden centers. (The pH reading of an alkaline soil is above 7.0 and the pH reading of an acid soil is below 7.0.) Rake to level the surface and also to remove any remaining rough material. After watering well, rake again to even the

to even the surface. The level of sandy beds should be kept 15 cm (6 in) lower than surrounding paths or grass to allow for better water retention. After planting, apply a layer of compost. Earthworms will take it to the roots, thus aerating the soil and eliminating the need for further digging.

For ease of watering your herbs, install a standpipe in your garden and make sure the tap and hose are nearby.

To simplify harvesting, make paths so that the centre of the bed can be reached from either side. Alternatively, beds should be no wider than an arm's length. The most attractive paths are made of weathered bricks, stepping stones or grass. Paths should be wide enough to manoeuvre a wheelbarrow comfortably. A bird bath and a sundial add interest to a herb garden. If possible, place a seat in a sheltered corner and take time to sit and enjoy your garden. Water in any form is always welcome in a garden and if you are not fortunate enough to have a stream running through your property, consider buying one of the easily installed water reticulation systems available at garden centres, shops and nurseries. Beautifully shaped flow bowls, when properly placed, allow for a gentle flow of water through a garden. Otherwise look for the Japanese bamboo water pipes that allow water to flow intermittently, and of course there is nearly always room to make a pond, even a very small one.

COMPOST

Compost is one of nature's gifts to gardeners, because it is the life-sustaining material of the earth. By making our own compost, we are returning to the soil some of that which we have taken out. If you also participate in a neighbourhood recycling scheme, there will be very little for you to put out for the rubbish collector.

Material which is suitable for making compost ranges from crumpled, wet newspaper, cardboard, egg cartons, wine-bottle sleeves made from repulped paper, egg shells and dead floral arrangements to unseeded weeds, prunings cut into smaller pieces, leaves, grass cuttings and fruit and vegetable peelings. Potato peelings are only included if they are free from eelworm (nematode). Fresh manure, especially poultry manure or that from a pigeon loft, gives added nutriment and also acts as a compost activator, thereby speeding up the process of decomposition. Other good activating agents are plants such as yarrow, nettle, dandelion, tansy or comfrey. It is not advisable when assembling a

ABOVE **PLACE COARSE MATERIAL SUCH AS TWIGS AT THE BASE OF THE COMPOST HEAP.**

OPPOSITE **A LAWN OF THYME AND CHAMOMILE IS LOVELY TO LOOK AT AND WONDERFULLY FRAGRANT.**

compost heap to add lime when using manure, as they have an adverse effect on each other. To test if a compost heap is working, insert an iron rod into the center of the heap after a week and withdraw it after about 5 minutes, when it should be quite hot to the touch. If not, loosen the heap to introduce more air. In the more temperate climates, compost does not heat up quite as quickly. It is therefore best to chop the material very finely.

There are several methods of making your own compost. The three-compartment method is tidy and is the most satisfactory method for a large garden. For a smaller garden either a compost heap, the tumbler method or a commercial compost-maker (*see* page 83) are alternatives you may wish to consider, depending on the available space and practicability.

THREE-COMPARTMENT METHOD
Make three adjoining compartments from wire, wooden slats or concrete slabs, leaving them open at the top and front. There should be gaps in the sides to allow for air circulation. For ease of turning the compost, a solid base is preferable, such as a cement slab or packed clay ground. Store all the material except the manure in Bin 1. When there is sufficient material, make a bed of small twigs in Bin 2, then layer the contents of Bin 1 with manure on top of this area. If there is any good soil available, spread a little between the layers. (I find that enough soil remains on the roots of weeds and dead plants.) Take care to spread the grass cuttings evenly, otherwise they tend to become rather slimy. Moisten each layer and compact the material lightly.

Keep damp but not soggy. Cover the compost with a sheet of plastic during heavy rain because excess water will stop the natural heating action which is necessary for break- down. After four weeks, or when the material begins to darken, fork the contents of Bin 2 into Bin 3, spreading evenly and damping down if necessary. This could take anywhere from four weeks to several months, depending upon the air temperature, the mix of materials and how finely they were chopped. Once the compost has a good, dark color, and the bulk of the contents are no longer indi- vidually recognisable, it should be ready and is best used within the next two or three months. Any remaining coarse material is then tossed back into Bin 2. Now the material which has been collecting in Bin 1 is layered in Bin 2 and the whole cycle is then repeated.

COMPOST HEAP
Place coarse material, such as twigs, at the base of the heap and layer all the material with any manure that is available. Damp down and cover with long grass or straw. Turn and restack every six weeks until ready.

TUMBLER METHOD
Cut an opening measuring about 20 x 20 in (50 x 50 cm) in the middle of a 45-gallon (200-liter) drum. Hinge one edge and, on the opposite side, weld a closure (like a hasp and staple) to form a flap that can be opened. Make an opening at each end of the drum and pass a strong rod through these openings so that the drum can be rotated. Mount the "tumbler" so that a wheelbarrow can be pushed underneath it. As plant material becomes available, put it into the drum through the hatch, together with the odd handful of manure. Sprinkle with water if necessary. Turn drum a few times after each addition. The inside heat (and that outside if the air is warm) should produce compost fairly quickly, but it will take longer in winter. Push a wheelbarrow under the drum, open the hatch and scrape out compost, returning to the drum material which has not yet decomposed.

COMMERCIAL COMPOST-MAKER
This is suitable for a small garden and can be obtained from garden centers or nurseries.

Whichever method you use when making compost, remember to add an activating agent (*see* page 80) to the plant material. (A natural activator is "recycled" beer, i.e. urine!) Well-made compost should not smell or attract flies. When you turn the compost, look for large, gray maggots. Destroy them immediately, as they will turn into big, hard, black-and-yellow beetles which feed on roses and dahlias.

SOWING, PROPAGATION AND PLANTING

The most usual methods of propagating herbs are growing from seed, taking heel or tip cuttings, layering, dividing roots or growing from suckers. To establish which method best suits a particular herb, refer to the cultivation entries under the individual herbs in Chapter 2.

GROWING FROM SEED
This needs care and patience as some herbs, such as parsley, take up to three weeks to germinate. The viability of seed varies. Some seed, like that of basil, keeps indefinitely, while other seed, such as angelica, needs to be sown as soon as it is ripe. If this is not practical, seeds may be kept in a sealed container in the freezer or in a dry, dark place.

The best sowing medium is a fine soil of which half should consist of sand. As a sandy soil is not very high in nutrients, the seeds grow strong roots in search of food.

SOWING IN TRAYS
Water soil in trays before sowing. For easier distribution of very fine seed, mix with a little dry soil and then sow. Fine seed should only be covered with a light dusting of soil. Larger seeds should be covered with soil to twice their thickness. With a flat piece of wood, press soil down firmly. Make sure the trays are level and the soil is evenly spread. Cover trays with a single sheet of newspaper and a piece of glass. Check each morning and, as soon as seeds have germinated, remove newspaper and cover seedlings with glass only (this helps to retain the moisture). Never allow the trays to dry out. Use a fine mist spray to water when necessary.

As seedlings develop, remove glass to allow in more air and light. When they are at the four- to six-leaf stage, lift carefully (an old kitchen fork is useful), separate and plant in deeper trays or small pots with good soil. Firm in gently and water with a fine spray, or dip a sponge in water and squeeze around the seedlings. Harden plants off gradually by moving them into the sunlight as they grow. Different plants do not take the same length of time to harden off. When they look strong and healthy, they are ready to be planted out.

SOWING DIRECTLY

Level the ground by raking and at the same time removing coarse material. Water the ground, then rake again if the wet ground has any uneven patches. Scatter seed or make long grooves; the latter allow for even sowing and prevent over-crowding of seedlings. Grooves (drills) are better for larger seeds. Most seeds sown directly must be protected from the elements in any way that is practical. Use a fine shadecloth, such as muslin or green gauze, anchored with bricks. As seedlings grow taller, the shadecloth is raised by increasing the height of the brick piles. A more elaborate method is to use wooden frames and different gauges of shadecloth.

GROWING FROM CUTTINGS

To propagate you will require:

✠ sharp pruning shears or a knife
✠ a general-purpose hormone rooting powder
✠ a tray or pot of coarse sand
✠ a piece of thin cane or a knitting needle
✠ a watering can with a fine rose

The average length of a tip or heel cutting is 4 in (10 cm). Strip all the leaves from the lower stem and, if there is any bud formation, nip this out. Dip the cuttings in water, shake, dip the ends into rooting powder and tap off the excess powder. In the tray or pot, make holes in the sand with the cane or knitting needle and plant the cuttings in the holes. The closer together they are, the better the growth. If you only have a few cuttings, place them around the edge of the pot, not in the center. Firm down and water. Keep in a warm, shady place. After about five to six weeks, gently lift a few of the cuttings. If they have developed a root system, transplant them into deeper trays, pots or bags of good soil. Firm down the soil and water the plants. Move them out into the sunshine gradually to harden them off and let them become sturdy before planting them out in the garden.

RIGHT *BUXUS* HEDGING IS USED TO SEPARATE THE DIFFERENT VARIETIES OF SAGE AND SANTOLINA IN THIS FORMAL ARRANGE-MENT OF HERBS, ALSO CALLED A PARTERRE.

GROWING BY ROOT DIVISION

Where indicated (*see* individual herbs in Chapter 2), lift the plants either in spring or in autumn. Shake off the soil and prise apart or cut through the root system with pruning shears. Each section should have both roots and foliage. Remove any old wood and dead leaves. Plant the sections in good soil, either directly in the ground or in pots or bags.

GROWING BY LAYERING

For this method you will require:

✠ a sharp knife

✠ hormone rooting powder

✠ strong wire hoops or half-bricks

Low-growing flexible branches are best for this method. Take the branch and make a small cut (not all the way through the branch) about 12 in (30 cm) from the tip or wherever practical. Dust cut with rooting powder. Gently bend the branch (while still attached to the mother plant) and bury the cut section, keeping the tip well exposed. Anchor the branch with wire loops or bricks. Keep well watered. After a few months a root system should develop. Sever the new plant from the mother plant and leave it for a week to recover from the shock. Lift and plant out.

GROWING FROM SUCKERS

When a sucker shows above the ground near a mature plant, expose the connecting root and cut through it. Leave it in position, cover with soil and water well. Leave it for at least a week by which time the sucker, which already has its own root system, should have recovered sufficiently to be lifted and potted or bagged in good soil. When the sturdy new growth appears, move it out into the garden.

PESTS AND DISEASES

Natural methods of controlling pests are a must, because the ecological cycle must not be broken. Managing a garden this way means that no insect or bug is completely eliminated and thus the cycle is kept intact. All creatures, from the smallest to the largest, are part of the chain. Fortunately herbs are susceptible to few pests and diseases, but watch out for:

LEFT **A BEAUTIFUL HERB GARDEN WITH ROSE TOPIARIES, SITUATED AT ALDERLEY GRANGE, GLOUCESTERSHIRE.**

ANTS

Mix 1 tsp (5 ml) borax and 4 tsp (20 ml) sugar with 8 oz (250 ml) warm water. Pour this mixture into saucers, jam jar lids or any other shallow receptacles. Place them in strategic positions around the house. Ants will drink it and then go back to their nests to die. Outdoors, trace them to their nests. Use the borax mixture to pour down or spray over nests.

APHIDS (GREENFLY, BLACKFLY)

These pests can be black, gray-pink, green or orange. They form a cluster near tips of plants and on undersides of mature leaves, suck the sap of plants and cause wilting. Spray plants with a soapy water solution every morning to suffocate the aphids. It is very important that the breeding cycle be broken, so you should continue spraying daily with the soapy water solution until no more aphids appear — this usually takes about three or four sprayings.

CATERPILLARS

Pick them off by hand. Shake plants such as mint and lemon balm to dislodge small green caterpillars, otherwise use wormwood spray or general insect spray (*see* page 88).

COTTONY CUSHION SCALE (AUSTRALIAN BUG)

These soft-scale pests occur in some countries, particularly in the southern hemisphere. They live off the sap of growing stems and may also be found on the undersides of mature leaves and in the joints of woody stems. They cluster in a dirty white, woolly mass of ridged bodies with orangey-brown heads. Brush off the "bugs" with an old toothbrush dipped in a mixture of half methylated spirits and half water, or use one of the general garden sprays (*see* page 88).

MILDEW

Mildew is a fungal disease which manifests itself as a grayish, downy deposit on the leaves. Sooty mildew looks like its name implies — a sooty covering on stems and the underside of foliage. Plants which do not have adequate sunshine or air circulation are most often affected. Spray the affected plants with sulfur dust (vine dusting powder) early in the morning, when the foliage is still slightly moist from the dew, or try any one of the general garden sprays (*see* page 88). Badly infected foliage should be cut out and destroyed.

RED SPIDER MITE

This is not a spider, but rather a mite which lives on the undersides of leaves and thrives in hot, dry conditions. As a preventative, spray undersides of leaves of susceptible plants with water every day (*see* individual herbs in Chapter 2). If, however, red spider does occur, dust the undersides of the leaves with sulfur (vine dusting powder).

RUST

Bright orange markings appear on the foliage of herbs such as mint and chives. If new stock is available, remove and destroy old plants and plant new ones in a different position. Otherwise, spray with a mild commercial copper spray after all the foliage has been cut down near to ground level and compost applied as a mulch. Destroy all affected foliage.

SCALE

Scale manifests itself as hard brown ovals which appear on the undersides of leaves or on woody stems. Scale attracts ants, so deal with them first (*see* page 87). If the plant is not too big, remove scale by brushing with an old toothbrush dipped in a mixture of half water to half methylated spirits. A mature tree will need to be treated by spraying, with horticultural oil, to be repeated after ten days. (This oil is non-toxic. It acts by covering scale with a suffocating film of oil.)

SLUGS AND SNAILS

There are natural ways of ridding the garden of these pests. If cabbage leaves are left face down overnight, slugs and snails will be waiting there to be disposed of the next morning. Hollowed halves of citrus fruit containing beer and placed in the garden are most effective traps, especially for slugs. Walk round the garden in the evening or early morning with half a bucket of strong lime or salt water. Drop snails into this to kill them. To protect seedlings, dip coarse string in creosote and lay it on the ground around the plants. Slugs and snails will not cross the string. Tobacco dust, sprinkled sparingly, is also sometimes used as a deterrent. If enough are available, crushed egg shells also work. Some garden snakes also consume these pests.

STINKBUGS (TIP WILTERS)

They are hard-backed gray bugs which exude a stinking fluid when touched. The younger bugs are brown. They cause extensive tip-wilting. A most effective way of dealing with them is to attach a firm piece of wood, about 20 in (50 cm) long, to an empty soup can with a nail. Pour a little paraffin into the can and slip it underneath the bug, then knock it into the paraffin in the can with another length of wood. This works quite well, as stinkbugs have a tendency to drop when disturbed. Lizards will eat them if they come into contact with them on the ground.

HOME BREWS TO KEEP HERBS HEALTHY

For these home brews to be really effective, they should be applied frequently, as the breeding cycles of the pests need to be broken. Keep an eye on the weather, as a shower of rain within 24 hours of spraying will nullify all your efforts. If you have a small garden, make up smaller quantities, but keep to the same proportions. These sprays may be used on plants which are to be used for culinary purposes. They should, however, be washed before they are eaten, because although the sprays are non-toxic, the soapy taste is unpleasant.

Nowadays, many garden centers stock proprietary brands of natural garden remedies which are both non-toxic and environment friendly.

GENERAL INSECT SPRAY

Crush three unpeeled heads garlic and 3 oz (90 ml) liquid paraffin. Place in a bowl, cover and leave to stand for 24 hours. Melt 1 TBS (15 ml) grated, oil-based soap in 17 oz (500 ml) hot water. Blend the garlic mixture with the soap mixture. When cooled, strain into a glass jar or bottle and seal. Keep it in the refrigerator. To use, dilute about 4 tsp (20 ml) of this solution in 4 pints (2 liters) of cold water. Spray every two weeks.

WORMWOOD SPRAY

Simmer 8 oz (225 g) wormwood leaves in 3½ pints (2 liters) water for half an hour. Stir, strain and leave to cool. Dissolve 1 tsp (5 ml) soap flakes in 17 oz (500 ml) hot water. Combine this with the wormwood water and spray plants frequently at the height of the caterpillar season.

RED PEPPER SPRAY

Chop an unpeeled onion and a head of garlic. Simmer the onion and garlic with 1 TBS (15 ml) cayenne pepper in about 2¾ pints (1.5 liters) water for 20 minutes. Cool the mixture, pour into a jar, seal, stand for six weeks and strain into bottles.

To use, mix 1 TBS (15 ml) of this mixture with 1¼ pints (750 ml) water. Add a little soap solution. Use as a general pest spray. It is effective against caterpillars.

COMFREY FOLIAR FEED
Before comfrey flowers, cut the leaves and pack them into an old bucket or similar container with holes in the bottom. Place a plate or a can lid on top and weigh it down with half a brick. Put a plastic plant pot in an old basin and stand the bucket on the pot. After three weeks there should be a quantity of brown fluid in the basin. Strain this and then bottle it.

Spray plants in the proportion of 1 TBS (15 ml) comfrey liquid to 1¾ pints (1 liter) water and a few drops of liquid detergent. (Put the remaining contents of the bucket on the compost heap.)

There are many other home brews you could make yourself. Most of them are improved with the addition of a little dissolved soap or a liquid detergent. This ingredient acts as a wetting agent which effectively enables the spray to stick to the foliage.

RIGHT *BUXUS* CAN BE USED FOR TOPIARIES AS WELL AS HEDGING. HERE IT IS COMBINED WITH SAGE TO ENHANCE AN ORDINARY PATHWAY.

CULINARY HERB GARDENS

For obvious reasons, it is desirable to have a culinary herb garden as near to the kitchen as possible. If this is not feasible in your case, you could plant a few of your favorite herbs in containers outside the door.

Where a backdrop is needed for the garden, plant one or more bay, elderberry and/or maidenhair trees. Bay, elderberry and myrtle can be pruned to form a tall hedge. Lemon trees also have their place in this kind of garden, especially if it is sheltered — plant one tree as the centerpiece or plant a row to form a backdrop. A stunning effect can be achieved by underplanting a group of lemon trees with lavender. If the garden is large enough, a few other fruit trees could also be introduced. Better still, if you have a walled garden, espalier the trees (train them to grow against the wall). When you plan to plant a windbreak or a garden division, you could use plants such as Dutch lavender, myrtle or common rosemary (the pink variety 'Majorca Pink,' where available, has a dense, upright growth which is ideal for this purpose).

For a semiformal look, grow low hedges for edging or dividing beds — use dwarf lavender, common origanum, winter savory or sweet marjoram. Low-growing hedges will need to be clipped twice a year and in between errant shoots will have to be cut back from time to time. Other hedging is pruned hard once a year.

When laying paths, make sure the beds will be accessible in all weather conditions. Consider having non-slip surfaces, as you may need to dash out in the pouring rain to collect herbs while you are busy preparing food.

For informal plantings, lay stepping stones so that herbs can be reached without damage to surrounding growth. Do not use rounds of wood, as they can become slippery. Depending on your own taste and that of your family, plant larger areas of the herbs most often used, but do not neglect the more unusual. Plant these in smaller quantities until you acquire a liking for them. Another good way of

---

CULINARY HERBS

PERENNIALS, TALL	BORAGE	ANNUALS, LOW-GROWING
BASIL	CELERY	BASIL
FENNEL (common)	CHICORY	CALENDULA AND CHERVIL
LAVENDER	CORIANDER	DILL (dwarf)
LEMON VERBENA	DILL	LETTUCE AND NASTURTIUM
PINEAPPLE SAGE	GARLIC	PARSLEY (flat-leafed)
ROSEMARY	ONIONS	SUMMER SAVORY
	ROCKET	
ANNUALS, TALL		EDGINGS AND GROUND COVERS
FLORENTINE FENNEL	BIENNIALS, MEDIUM HEIGHT	BASIL (dwarf)
	CARAWAY	FRENCH SORREL
PERENNIALS, MEDIUM HEIGHT		CHAMOMILE
ANGELICA	PERENNIALS, LOW-GROWING	MARJORAM (creeping and pot)
BERGAMOT	CHIVES	PARSLEY (curly)
LAVENDER	GARLIC CHIVES	THYME VARIETIES
LOVAGE (dies back)	FRENCH SORREL	WINTER SAVORY (dwarf)
MARJORAM AND SAGE	LAND CRESS	
	LEMON BALM	OTHER
ANNUALS, MEDIUM HEIGHT	MINT	ANNUAL NASTURTIUMS — climbers
ANISEED	THYME VARIETIES	(among trees)
BASIL VARIETIES	WINTER SAVORY	RASPBERRIES (in the background)

gardening with herbs would be along the lines of a French potager, where herbs are grown in neat lines side by side with vegetables. If this suits you, plant some vegetables with foliage color variations for eye appeal, such as Swiss chard with red veining, purple broccoli and chicory, red cabbage, lettuces, eggplant and peppers (red, orange, yellow and green). If you do not want vegetables in the garden, bear in mind the many variations of foliage, texture and shape as well as the lovely flower colors of herbs, and so make full use of them to make an attractive and practical garden.

BELOW **COMBINING HERBS AND VEGETABLES IN THE GARDEN, ESPECIALLY THE KITCHEN GARDEN, CAN BE A VERY GOOD IDEA. BESIDES BEING USEFUL, IT IS ALSO DECORATIVE.**

FRAGRANT HERB GARDENS

All herb gardens are fragrant, but for a heady concentration, plant only herbs with a high volatile oil content (*see* table below) and surround them with hedges of lavender, myrtle, rosemary or roses. To get the most pleasure out of a fragrant herb garden, there will need to be paths or stepping stones, so that herbs can be touched or brushed against for the fragrance to be enjoyed. In any but formal gardens, low, ground-hugging herbs should be allowed to grow through paths. You could leave gaps in the paving for planting chamomile, low thymes and penny-royal. If there are steps in a garden, grow these herbs under the risers and down the sides. When they are crushed underfoot, the aroma will be released. Use archways to train roses, honeysuckle or jasmine at the entrance or, if the garden is symmetrical in design, use several arches where the paths meet in the center. For an alternative centerpiece, grow a lemon tree in a container. It can be pruned to form compact growth while still producing fruit.

Heat brings out the fragrances of plants. To enjoy the fragrance even on the hottest day, make an arbor of shaped bay or elder to provide shade for a seat. A bower of jasmine, roses and/or honeysuckle would serve the same purpose. Imagine sitting, surrounded by scents, listening to the bees and, possibly, the sound of water.

HERBS FOR A FRAGRANT GARDEN

BACKGROUND

BAY (as a tree, free-growing or as a high hedge)
ELDER (as a tall shrubby tree, free-growing or as a high hedge — not suitable for a windbreak)
JUNIPER (shrublike or as a tree, depending on climatic conditions)
LEMON (in sheltered gardens)
MYRTLE (free-growing or as a high hedge)

HEDGES FOR SURROUNDING GARDEN OR AS A WINDBREAK

COLEONEMA (where available)
LAVENDER (tall)
MYRTLE
PELARGONIUM (free-growing)
ROSES (entwined and layered or clipped)

LOW HEDGES FOR DIVIDING OR SURROUNDING BEDS

BOX VARIETIES *(Buxus)*
LAVENDER (tall)
MARJORAM (common)

MARJORAM (sweet)
ROSEMARY
SANTOLINA
SOUTHERNWOOD
THYME (common)

CREEPERS

HONEYSUCKLE
JASMINE
ROSES

BIENNIALS

CLARY SAGE (center or back of bed)

BIENNIALS, TALL

EVENING PRIMROSE
LAVENDER VARIETIES
LEMON VERBENA
PELARGONIUM (rose and lemon)
ROSES
ROSEMARY

PERENNIALS, MEDIUM HEIGHT

BERGAMOT
BUCHU (in a dry, hot position)
LEMON BALM

MARJORAM
MINT
PELARGONIUM (lemon-scented 'Fingerbowl')
PEPPERMINT PELARGONIUM (shade)
PINEAPPLE SAGE
SOUTHERNWOOD
TANSY
THYME VARIETIES

ANNUALS, MEDIUM HEIGHT

BASIL VARIETIES
MEADOWSWEET (shade)

PERENNIALS, LOW-GROWING

CHAMOMILE
LAVENDER (dwarf varieties)
MARJORAM (creeping and pot)
MINT (e.g. pennyroyal)
ROSEMARY VARIETIES
SOAPWORT
THYME VARIETIES
VIOLETS

ANNUALS, LOW-GROWING

BASIL (dwarf)

CONTAINER HERB GARDENS

There are many reasons for growing herbs in containers. If the herb area is far from the house, planting frequently used culinary herbs in containers near the kitchen makes for ease of use. Patios, balconies and steps can be utilized as growing space. If the available ground is not suitable for cultivation, containers can be used to advantage, but remember when placing them under trees to keep tender plants away from the drip area, as they will take a battering in wet weather.

To create a background or soften a wall on a balcony or patio, make provision for a creeper by fixing wires to the wall or erecting a trellis. Remember to allow for the space the container will occupy. If a patio is open to a garden, part of it could be enclosed with fencing such as picket or trellis. A climbing or rambler rose, honeysuckle or a jasmine would provide cover and fragrance (use a large container). A good deciduous creeper such as hop would leave the area open to sunshine in winter. If space permits, a small water feature would be a good place to grow watercress.

Place small pots or troughs on steps or outside stairways, with suitable saucers to prevent staining by dripping water. Window boxes are also suitable for growing herbs. They must be properly secured and the supports must be strong enough to hold the filled containers. Drip collectors are even more important if window boxes are above walkways.

To grow many herbs in a small space, stack containers in pyramids in corners or around pillars. Use bricks or logs to lift planters. Plant up anything that will hold soil, as close planting and grouping will cover containers. Containers could include anything from washing machine drums and toilet tanks to old clay pipes and chimney pieces, though most people prefer a variety of treasured clay pots.

Group containers of varying shapes and sizes together for an interesting effect, but if a planter is particularly pleasing, it should stand on its own. Depending on climatic conditions, a large container, such as a half barrel, could be planted up with a bay tree to provide a focal point. Do not use too many small pots on the same level, as the result can look messy. There is an art to arranging pots, so stand back, look at the grouping from all angles and then make adjustments.

Use pebbles, broken brick, china or small stones in the bottom of a container for drainage. Place planters on tiles or bricks so that drainage holes do not become blocked. When filling containers, use a wheelbarrow, as soil can be taken up to large containers and you won't have to move them when they are full and heavy. Mix moistened garden soil with compost and add a handful each of milled seaweed, bone meal and hoof-and-horn meal to each barrow load. Do not overfill containers, as the plants have their own soil which will take space, and allowance must also be made for watering.

Consider heights and spread when grouping plants. Soften edges of containers with herbs that creep, hang or droop, such as winter savory, low-growing varieties of rosemary, creeping golden marjoram, nasturtiums, catmint, salad burnet, curly parsley and thyme.

ABOVE LEFT **LAVENDER, SAGE, BASIL AND PARSLEY ARE ALL SUITABLE HERBS TO GROW IN CONTAINERS.**
ABOVE RIGHT **A NOVEL CONTAINER IN WHICH TO CULTIVATE HERBS IS AN OLD WHEELBARROW.**

To keep containers looking attractive, grow annuals in mixed plantings with perennials so that there are no spaces left when the annuals die off. Alternatively, you could plant annuals in separate pots so that they can be removed when they are past their prime.

Hanging baskets make maximum use of space. Plastic hanging "baskets" are sold at garden centers and shops, but wire baskets with side plantings give a softer effect. Also available are attractive hanging clay and ceramic containers.

To plant up a wire basket, purchase a commercial liner or line with sphagnum moss or coir and then a sheet of strong plastic. Place some form of drip collector in the bottom of the basket. To make the job easier, perch the basket on a bucket. Half fill the basket with good potting soil, then make a few holes through the plastic and gently pull a plant (such as curly parsley, a creeping thyme or catmint) through each hole, root first, and cover with soil. Plant chives, garlic chives, dwarf dill or celery in the center and surround with plants like dwarf bush basil, opal basil, nasturtium and/or dwarf winter savory. Top up with soil, leaving space for watering. The choice of herbs is yours, but will also depend on the size of the basket. The one snag with hanging baskets is that they tend to dry out very quickly and so need extra care. If a basket should become very dry, lift down and soak in a bowl or bucket of water until soil stops bubbling. Allow to drain before rehanging. Keep the plants in good shape by constant harvesting or trimming, and feed them once every two weeks.

Another form of container gardening is a raised bed or hollow wall. If it is on a non-porous base, such as a patio, make drainage holes near the bottom of the wall or bed. To prepare a raised bed for planting, place a layer of broken brick, china or clay pot, pebbles or stones at the bottom of the cavity, then fill it with coarse sand to about a third of the depth before filling it up with good soil. Planting is exactly the same as for other containers.

Herbs in containers need extra care and attention, as they tend to dry out quickly, and they should regularly be fed with a liquid fertilizer. For the best results, try using two different formulas alternately.

The drainage holes of containers can become blocked and the plants can then be waterlogged. To remedy this, tip the container on its side and clear the holes. Place the container upright on bricks or tiles after it has drained properly.

Most herbs lend themselves to being planted in containers, provided the size is correct, but I would steer clear of large plants like elder. Only after due consideration of all factors should you make your decision as to what to plant.

INDOOR HERB GARDENS

This is not the ideal way of growing herbs, but sometimes there is no alternative. It is a good way to overwinter herbs. A windowsill is a good position, but take care that the midday sun coming through the glass, especially in winter, does not burn the plants. Plants need light and, when days are short, you may have to resort to artificial lighting some of the time.

One way to grow herbs indoors is to remove the curtains and secure strong wire or metal frames down each side of the window. The frames should stand slightly away from the wall to prevent damp. These frames, with brackets or circles to hold plant pots, will allow air and light to reach the herbs.

A table or an old tea trolley could also be used to hold plant pots. This makes it easy to move herbs to give them the light and air they need. A good position would be in front of a window or a glass door. Keep plants out of drafts. For even growth, turn containers slightly each day.

The size of the container is important. It is useless to plant parsley in a 5 in (12 cm) pot when the root is 6 in (15 cm) long, and then wonder why the plant is not thriving. Perennial herbs grown indoors may not last as long as those grown outdoors. However, they do improve if you give them space to develop. Containers require dishes to prevent water dripping on floors and furniture. Garden centers and plant shops stock plastic containers with built-in anti-drip sections.

The question "How much water and how often?" is frequently asked. The finger test helps. Stick a finger into the soil up to the first joint. If it feels dry, water the plant. If it is very dry, dunk the whole pot in a bucket of water until it ceases to bubble, then remove and drain. Do not overwater, as more plants have died this way than from thirst. Fertilize every two weeks with seaweed or fish emulsion or other liquid plant food, mixed in prescribed proportions. Do not overfeed, as this could cause a harmful buildup in the soil. Some fertilizers have a strong smell, but this soon dissipates.

Indoor plants are prone to disease, so keep an eye on them. Do not allow dust to gather on foliage — spray regularly with water, using a fine jet. If plants cannot be taken outside, place them on newspaper or in the bathtub to do this.

Suitable herbs for an indoor garden are basil, bay, chervil, chives, dwarf dill, coriander, lettuce, land cress, lemon balm, sage, mint, sweet marjoram, nasturtiums, savory (winter and summer) and thyme. Several herbs can be grown together, if they are compatible, but mint should be planted on its own.

RIGHT **THIS WINDOW BOX CONTAINS A MIXED PLANTING OF LAVENDER, SAGE, PARSLEY, ROSEMARY, BASIL AND FENNEL.**

MEDICINAL HERB GARDENS

In times gone by, all the herbs for medicinal use were gathered from the wild (this is still done today to a certain extent). However, this method of gathering herbs was not always convenient, so the relevant plants and seeds were gradually collected and grown in places where they would be more readily accessible, as in the case of monastery gardens. These gardens were often walled or cloistered and they were laid out in a formal pattern for easy harvesting. The herbs were many and varied. Nowadays we would mostly grow herbs that are practical to use in the home, and others purely for historical interest, or as specimens in the case of herbs which are grown on a large scale for commercial harvesting. Some writers advocate growing groups of particular herbs for treating specific complaints. I disagree with this, unless you happen to have a really large garden, because any particular herb may be used to treat many different complaints. With the wide variety of plants available, the form of a medicinal garden is of your choosing.

RIGHT **THE CHELSEA PHYSIC GARDEN IN LONDON IS AN EXAMPLE OF A FORMAL MEDICINAL HERB GARDEN. THIS IS A VIEW OF THE HERB GARDEN AND PATHS.**

HERBS FOR A MEDICINAL GARDEN

TREES	**ANNUALS, TALL**	LUNGWORT
ELDER	CAYENNE	MINT
JUNIPER		RIBWORT
LEMON AND LINDEN	**BIENNIALS, MEDIUM HEIGHT**	ROSEMARY
MAIDENHAIR	CARAWAY	SOAPWORT
		VALERIAN AND VERVAIN
HIGH HEDGES OR WINDBREAKS	**PERENNIALS, MEDIUM HEIGHT**	
JUNIPER	BASIL	**ANNUALS, LOW-GROWING**
	COMFREY	BASIL
SURROUNDING HEDGES	ECHINACEA	CALENDULA
BARBERRY	GOLDENROD	NASTURTIUM
LAVENDER	LAVENDER	
ROSES AND ROSEMARY	RED CLOVER	**PERENNIAL EDGING**
	ROSEMARY	CHAMOMILE
LOW DIVIDING OR	RUE AND SAGE	THYME VARIETIES
BORDER HEDGES	ST. JOHN'S WORT	VIOLET
LAVENDER	THYME (common)	
ROSEMARY		**SHADE**
RUE	**ANNUALS, MEDIUM HEIGHT**	ANGELICA
	CLEAVERS	
BIENNIALS, TALL	DILL	**DAMP**
MILK THISTLE	FLAX (LINSEED)	HORSETAIL
MULLEIN		
	PERENNIALS, LOW-GROWING	**DRY**
PERENNIALS, TALL	ALFALFA AND FEVERFEW	ALOE
ELECAMPANE	HOREHOUND	BUCHU AND BULBINE
FENNEL	LADY'S MANTLE	HOP (needs support)
LAVENDER	LAVENDER	STINGING NETTLE (confine roots)
ROSEMARY	LEMON BALM	RASPBERRIES (in the background)

FORMAL HERB GARDENS

In the 10th century, formal herb gardens in Europe and the Middle East were planted in squares or in circles divided to look like spoked wheels. In the grounds of large houses and stately homes, these gave way to very formal knot gardens, designed to be seen to the best advantage from the upper floors of the houses or the raised terraces surrounding them.

The main features of a formal herb garden are hedges and topiaries, which entail close clipping (very time- and labor-consuming). For topiaries, grow 'McConnell's Blue' rosemary (where available), box and myrtle. Lemon trees, clipped and pruned to form rounds, will still bear fruit if this is done judiciously. In a small formal garden, I have seen rosemary which has been pruned, wired and clipped to form a tall column. Use 'Miss Jessop's Upright', which is available in some countries, or else common rosemary.

A formal herb garden must be symmetrical in layout, using low hedges to make compartments. Herbs for this hedging could be box, rue, lavender, compact rosemary, dwarf myrtle and santolina (*S. chamaecyparissus* or *S. viridis*). The compartments can be planted with one or more kinds of herb, but nothing must be allowed to grow rampant. Variegated forms of herbs could play their part to advantage. Do not plant large areas of any one annual, as this will lead to unsightly gaps.

A centerpiece is important. Depending on the size of the garden, it could be a gazebo, a lemon or a bay tree, a large ornamental planted container, a birdbath, a sundial or a pond. Seating should be placed along the outside edge or tucked into corners so as not to disturb the overall pattern. Matching pots of clipped herbs could be used to line the steps leading down to the garden.

A formal herb garden must be kept under control at all times; if not practical, then grow herbs informally.

RIGHT **THIS GARDEN AT CRANBOURNE MANOR IN ENGLAND IS AN EXAMPLE OF A TRADITIONAL, PLANNED, FORMAL HERB GARDEN. IT FEATURES ELABORATE TOPIARIES AND HEDGE–SHAPING IN A SYMMETRICAL DESIGN AND THE SUNDIAL FORMS A STRONG FOCAL POINT IN THE CENTER.**

IV

HARVESTING, DRYING & STORING
HERBS

"The time when the entire Plant is in its most
full Perfection is when it is in the Bud when the heads are formed
for flowering but not a single Flower has yet disclosed itself."

(SIR JOHN HILL)

HARVESTING, DRYING & STORING HERBS

As most herbs deteriorate quickly, it is advisable to attend to them as soon as possible after harvesting, and to have the necessary equipment and material ready. To prevent mold, always make sure that no trace of moisture remains when drying herbs. When they are completely dry, the herbs should be stored in airtight containers to keep them dry.

HARVESTING HERBS

When gathering the leaves and flowers of herbs from the wild, it is always vital to seek permission to do so from the landowner, as you may be trespassing on private land. Never dig up whole plants, take care not to destroy them and never take all of any one kind of herb from one specific place. It is not always very wise to gather plants from the roadsides where they could have been polluted by traffic fumes. Pick only the quantity of any herb that you will have enough time to deal with, using only good implements such as sharp scissors, pruning shears or a knife to prevent damage to the plants.

The best time of day to harvest any flowers and foliage is during mid-morning, after any dew has had time to evaporate and before the heat of the day has caused the volatile oils of the plants to evaporate.

Mature roots are usually lifted in autumn, when the stems and the foliage of the plant are no longer draining the nutriment from the roots. Harvest roots only from the garden, because you should not dig up whole plants from the wild. The foliage and the stems are usually cut before the plant flowers, because this is the time when they have the maximum oil content. They are then bunched and hung up in a warm place to dry. The flowers are cut when they are fully open and they are then tied into bunches and hung for drying.

When harvesting herbs from the wild, make sure that you are collecting the correct plant, as there are highly toxic herbs which look very similar to some of the useful herbs.

DRYING HERBS

Wooden frames covered with a fine mesh or any other loosely woven material are used when drying roots as well as loose flowers and foliage. Bunches of flowers and foliage can be hung from hooks. To save space and create good drying conditions, a frame of wooden slats that can be pulled up to the ceiling with the aid of pulleys is a very good idea. A mesh covering would do for flat drying, and bunches of flowers or foliage could also be hung from the slats.

Paper bags or deep trays are used for catching dried seeds. Small quantities of flowers or leaves could be spread out on newspaper and placed on any suitable surface. One writer has suggested the use of an open drawer. (Most people never have an empty drawer in the house!) Muslin or any other suitable material is needed to keep dust off culinary and medicinal herbs.

Roots can either be rinsed or they can be brushed clean of all traces of soil, and the larger ones can sometimes be sliced to facilitate drying. Spread the roots out on racks to dry.

Large leaves are spread out on racks. For culinary and medicinal use, first rinse the leaves in lukewarm water to remove any dust and foreign matter, then shake them dry and drape with muslin to keep them dust-free.

Flowers such as lavender are bunched and hung up to dry.

PREVIOUS PAGES **HERBS BEING HARVESTED.**

INSET ON THIS PAGE **A LAVENDER BASKET.**

RIGHT **A DRY, WARM SHED PROVIDES AN IDEAL WORKING SPACE.**

PRESERVING HERBS FOR CULINARY USE

CULINARY OILS AND VINEGARS

SUITABLE HERBS ARE nasturtiums (leaves and seeds), common and garlic chives (foliage and flowers), juniper (berries), rosemary, lavender, basil, cayenne, tarragon, garlic, green ginger, fennel, dill, sage and thyme.

Pack a wide-mouthed glass jar lightly to three-quarters of its capacity with the chosen herb or herbs. For vinegars, use cider or wine vinegar. Suitable oils are maize, sunflower or olive oil. Fill the jar with vinegar or oil and cover with plastic wrap. For vinegar, stand the jar on a windowsill or in any sunny place. Oil should be kept out of the sun, otherwise it could become rancid. After ten days, strain and taste. If not sufficiently potent, return to the jar with more fresh herbs and top up with oil or vinegar. When ready, strain and pour into suitable bottles with a sprig or two of the herb used.

CRYSTALLIZING

TO CRYSTALLIZE rose petals, violet or borage flowers and mint leaves, coat petals and leaves with lightly beaten egg white, using a small paintbrush. If dipping leaves and flowers into egg white, do not overdo it. Dust lightly with caster sugar and lay on baking trays lined with waxed paper. They can be sun-dried, but drying in a warm oven is best. When crisp, remove from the paper and store in an airtight container.

Angelica requires a different method. Ideally, stems should be as thick as your thumb, though I have also used thinner ones. Cut the stems into manageable pieces. Cook gently until just tender, then drain. Using a sharp knife, remove the paper-thin outer skin. Weigh the stems. For each 1 lb (450 g) of stems you will need 1 lb (450 g) sugar and 8 fl oz (250 ml) water. Lay the stems in a dish and cover with the sugar. Leave them for approximately 48 hours. Now pour the resulting syrup with the water and stems into a saucepan. Stirring gently, simmer until the stems are clear and all the syrup has been absorbed. Place stems on a rack in a warm oven until crisp on the outside. Store in an airtight container.

Petals of flowers such as calendula and roses are carefully separated and spread to dry. Other flowers are scattered loosely on frames. For potpourri, flowers such as mullein are dried face down. Use only fresh flowers without any discoloration.

Seeds are easier to dry when part of the stem is retained. Cut and bunch, then hang, head down, in paper bags in which air holes have been made near the top. Alternatively, hang, head down, over deep trays into which seeds will drop for collection. Dip stems of seeds for culinary or medicinal use in hot water to remove dust and foreign matter, shake dry, then hang and, if necessary, cover with muslin. *Do not* dip seeds to be used for sowing. Dry herbs in a warm, dry place out of direct sunlight. If weather is unfavorable, dry in a

warm oven at 122°F (50°C), with the door slightly ajar. Do not hang herbs in a steamy kitchen or in a garage where there are exhaust fumes. An attic or dry cellar is ideal.

STORING HERBS

To store the herbs that you have harvested, it is necessary to have a supply of airtight containers, preferably made of dark glass or ceramic. Labels are very important for naming and dating the containers. It is not always easy to recognize dried herbs at first glance and, as many of the herbs may lose their potency with time, the date must be noted. Do not keep dried herbs for longer than a year.

When the foliage is crisp and completely dry, strip it from the stems and pack it in jars. Lavender flowers are removed from the stems for storage when they are dry. Other loose dried flowers are placed in large jars or crocks until they are required. Seeds are shaken loose from the flower heads into the bag or on to the tray. If there are husks to be winnowed, as in the case of rocket, do this outside where there is a very gentle breeze, over a piece of sheeting.

All plant material must be perfectly dry before storing, as the slightest trace of moisture will inevitably cause spoilage.

If any herb needs a specific treatment, such as freezing, salting, etc., this information will be found under the entries for the individual herbs (*see* Chapter 2).

V

FRAGRANT USES FOR HERBS

"Heaven is not only above your head, it is under your feet as well."

FRAGRANT
USES FOR
HERBS

THERE ARE MANY DIFFERENT WAYS IN WHICH HERBS MAY BE USED TO IMPART FRAGRANCE. THE MOST POPULAR FRAGRANT USE OF HERBS IS IN POTPOURRI, A BLEND OF DRIED HERBS AND ESSENTIAL OILS. YOU COULD ALSO MAKE A COMFORT BAG, A TUSSIE MUSSIE, A LAVENDER BASKET OR AN HERB PILLOW. FRAGRANT HERBS ARE IMMENSELY VERSATILE, SO USE YOUR IMAGINATION AND ENJOY THE PERFUME.

PEOPLE USED TO LIVE under far from hygienic conditions, and disguised smells instead of getting rid of the cause. In those days, when the state of floors left much to be desired, they were covered with rushes, which were lifted with the dirt and replaced periodically. To cover up smells and deter fleas and other vermin, rosemary, tansy, lavender, southernwood and other herbs were used. The more affluent people used herbs such as sweet flag, which was not so freely available at that time.

To freshen elaborate clothing which could not be washed, herbs were allowed to smolder and the fragrant smoke penetrated the garments arranged around the fireplace. As we do to this day, herbs were chosen and used to impart perfume to clothes and linen and to repel moths. And with the many ways of using garden and hedgerow herbs, how pleasant it is to enter a home where natural fragrances prevail.

TUSSIE MUSSIE

As a fragrant and long-lasting present, a tussie mussie is ideal. It is a posy of about a hundred stems of herbs and, when it begins to fade after a week in water, the stems are mopped dry and it is hung upside down to dry. It becomes a pretty, long-lasting table decoration, or may be hung in a wardrobe.
To make it you will need:
✠ sharp scissors
✠ pruning shears
✠ florists' tape

✠ 1 yd (1 m) ribbon
✠ a small glass jar or vase
✠ one rosebud or carnation flower
✠ about ten stems each of at least eight different herbs

Among the most suitable herbs are mints and thymes in flower, lavender flowers and foliage, rosemary, rose, lemon and peppermint pelargonium leaves, santolina flowers and foliage, and flowers and foliage of marjoram or any herb you find suitable. To add extra softness to the posy, include flowers of parsley, celery or fennel.

Cut 6 in (15 cm) stems and strip off foliage to about 2 in (5 cm) from the top (save this to dry for potpourri). Cut 1½ in (4 cm) pieces of florists' tape on a slant, then take, for example, a lavender flower and a stem of santolina foliage and bind together with a piece of tape. Prepare all the herbs in the same way, except the pelargonium leaves and the rosebud.

To form the center, bind four or five small rose or lemon-scented pelargonium leaves evenly around the rosebud. Arrange the pairs of herbs in circles of the same combinations around the center.

As posy holders aren't always easy to obtain, I usually finish off the tussie mussie with a circle of about six large peppermint or rose pelargonium leaves. Tape securely and tie with ribbon, making a bow. Trim stems and place posy in a vase. Change water daily.

PREVIOUS PAGES
A FRAGRANT SUMMER GARDEN ENHANCES YOUR HOME.
RIGHT **HERBS ON A WINDOWSILL IN THE KITCHEN WILL ELIMINATE COOKING ODORS.**

Potpourri

This is a comparatively simple way of introducing the fragrance of herbs to the home. To make it, you will need to collect and dry scented flowers for fragrance as well as some pretty ones for color. The combination of scents and colors is a matter of availability and your own personal choice.

When drying rose petals, include some rose leaves too, as they turn a lovely soft shade of green when they are dried.

Any dried sweet or spicy-scented foliage should be stripped from the stems, which are then discarded. Spices such as anise, cinnamon and cloves are often added to mixtures of herbs used for potpourri. They also help to "fix" the scent. Other fixatives include chopped or minced dried citrus pith and peel. After squeezing the fruit, collect all the peels and then store them in plastic bags in the freezer until you have enough to make a worthwhile amount. Mince or chop the peel finely and spread it out on trays to dry in the sun or in a cool oven. When the chopped peel is evenly and crisply dry (but not frizzled), store the peel in closed jars until required.

Whole coriander seed and the leaves of the Inca marigold (where available) are two other ingredients which can also act as a fixative and be used to hold the volatile oils.

In many potpourri recipes the use of orris root as a fixative is advocated. This is the powdered root of the Florentine iris. It may be purchased, but it is sometimes difficult to find and a good powder can also be expensive.

Essential oils are added for long-lasting fragrance. As these are expensive, buy only two or three of those that appeal to you and will complement the herbs being used.

To mix potpourri, spread an old cotton sheet on the floor and pile on pretty and fragrant flowers and foliage. Tip the chopped peel on top, as well as any spices you may be using. Add the oil to the peel drop by drop. To 6–8 lightly packed cups of dried material add 1 cup of dried peel and about 10 drops of oil, depending on the strength of the oil. Oils are concentrated, so do not waste them by being over-generous. Stir with your hands to blend ingredients. (Do not wash the now fragrant sheet, but fold it and put it away for future use.) Pack into a large glass or pottery container, seal and leave to

mature for four or five days. Open the container and test for fragrance. If the fragrance is not strong enough, tip out onto the sheet and add some more peel with a little oil. Blend the ingredients again and repack in the jar. It will be ready in about two weeks.

ABOVE **POTPOURRI IS MADE FROM A MIXTURE OF DRIED HERBS AND ESSENTIAL OILS. USE A SELECTION OF FLOWERING HERBS TO ADD MORE COLOR.**

Potpourri is put into pretty pots or jars with lids and placed around the house away from sunlight. Leave the jars open when more fragrance is desired and close them when you are away from home to preserve the scent.

To refresh potpourri, add a few drops of the desired oil to a small quantity of dry, minced citrus peel and stir into the existing mixture. When your potpourri becomes dusty and crumbly, discard and start afresh.

If you wish, make a potpourri with a color scheme, adding appropriate oils. If you use your imagination, there is no end to the interesting combinations and textures for a pleasing, crisply fragrant mixture. To make a lemon-scented

potpourri, use dry lemon verbena, lemon pelargonium, lemon grass, sweet marjoram, yellow and white flowers such as chamomile, mullein, santolina, feverfew, rose petals and foliage, and blend with minced citrus peel and lemon verbena and clove oil. Be discreet with the clove oil.

COMFORT BAG

A comfort bag is just that — the ideal gift for someone confined to bed. Trim the edges of a 10 in (25 cm) square of soft material like silk or fine cotton with pinking shears or finish with a rolled seam. Place soothing dried herbs, such as hops, lavender and chamomile, in the center of the material. Gather up and tie into a loose bundle with soft ribbon. The patient is comforted by holding the bag to the cheek and breathing in the fragrances. To renew the fragrance, untie the bag and add more herbs or a few drops of lavender oil.

Another way to give a hospital patient the pleasure of herbs where space is at a premium is to tie a bundle of fragrant foliage to the bed head with a length of ribbon.

HERB PILLOW

An herb pillow is a more time-consuming but longer-lasting gift to make for someone special. Stitch a pillow lining of cotton or linen and stuff this lining loosely with dried herbs and pillow stuffing (natural or synthetic) in equal parts, or use only herbs. Stitch up the end of the case. Make an attractive outer cover with pretty material and trimmings. An herb pillow is not usually very big, but the size of the pillow is a matter of personal choice. If your herb pillow is to be used as a sleep pillow, it should contain calming and sleep-inducing herbs such as lavender, hops or chamomile.

WEDDINGS

A wedding is a wonderful occasion for making the most of the fragrance of herbs. If the church is to be decorated, make up small, simple bunches of flowering and foliage herbs to tie on to the aisle pews. Depending on the style of the bride's gown, she could carry a bouquet incorporating herbs (such as a loosely constructed tussie mussie, perhaps). Small, tight tussie mussies would then be appropriate for the bridesmaids. These bouquets could later be dried for keepsakes.

Instead of paper confetti, use environment-friendly rose petals or a mixture of flowers and herb foliage. Rose petals may be collected over a few days and will keep well in the refrigerator in paper bags if they are removed from the calyx. If you are using dried petals and foliage, you will need a fair quantity, so ask friends to collect and dry them for you. A fragrant potpourri mix without a fixative works very well,

though some guests may slip a handful into their pockets and handbags!

The table arrangements could be made of herb flowers and foliage instead of the conventional arrangement of blooms. This, of course, would depend on seasonal availability.

HERBS IN THE HOME

To make attractive gifts for friends and family members (or for your own use), there are many ways in which you could use herbs. You could, for instance, make herbal *coat-hanger covers.* Stitch a loose lining in the shape of a hanger, cover a hanger with the lining, stuff the lining with dried herbs, sew up and then cover with a suitable material. Finish the hanger with a pretty ribbon bow or a tiny posy of artificial flowers.

To prevent moths from damaging your clothing or stored blankets, make small, flat *moth-repellant sachets* of lavender, mint, santolina, southernwood and/or bay.

As heat will bring out the fragrance of herbs, make *place mats* and pads for hot dishes with dried herbs of your choice added to the stuffing material.

To make a *centerpiece* for a dinner table, arrange fresh herbs in a low bowl and place a lit candle in the center to accentuate the fragrance. The herbs make a good talking point.

Small herb sachets slipped into a *hot water bottle cover* will give warmth and extra comfort on cold nights.

To have *fragrant linen,* use lavender, rosemary or lemon verbena on their own, or bags of mixed aromatic herbs. For placing between folded clothes or piles of linen, the much flatter sachets are more practical. Make sachets, pillows and bags of fine material and fill them loosely with dried herbs of your choice, so that the fragrance is evoked by gently rubbing the herbs together.

ABOVE **USE HERBS TO DECORATE THE CHURCH FOR A WEDDING WITH A DIFFERENCE.**
ABOVE OPPOSITE **HERB PILLOWS GIVE FRAGRANT COMFORT TO PATIENTS CONFINED TO BED.**
BELOW OPPOSITE **DRIED HERBS AND ESSENTIAL OILS ARE USED TO MAKE A COMFORT BAG.**

When lighting a *fire* in winter, add dried stalks of herbs such as lavender or rosemary which have been saved from pruning.

The flavor of *food cooked over the coals* is improved when cuttings of rosemary, lavender, marjoram, etc., are burnt.

To improve commercial wax *furniture polish,* scrape the wax from the container and melt gently in an old saucepan. Stir in 7 oz (200 g) crushed lavender flowers and/or lemon balm leaves for every 14 fl oz (400 ml) wax. Amounts need only be approximate. Remove from heat and leave for about 12 hours. Reheat wax until liquid, strain through a cloth and pour back into the container. Fold the used herbs into the cloth and use this to apply the polish to furniture or floors. This means that none of the wax is wasted. Lemon balm, crushed and rubbed on furniture, is in itself good for wood.

To make an *herbal bath oil,* you will need unscented technical oil (cosmetic oil) from a drugstore or the more expensive almond or apricot kernel oil, a wide-mouthed glass jar and plastic wrap to cover the jar opening. Use herbs of your choice, such as scented pelargonium leaves, lavender, rose petals, lemon verbena, sweet marjoram, rosemary and yarrow.

Gather enough herbs to fill three-quarters of the jar. Tear up larger leaves. Pour oil over herbs to fill jar and cover the opening with plastic wrap (the lids tend to get tacky). Leave on a sunny windowsill or any warm place for a week or two.

Strain oil through muslin or old, clean tights, squeezing out every drop. If the fragrance is not quite strong enough, infuse again with fresh herbs and top up with more oil. Pour into attractive bottles, together with a sprig or two of the appropriate herb for eye appeal, and seal with a lid or cork. Label bottles clearly as bath oil. Protect labels from oil and keep them clean by brushing with clear nail polish.

Vinegars for baths or *hair rinses* are made in the same way, substituting a good white wine or light cider vinegar for the oil. Pour 2 TBS (30 ml) into bath water for a refreshing bath.

Another way to have a herbal bath is with a *bath bag.* Place a handful of fresh or dried herbs (*see* page 170) in the center of a square of muslin or thin cotton material, add a small handful of oatmeal and then tie up, leaving a length of cord to attach the bag to the hot water tap. Run the bath water through the bag. While bathing, remove the bag from the tap and use it for a body rub. Rinse after use and hang it over the bath to dry, as it may be used a few times. A collection of bath bags made up with oatmeal (to soften the skin) and dried herbs makes a lovely gift. Use lemon-scented or spicy herbs if the gift is for a man.

One drop of good essential oil on a *light bulb* will perfume a whole room. To induce sleep or calm a restless child, use a drop of lavender oil on the light bulb of the bedside lamp. Look out for and purchase ceramic herb burners, the heat for which is produced by a cleverly wired light bulb or by burning short plump candles.

Place a few of your favorite herbs in the *vacuum cleaner bag.* As the air comes out, so does the scent.

A *lavender basket* is a fun addition to any gift. Use it in a cupboard, wardrobe or drawer for fragrance. It is important that the basket should be made while the lavender stems are still fresh and pliable.

To make it you will need:

✣ 13 or 15 long-stemmed, long lavender heads
✣ 1 yd (1 m) narrow, lavender-coloured ribbon
✣ another ½ yd (45 cm) of the same ribbon for a bow
✣ a small piece of adhesive tape

Bunch the lavender close to the heads and tie the bunch firmly with the ribbon, leaving the longest possible end. Now gently bend the stems back over flower heads, so as to cover them. Bring the length of ribbon from the center and proceed to wind it under and over the stems in a basket weave, keeping the whole inverted bunch as compact as possible. Continue until flower heads are completely encased. Wind ribbon around stems and cut off any surplus. Secure with adhesive tape. Trim stems to an even length and finish with a ribbon bow.

When using your *clothes dryer,* tie your favorite herbs in an old stocking and toss it in among the clothes.

Herbs under a *carpet* or a *rug* will, when walked on, give off fragrance. This is like the strewing of herbs in days gone by — those, however, were used to cover up unpleasant smells.

Pop a handful of herbs of your choice into a warm *oven* after cooking, in order to clear the kitchen of any lingering cooking odors.

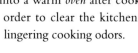

RIGHT **BATH BAGS, HERBAL OILS AND BATH RINSES CAN ALL BE USED TO MAKE YOUR BATH SOOTHING AND RELAXING.**

VI

HERBAL
HEALING

"Let food be your medicine and medicine your food."

HERBAL
HEALING

The use of herbal (plant) medicine to treat disease is known as herbalism. Herbal medicine is not a cure for disease, but rather works on the principle of helping the body heal itself. It helps the body achieve homeostasis by encouraging the elimination of toxins and by stimulating or calming the various organs or systems.

HERBALISM

Herbalism is widely practiced in many parts of the world, both by traditional or indigenous healers, who play a major role in health care in isolated parts of the world, and also by trained herbalists in the West, who form a part of complementary medicine (which is of course complementary to orthodox Western medicine). The traditional or indigenous healer's knowledge of plants is often very impressive and has usually been gleaned from many generations of experience. (In her novel, *The Clan of the Cave Bear,* Jean Auel gives a very good idea of how certain plants might have been used as medicine in the early days of mankind.)

Previously scorned by practitioners of orthodox medical science, the role of traditional healers has recently been re-evaluated, with the World Health Organisation (WHO) recognizing the importance of their contribution to the health care of millions of people.

With the recent crises of AIDS, cholera, the increased incidence and spread of malaria, the possible re-emergence of smallpox and the appearance of alarming mutant viruses, the world is now starting to take a more serious look at herbalism. Herbal medicine might have some really excellent answers to many of our most serious health problems, and scientists are beginning to investigate the possibility that many of their most perplexing medical problems might well be solved by traditional healers. Research into

plant medicine is now taking place more than ever before in the history of medicine.

In the West, herbalism has lately experienced a revival after its earlier almost total demise as a form of indigenous healing (*see* Herbalism in the past, page 121). In his book, *Of Men and Plants,* Maurice Mességué gives a very interesting account of some of the struggles that can face a herbalist in Western society, and even though he experienced his problems earlier this century, many herbalists today still have trouble being accepted into the health care systems of several Western countries.

In Britain, the School of Phytotherapy and Middlesex University are two institutions which both offer excellent academic courses in medical herbalism. Today, the qualified herbalists in Britain are all members of the National Institute of Medical Herbalists and as such they are recognized by the letters MNIMH or FNIMH after their names. The members of the Institute practice herbalism in many other parts of the world where they are also officially recognized. At present, the School of Phytotherapy has students who have come there from all over the world to study herbalism, as most of the other countries in the world have no organized official training in herbalism.

RIGHT **PREPARATION OF TRADITIONAL CHINESE HERBAL MEDICINE TODAY.**
INSET ON THIS PAGE **THE CHINESE GODDESS MA-KOU GATHERING MEDICINAL HERBS.**

HERBALISM AND OTHER COMPLEMENTARY THERAPIES

Ever since humans have lived on this planet, plants have been used medicinally. Herbalism is the oldest known form of medicine. It would not be far-fetched to say that if it were not for herbal medicine, our survival would have been uncertain. In the past, herbal remedies were the only answer to cure fevers and heal the injuries of battle and childbirth.

Other therapies which evolved from herbal medicine are homeopathy, aromatherapy, naturopathy, Bach flower therapy and anthroposophic medicine. They each have their own philosophies, with plants forming the cornerstone.

Herbalism is a discipline on its own. It makes use of all parts of the plant, including resins, flowers, oils, seeds and roots. Herbal medicine can be made from any plant with chemical constituents which have medicinal properties, such as succulents, trees, shrubs and grasses, and not only from herbs such as parsley and thyme. Therefore the word "herbal" is a bit of a misnomer, and the term "plant medicine" is more appropriate. The active constituents are extracted from the plant material in various ways and the medicine is used in its natural form.

TOP **EDWARD BACH, WHO DEVISED THE BACH FLOWER REMEDIES.**
ABOVE **HIPPOCRATES, KNOWN AS THE FATHER OF MEDICINE.**
OPPOSITE TOP **NICHOLAS CULPEPER, AUTHOR OF** *COMPLETE HERBAL.*
OPPOSITE BOTTOM **SAMUEL HAHNEMANN, GERMAN DOCTOR AND ORIGINATOR OF HOMEOPATHY.**

HERBALISM AND HOMEOPATHY

People sometimes confuse herbalism with homeopathy, but although they both work to achieve homeostasis and subsequent healing without suppression of symptoms, the actual way in which they function in the body is quite different.

Homeopathy was the brainchild of the German doctor Samuel Hahnemann (1755–1843), but by then Hippocrates had already observed the phenomenon of "Like Cures Like."

Homeopathy uses many different animal, mineral and synthetic materials as well as plants, and it works on three principles: the Law of Similars, the Principle of the Small, Infinitesimal Dose, and the Principle of Individualization.

A homeopathic remedy is chosen according to the Law of Similars. This law works on the basis that "Like Cures Like." The symptoms observed in the patient are matched up with the effects caused by a substance. A bee-sting, for instance, would cause redness, heat and swelling, therefore Apis (from the honey-bee) is given to a patient to treat a condition where these symptoms predominate.

The given remedy is diluted, often to the extent that no molecular evidence of the original substance is detectable, the rationale being that the energy of the original substance will stimulate the vital forces of the person it is given to. It is also succussed (shaken regularly) in order to impart energy. Finally, the remedy is not only carefully chosen to match the symptoms, but also to match the mood, emotional state and even the personality of the individual patient. (This is only a brief outline to give you an indication of the complexity of homeopathy.)

In herbalism, the remedy is chosen to fit the whole picture as revealed by questioning and clinical examination. Some individualization is applied, but it is not as critical as in homeopathy. An herbalist chooses an herbal remedy based on knowledge of the chemical constituents of the plant and its effect on the body's physiology. It is not diluted, but given in concentrated form, in small doses.

Another offshoot of herbalism occurred when Edward Bach devised the 38 Bach Flower Remedies in the 1930s. Bach was an orthodox medical doctor who gave up his practice to research the qualities of certain flowers and trees, particularly their healing forces. He found that certain plants were ideal to alleviate certain emotional disorders and devised the Bach Flower Remedies and also Rescue Remedy. In common with homeopathy, these remedies are matched to the personality and the emotional state of the patient, and there are no side effects.

HERBALISM IN THE PAST

The earliest records of herbal medicines originate from China and Egypt. From Egypt, this knowledge spread to Greece, which was the birthplace of Hippocrates, the father of medicine. He was the first to recognize that disease was a natural phenomenon and not influenced by evil spirits, as was popularly believed. He recognized one of the most important principles of homeopathy — that "Like Cures Like" — and he also had the insight to say, "Let food be your medicine." Hippocrates was open-minded and unbiased towards what we today label "complementary medicine."

Herbalism was actively practiced in medieval Europe and several works, uninfluenced by the Greek writings, were

produced. The most famous book was Nicholas Culpeper's *Complete Herbal*, which first appeared in 1653, edited reprints of which are still available today.

Herbal medicine was linked to myths and magic, and often involved mysterious rituals. There was the Doctrine of Signatures, a highly unscientific way of categorizing plants according to their resemblance to parts of the human body. (Strangely enough, the Doctrine of Signatures was not too inaccurate, and many plants used in this way have subsequently been shown to have the desired effects because of their chemical constituents.)

The Church was quite alarmed about the "witchcraft" that was evidently linked to the use of herbal medicine. The famous medieval witch hunts began, and thousands of innocent people were burned at the stake, some only because they drank herbal tea and owned a black cat.

As herbal medicine slipped into disfavor, medical science was progressing. Herbalists were labeled as nothing more than cranks. In the 19th century, a revival of interest sprang up in North America, where the indigenous people sparked the curiosity of immigrant Americans. A lot of information which was gleaned from the Native Americans was taken back to Europe. Unfortunately, quackery was prevalent and outrageous claims were made, both in America and Europe. Many herbalists were arrested or even imprisoned. Even today, herbalism often evokes the image of a quack bearing bottles containing mysterious and useless potions.

Orthodox medicine today is predominantly a chemical-based system, with very little acknowledgment of plant medicines, despite the fact that many pharmaceutical agents are derived from plants. Some research institutions, notably in Germany, are taking a serious look at plants, both to use them in the pharmaceutical industry and to examine the chemical constituents to see how they assist in healing.

HERBALISM TODAY

Herbalism now stands at the crossroads — between crude and sophisticated, traditional and modern — trying to find a niche in a world fairly hostile to the idea that "herbs" can be of value in medicine. The U.S. Food and Drug Administration (FDA) is battling demands for herbal medicine, placing obstructive legislation in the path of progress.

In Europe the picture is brighter. With a lot of research supporting herbal medicine, most European countries have some form of herbalism entrenched in their health care systems. Germany seems the most advanced, with orthodox doctors prescribing both herbal and allopathic medicine. Britain has set high standards for herbalists — most are members of the National Institute for Medical Herbalists.

Despite the acceptance of herbalism in most European countries, many storms are still brewing over legislation for standardization and registration of herbal products, and differences in marketing. At least European countries now agree that phytopharmaceuticals are both acceptable and necessary.

In other countries with divisions between underdeveloped and developed cultures, traditional healers are more readily accepted in accordance with recommendations by the World Health Organisation (WHO), which has recognized that for millions of people, orthodox medicine is out of reach.

THE BENEFITS OF HERBAL MEDICINE

IT IS GREEN MEDICINE

Herbal medicine is environment-friendly in its manufacture as well as its disposal. The cultivation of medicinal plants is usually well controlled. No artificial fertilizers, pesticides or herbicides are used, as these may contaminate the product. Many herb growers are now using biodynamic or organic methods, i.e., growing herbs without using chemicals.

Manufacturing herbal medicine is relatively simple. Though the manufacture of phytopharmaceuticals is sophisticated, it is not a source of pollution — a spillage of herbal tincture would not harm the environment. If disposal of the product is required, it will not poison water supplies.

IT IS INEXPENSIVE

Even today, herbal remedies are relatively inexpensive, and an herbal infusion is still the cheapest form of medication. In parts of the world where most of the population is very poor, herbal medicine is the only affordable option.

IT IS HUMAN-COMPATIBLE

Plants form the bulk of our food and drink and we cannot survive without them. Human body cells can cope with plant chemicals, as they are used to them and have evolved to metabolize them. Side effects of herbal medicine dispensed by a qualified herbalist are unusual and, if they do occur, generally not dangerous. Often, side effects are the result of incorrect dosage in self-medication, or overuse by people believing that, because it is natural, it must be safe.

THE DANGERS OF HERBAL MEDICINE

From time to time, one reads about poisoning as the result of the ingestion of a noxious plant, or about the carcinogenic properties of certain medicinal plants. These dangers are real enough if someone ingests unidentified plants, herbs that have been adulterated by unscrupulous dealers, or takes an overdose of a potentially harmful herb. Many plants that are used on a daily basis have the potential to poison or harm when taken in excess. These include drinks such as tea and coffee, foods such as carrots or green potatoes and drugs like tobacco, alcohol and *Cannabis sativa* (marijuana). Tobacco and alcohol are responsible for shocking numbers of fatalities every year, yet people are free to consume as much as they wish. When it comes to herbal medicine, however, even a hint of a toxic or carcinogenic compound can result in its being banned. This is one of the ironies of life, and perhaps an example of deliberate, self-serving manipulation by powerful interest groups.

Many herbs have traces of potentially toxic substances, and will cause harm if consumed regularly in large quantities. It is not safe to take any medicine on a long-term regular basis without the guidance of a qualified person. Just because a herb is natural, it does not mean it is safe.

USING HERBAL MEDICINE

✠ Don't treat serious chronic conditions yourself. You might only have half the picture and neglect other aspects. The only way to use herbal medicine is to consult a herbalist.
✠ Consult a reputable herbalist. For example, in Britain, the letters MNIMH or FNIMH after the name indicate registration

with the National Institute of Medical Herbalists. Britain and Ireland are the only European countries where unregistered herbalists are allowed to practice. In other parts of the world regulations differ, but the golden rule applies: ensure that a herbalist has a sound background and a good reputation.

✠ If your knowledge of herbal medicine is not too good, educate yourself. There are excellent books on the subject. If you need guidance, find an herbalist and register with him or her. A good herbalist is there to advise and educate you as well as to improve your state of health.

✠ Get to know the relevant plants intimately, especially if you want to grow your own supply of herbs for medicinal purposes or pick them from the wild. You should know what they look like and what their botanical names are. Find a good source of reference to crosscheck and make sure of the correct identification.

✠ When buying a plant for medicinal use, don't blindly trust the labeling at your nursery. Nurserymen can make mistakes, and many herbs are wrongly labeled.

✠ Don't use an herb for more than a week without checking, either with your herbalist or a good reference work.

✠ Don't believe every claim made for herbal medicine. Drugstores and health-food stores are often as guilty of using wild claims to promote their herbal products as the media are.

Check with your herbalist if you are not sure.

✠ Don't treat your illness by using an herb recommended by a lay person. Just as you should never take any medication from an unqualified person, a friend or neighbor's advice on herbal medicine could be quite wrong for you.

✠ To be on the safe side, use a combination of different herbs, choosing those with similar therapeutic actions.

Herbal medicine is perfectly safe when used correctly. Paracelsus, born in 1493 and known as the Father of Modern Science, is reputed to have said, "It is the dosage which decides whether a substance is a poison or a medicine."

ABOVE **A MAN SELLING HEALING HERBS FOR ALL AILMENTS AT AN INDIAN OCEAN ISLAND MARKET.**

CONSULTING AN HERBALIST

Go to an herbalist with a good reputation. Ask what training he or she has received. Beware of advertizing that promises cures. The body heals itself; an herbalist is merely a facilitator.

The first visit can take an hour or longer. The herbalist will take a medical history. If he or she is a registered herbalist or homeopath, a physical examination may also be done.

Don't be alarmed if the herbalist asks personal questions and probes your state of mind. This is an essential part of finding out about the whole person. The herbalist will explain which herbal medicine he or she is going to dispense and why, and instruct you how to take it. Changes in lifestyle and diet may be necessary, depending on the herbalist's approach.

HERBS AND PREGNANCY

Many herbs stimulate the uterus and should therefore be avoided by women who are of childbearing age and trying to become pregnant, as one is often unaware of a newly started pregnancy. These herbs (*see* below) should also not be taken during pregnancy. Pregnant women can, however, enjoy herbs in their food, especially dark, leafy greens.

Avoid the following herbs in therapeutic doses during pregnancy — do not take in tincture form, infusion or decoction:
ALOE VERA ANGELICA AUTUMN CROCUS BARBERRY BLACK COHOSH CELERY SEED CINNAMON DEVIL'S CLAW GOLDENSEAL HYSSOP JUNIPER MALE FERN

MANDRAKE PARSLEY SEED PENNYROYAL POKEWEED ROSEMARY RUE SAGE SOUTHERNWOOD TANSY THUJA WORMWOOD YARROW

The following herbs are useful during and after pregnancy:
✠ Chopped PARSLEY, CELERY, LAND CRESS and ROCKET — take in moderate amounts for vitamins and minerals
✠ RASPBERRY LEAF — to tone the uterus, but should *never be used* during the first trimester of pregnancy
✠ CHAMOMILE, GINGER, PEPPERMINT — for morning sickness
✠ GOLDENSEAL — during labor to assist the uterus (*never take during pregnancy*)
✠ ST. JOHN'S WORT oil with added lavender oil — to heal the perineum after birth
✠ OATS — use oat tincture for postpartum depression
✠ FENUGREEK, FENNEL, CARAWAY and MILK THISTLE — to promote milk production
✠ SAGE — for reduction of milk flow during weaning
✠ FENNEL — for baby's colic
✠ CABBAGE LEAVES (bruise and apply externally) and ECHINACEA (take tincture internally) relieve the pain of mastitis
✠ CALENDULA CREAM — for diaper rash and cracked nipples

HERBS AND CANCER

Many plants have anti-tumor properties, but no one plant can provide a cure for cancer. Plants are being investigated by scientists in the hope of finding a cure, but most are rejected, because of toxicity or disappointing results when tested. So far there is no proven plant cure, but many plants are used in a holistic fight against cancer.

Herbal medicine can be supportive to cancer sufferers, and can be combined with orthodox medical treatment.

Many cancer victims have tried herbal "cures" without success, and this has led to the warning, "beware of quack cures!" A good herbalist will not promise a cure, but can offer support therapy and improve the body's immune system.

HERBS AND THE PREVENTION OF ILLNESS

Many herbs can help to prevent illness. It is possible to remain well by following a healthy diet, combined with fresh air and sufficient exercise, low stress levels and the use of certain herbs which help with detoxification and improve the immune system. Some herbs have strengthening and tonic properties, while others contain both vitamins and minerals. These herbs are listed under the descriptions of medicinal herbs (*see* pages 130–147).

HERBS AND CHILDREN

Herbal medicine is eminently suitable for children and even for babies. It is both gentle and supportive. Many herbs have a febrifuge or diaphoretic action, and will lower a fever by encouraging perspiration. Other herbs will help to fight infection. As children often have violent infections, resulting in a high fever lasting for as little as one day, herbal medicine helps the body fight off the problem without suppressing the body's own efforts.

Children become irritable during illness, especially when they are very young, and calming herbs such as chamomile or lemon balm will safely soothe them. Herbal medicine helps children develop a strong immune system, as it does not suppress symptoms and will not upset any of the balances in the body, but will support and strengthen it.

THE PREPARATION OF HERBAL REMEDIES

AS THIS IS ONLY A GENERAL GUIDELINE FOR THE PREPARATION OF REMEDIES, CONSULT

THE TABLE OF AILMENTS ON PAGE 128 TO FIND OUT WHICH HERB

TO USE FOR A SPECIFIC COMPLAINT AND HOW TO USE IT.

PREPARATIONS FOR INTERNAL USE

FRESH HERBS AND HERB JUICE

Eat herbs raw in salads. Some herbs, such as stinging nettle and celery leaves, can be juiced and taken neat, 4 tsp (20 ml) at a time, or combined with carrot, apple and celery juice.

INFUSION

Leaves and flowers are usually infused, sometimes other parts of the plant.

A standard infusion is prepared with 1–2 tsp (5–10 ml) dried herb per cup of boiling water, infused for 10 minutes before straining. Do not leave for too long, as it can become bitter and too strong. Make it in a pot with a lid to prevent evaporation. Drink hot or cold, but for influenza, colds and bronchitis, hot is best. It must always be used on the day of preparation.

If using fresh herbs, use double the amount of herb.

✠ The standard dosage for an infusion is 8 fl oz (250 ml) three times a day.

DECOCTION

Roots, bark and seeds are usually prepared in this way.

Use 1–2 tsp (5–10 ml) of herb per cup of cold water, bring gently to the boil in a saucepan with the lid on and simmer for about 10 minutes. It must be used on the day of preparation.

✠ The standard dosage for a decoction is 8 fl oz (250 ml) three times a day. If the herb is very bitter or strong, use 4 tsp (20 ml) three times a day.

TINCTURE

A tincture is an alcoholic extraction of a herb. Alcohol is used, as it dissolves the active constituents out of the plant matter, and also acts as a preservative. Tinctures remain viable for up to two years. Recipes vary according to the toxicity and constituents of the plant. Some require stronger alcohol, and others use different proportions of herb to alcohol, but this standard recipe may be used.

Use any part of the plant to make a tincture. Place 4 oz (100 g) dried herb in a glass jar with a tight-fitting lid and add 17 oz (500 ml) vodka or spirits (45% proof). Leave for two weeks, shaking occasionally, then strain through a cloth into a brown glass bottle. Keep tightly stoppered.

✠ The standard dosage for a tincture is 15 drops three times daily. (You may also use cider vinegar instead of alcohol. Never use industrial alcohol, as it is toxic, or spirit vinegar, as it is not good for your health.)

HERBAL WINE

Wine is used in much the same way as spirits for making a tincture. A sweet, fortified wine or a red wine with a good alcohol content (12%) is best.

Cover 4 oz (100 g) of chosen herb with 1¼ pints (750 ml) wine. Leave for a week before straining. Herbal wine does not last as long as a tincture, and is best used within a month.

✠ The standard dosage for herbal wine is 4 tsp (20 ml) once or twice daily.

SYRUP

Sugar is a good preservative and is ideal for cough mixtures, especially as some herbs for coughs are very bitter.

Prepare 17 oz (500 ml) of an infusion or decoction of the required herb. Strain, add 14 oz (400 g) of brown sugar (or a honey and sugar mixture) and heat gently until sugar dissolves. Pour it into a clean glass bottle, seal and store in the refrigerator.

✠ The standard dosage is 1 tsp (5 ml) three times daily. For a serious cough, consult your herbalist.

CAPSULES

Some people prefer to take herbal medicine in dry, powdered form. One can simply stir the powder into water, but taking it in capsule form is convenient. Empty capsules can be bought at some chemists or health shops.

Place the powdered herb in a dish. To fill capsules, scoop both halves towards each other through the powdered herb and fit the halves together.

✠ The standard dosage is two capsules, three times daily, depending on the herb used. When in any doubt, consult your herbalist.

PREPARATIONS FOR EXTERNAL USE

OIL INFUSION

This can be made in two ways — the hot or cold method.

For the hot method, fill a jar with fresh herb and cover with oil (olive, almond or sunflower — not mineral oil). Place the jar up to its neck in a saucepan of water, bring to a medium temperature and simmer for about 2–3 hours. Strain through filter paper or a cloth into a brown glass bottle.

Use the same method when making a cold infusion, but place the jar on a sunny windowsill for two to three weeks instead of heating the oil. The process can be repeated to make the oil stronger.

CREAM

A cream is a blend of oil, beeswax and water.

Melt 2 oz (50 g) wax in a double boiler. Add 8 fl oz (250 ml) olive or other vegetable oil and blend in. Add 2 oz (50 g) of herb. For lighter cream, add a little water, mixing well. Simmer for 20 minutes. Add a drop of tincture of benzoin as a preservative. Strain through a cloth into sterilized jars and seal.

The easiest way is to buy an aqueous (water-based) cream from a drugstore, melt it down with the herb, simmer for 30 minutes, strain and pot. You will need enough liquid to cover the herb during simmering. Alternatively, add herbal tincture to an aqueous cream, stirring to a good consistency.

OINTMENT

Ointment does not penetrate the skin like cream, but covers and protects it. Petroleum jelly is a good base, and the method is the same as for cream.

Melt petroleum jelly in a double boiler, add plenty of herbs, making sure that the melted petroleum jelly covers the herbs. Simmer until herb material is crisp. The herbs may settle to the bottom of the dish. Add more to make ointment stronger. Strain into sterilized jars while hot.

SUPPOSITORIES

These are best made in advance, ready for use when required.

Blend equal quantities of finely powdered herbs (refer to Table of Ailments on page 128) with cocoa butter, place the mixture into bullet-shaped moulds made out of foil, and refrigerate. Remove the foil before use.

COMPRESS

This is a very good way of dealing with an external complaint, such as a sprain.

Soak a cloth in a hot decoction of herb, squeeze most of the liquid out and apply the hot cloth to the affected area. Once it has cooled, repeat the process until relief is obtained. Tinctures of other herbs, even essential oils, can be added to the liquid.

POULTICE

Often used in the past, poultices are now regarded as old-fashioned, but are very effective for boils, abscesses, chest infections and sprains or injuries.

Mix chopped herb or powdered seeds with boiling water to make a pulp. Place pulp in a piece of cloth and apply to affected area while quite hot. It will stay hot for a long time, and should be replaced when cool. A thin layer of calendula cream protects skin and prevents the poultice from sticking.

BATH

Prepare an herbal bath by adding a strong decoction of the herb, or essential oils, to the bath water. This can be used for feet only, as a sitzbath (where one sits with only the hips and buttocks in the water), as a normal bath for relaxation, cleansing or stimulation, and as a bath to calm a baby, for instance.

Cover a cupful or more (depending on the size of the bath) of the herb with water and simmer in a pot, with the lid on, for 15 minutes. Strain and add to the bath. Only a few drops of essential oil are required for a bath. One can also use a few tablespoonfuls of herbal tincture.

POWDER

Powdered herbs can be applied to weeping eczema or ulcers. The powder must first be placed in gauze. It can also be used as snuff for sinus.

STEAM/INHALANT

Use steam for skin problems like acne, or an inhalant for bronchial problems, e.g. sinusitis and laryngitis. Use a strong decoction, one or two drops of essential oils or 2 tsp (10 ml) of tincture and add to boiling water.

TABLE OF AILMENTS AND SUGGESTED HERBS

THIS TABLE SERVES AS A GUIDE ONLY. MOST OF THE SUGGESTED HERBS ARE DESCRIBED IN THIS BOOK, FOR YOU TO STUDY FURTHER. REMEMBER THAT THE BODY HEALS ITSELF! HERBS, WHEN WISELY CHOSEN, ASSIST THE BODY IN ITS HEALING EFFORTS. OFTEN, THOUGH, HERBS ARE NOT ENOUGH, AND CHANGES IN DIET AND LIFESTYLE ARE NECESSARY FOR A TOTAL HEALING PROCESS. PLEASE REFER TO PAGE 124 FOR HERBS WHICH SHOULD NOT BE TAKEN DURING PREGNANCY.

ABSCESSES
INTERNALLY: cleavers, echinacea (infusion, tincture); garlic (raw, capsules)
EXTERNALLY: fenugreek (poultice)

ACNE
INTERNALLY: burdock, cleavers (infusion)
EXTERNALLY: lavender (oil), calendula (tincture)

ANEMIA
INTERNALLY: stinging nettle (tincture, juice, infusion)

ANXIETY
INTERNALLY: lemon balm, passion flower, chamomile, valerian (tincture, infusion, tablets)
EXTERNALLY: lavender (bath, compress on forehead)

ASTHMA
INTERNALLY: elecampane, sundew, thyme (infusion, syrup)
EXTERNALLY: sage (burn to inhale smoke); thyme (steam inhalation)

BLOOD PRESSURE, HIGH
INTERNALLY: garlic, hawthorn, linden blossom, yarrow (tincture, infusion)

BLOOD PRESSURE, LOW
INTERNALLY: rosemary (tincture, infusion)

BOILS See abscesses

BRUISES
INTERNALLY: Arnica D6 (tablets, homeopathic); St. John's wort (tincture, infusion)
EXTERNALLY: arnica (tincture, cream)

BURNS
INTERNALLY: Rescue Remedy (Bach flower remedy)
EXTERNALLY: comfrey (cream); aloe (juice); St. John's wort, lavender (oil)

CHEMOTHERAPY
INTERNALLY: fenugreek (tea); milk thistle, Siberian ginseng (tincture, infusion)

CHILBLAINS
INTERNALLY: cayenne, ginger, rosemary (tincture)
EXTERNALLY: eucalyptus (oil); slippery elm and cayenne (poultice)

COLDS
INTERNALLY: echinacea, elder, eyebright, ginger, peppermint, yarrow (infusion, tincture)
EXTERNALLY: thyme (steam inhalation)

COLIC
INTERNALLY: caraway, chamomile, fennel, ginger, peppermint, wild yam (infusion, tincture)
EXTERNALLY: chamomile (bath)

CONSTIPATION
INTERNALLY: linseed (as is); aloe, senna (capsules)

COUGHS
INTERNALLY: aniseed, coltsfoot, elecampane, garlic, mullein, ribwort, thyme, white horehound (syrup, tincture, infusion)
EXTERNALLY: thyme (steam inhalation)

CRAMPS
INTERNALLY: black cohosh, hop, skullcap, valerian (tincture, infusion)
EXTERNALLY: rosemary (massage with oil infusion)

CYSTITIS
INTERNALLY: birch, buchu, echinacea, goldenrod, ribwort (tincture, infusion)

DEPRESSION
INTERNALLY: oats, rosemary, skullcap, St. John's wort (infusion, tincture)
EXTERNALLY: rosemary and lavender or bergamot (bath)

DETOXIFICATION
INTERNALLY: birch, dandelion, stinging nettle (infusion)
EXTERNALLY: pine (bath); sage, thyme (compress)

DIARRHEA
INTERNALLY: agrimony, lady's mantle, meadowsweet, ribwort (infusion, tincture)

DIVERTICULITIS
INTERNALLY: caraway, chamomile, echinacea, willow bark (infusion, tincture)
EXTERNALLY: peppermint (poultice)

DYSPEPSIA
INTERNALLY: chamomile, ginger, meadowsweet, peppermint (infusion)

EARACHE
INTERNALLY: echinacea, ribwort (infusion, tincture)
EXTERNALLY: mullein (oil)

ECZEMA
INTERNALLY: burdock, cleavers, stinging nettle, red clover (infusion, tincture)
EXTERNALLY: chickweed (cream); oats (bath); pansy (tincture of *Viola tricolor*, smaller than garden pansy)

EYE INFECTION
INTERNALLY: echinacea, eyebright (infusion, tincture)
EXTERNALLY: calendula, eyebright, fennel, meadowsweet (infusion)

FEVER
INTERNALLY: lemon balm, elder, ginger, yarrow (hot infusion)

FLATULENCE
INTERNALLY: caraway, fennel, ginger, meadowsweet, peppermint (infusion, tincture)

FUNGAL INFECTION
INTERNALLY: garlic (raw, capsules); olive (oil); calendula, goldenrod, goldenseal, thyme (tincture, infusion)
EXTERNALLY: calendula (oil infusion); myrrh, thyme (tincture)

GASTRITIS
INTERNALLY: slippery elm (powder in capsules); chamomile, marsh mallow, meadowsweet (infusion)

HEMORRHOIDS
INTERNALLY: horse chestnut, lady's mantle, tormentil (tincture)
EXTERNALLY: ribwort, witch hazel (ointment)

HALITOSIS
CHEW: cloves, dill, peppermint; check teeth and digestion

HAY FEVER
INTERNALLY: echinacea, elder, *Ephedra,* goldenrod, goldenseal (infusion, tincture)
EXTERNALLY: for itchy eyes, use as for eye infection

HEADACHES
INTERNALLY: feverfew (tablets); chamomile, valerian, willow bark (infusion, tincture)
EXTERNALLY: lavender (compress)

INFLUENZA
INTERNALLY: echinacea, elder, garlic, ginger, willow bark, yarrow (infusion, tincture)
EXTERNALLY: rosemary (spirits — in rubbing alcohol — or oil for muscles)

INSOMNIA
INTERNALLY: lemon balm, chamomile, hop, passion flower, valerian (tincture, infusion)
EXTERNALLY: hop (pillow); lavender (bath)
FOR BABY: chamomile (bath)

LIVER COMPLAINTS
INTERNALLY: gentian, dandelion root, milk thistle (tincture, infusion)

MENOPAUSE
INTERNALLY: black cohosh, chaste berry, St. John's wort (infusion, tincture)

MENSTRUAL PROBLEMS
INTERNALLY: Painful periods — black cohosh, chamomile, feverfew, hop, valerian (infusion, tincture)
Heavy periods — lady's mantle, shepherd's purse (infusion, tincture)

NAUSEA
INTERNALLY: chamomile, cloves, ginger, peppermint (infusion)

PRE-MENSTRUAL TENSION
INTERNALLY: evening primrose (oil); chaste berry, skullcap, St. John's wort, valerian (infusion, tincture)

PROSTATE
INTERNALLY: buchu, horsetail, saw palmetto (infusion, tincture)

RHEUMATISM
INTERNALLY: birch, buchu, celery seed, devil's claw, feverfew, juniper, willow bark (infusion, tincture)
EXTERNALLY: arnica (oil or cream); rosemary (oil infusion with added juniper oil)

RINGWORM
EXTERNALLY: calendula (tincture); garlic, tea tree (oil)

SINUSITIS
INTERNALLY: elder, eyebright, goldenrod, goldenseal (infusion, tincture)
EXTERNALLY: eucalyptus (oil — as a steam inhalation and also rubbed directly over sinuses)

SORE THROAT
INTERNALLY: echinacea (tincture, infusion); garlic (raw, capsules); agrimony, myrrh, sage (gargle with an infusion)

SUNBURN
EXTERNALLY: calendula (oil); aloe (juice); St. John's wort (oil, with a few drops of eucalyptus)

ULCERS (PEPTIC)
INTERNALLY: cabbage (juice); linseed (tea); meadowsweet (infusion); slippery elm (powder in capsules)

ULCERS (LEG)
EXTERNALLY: calendula (oil); comfrey root (powder)

VARICOSE VEINS
INTERNALLY: horse chestnut (tincture)
EXTERNALLY: calendula, witch hazel (compress)

WARTS
INTERNALLY: thuja (tincture)
EXTERNALLY: dandelion (fresh juice applied several times daily); garlic (slices under a bandage); greater celandine (fresh juice)

WORMS
INTERNALLY: garlic, pomegranate, pumpkin seed, wormwood (tincture)
EXTERNALLY: aloe (ointment — apply around anus at night)

WOUNDS
INTERNALLY: echinacea (tincture); Rescue Remedy (for shock)
EXTERNALLY: calendula, chickweed, comfrey, elder (cream); calendula (tincture, as an antiseptic); St. John's wort (oil)

ALPHABETICAL LISTING AND DESCRIPTION
OF MEDICINAL PLANTS

THE FOLLOWING DESCRIPTIONS have been researched from well-respected works as well as drawing on the author's own knowledge. While every care has been taken to ensure that the material is factual and correct, the author accepts no responsibility for problems which may arise as a result of self-medication.

Pregnant women, lactating women and women of child-bearing age who may be pregnant are warned that therapeutic doses of herbs could cause miscarriage or problems to the nursing infant.

The standard dosage for all the listed herbs is 1 tsp (5 ml) dried herb per 8 oz (250 ml) boiling water for infusions or decoctions, or 15 drops of tincture three times daily. These dosages are quite low, to ensure safety. If higher doses are required, consult an herbalist.

YARROW

BUCHU

AGRIMONY

Achillea millefolium

YARROW

CAUTION

Yarrow should not be used during pregnancy. It should also not be used for any bleeding disorders that have not been professionally diagnosed. Do not use for longer than two weeks without consulting your herbalist for advice. Yarrow can sometimes cause contact dermatitis in sensitive people.

PARTS USED

Fresh or dried whole flowering plant, except the roots

THERAPEUTIC ACTION

Yarrow is reputed to have received its botanical name from Achilles, who knew of its effectiveness in staunching bleeding. At that time it was an important part of the first-aid kit for soldiers in battle. It contains azulene, a healing agent also found in chamomile. Yarrow can therefore be used for bleeding disorders such as bleeding hemorrhoids, menstrual problems and nosebleeds (*see* Caution above). Yarrow promotes perspiration and will help break a fever. It blends well with peppermint and elderflower as a tea for colds and flu. It has an antiseptic action too, and will be of benefit in mild cystitis. It has a bitter tonic action on the liver that will promote good digestion. It improves circulation by acting as a peripheral vasodilator, with resultant lowering of high blood pressure. Yarrow is a truly remarkable plant.

ADMINISTRATION

INFUSION (the dried or fresh plant); TINCTURE (use as indicated on the bottle, or on advice from your herbalist); FRESH LEAF (for nosebleeds or cuts)

Agathosma betulina

BUCHU

CAUTION

In cases of recurring cystitis, it is advisable to establish the underlying cause of the illness rather than to self-medicate. Consult your doctor or herbalist in this regard.

PARTS USED

Leaves

THERAPEUTIC ACTION

Mainly used for the treatment of certain bladder problems, this herb, which has its origin in South Africa, has been exported to several other countries ever since the 19th century. Buchu has an antiseptic action on the urinary system, and it is most beneficial in the amelioration of inflammation of the urethra (urethritis), as well as cystitis and mild prostatitis. It is also very useful as a diuretic and, as such, it can be a useful herb in the treatment of rheumatism. Buchu combines very well with several other herbs, adding a good refreshing flavor.

ADMINISTRATION

INFUSION; TINCTURE (buchu brandy); COMPRESS (buchu vinegar compress for sprains)

Agrimonia eupatoria

AGRIMONY

PARTS USED

Whole flowering plant, except the roots

THERAPEUTIC ACTION

In ancient Greek times, this plant was one of the best known healing plants, and it was used extensively for healing the wounds which were sustained in battle. After a long period of disuse, agrimony once again experienced a revival in the Middle Ages. Its main medicinal action is as an astringent, and this makes it an extremely effective gargle for a sore throat and also for cases of laryngitis. Its astringency makes it an excellent remedy for diarrhea, especially in the case of children, as its action is very mild. It also has a bitter tonic action on the liver and is very useful for digestive disorders and jaundice.

ADMINISTRATION

INFUSION (use for a sore throat, either to drink or as a gargle); TINCTURE; CREAM (for skin ulcers and sores); BATH (for eczema and scrofulous conditions)

Alchemilla vulgaris

LADY'S MANTLE

CAUTION

Do not use lady's mantle for undiagnosed bleeding disorders for a period of more than about two weeks.

PARTS USED

Leaves

THERAPEUTIC ACTION

This plant has astringent properties and is therefore most efficacious in cases where severe bleeding occurs. In herbalism it is specifically and mostly used for the treatment of menstrual disorders, such as heavy menstruation, and for leucorrhea and menopausal problems. As it is an astringent herb, it can also successfully be used for the relief of a sore throat, laryngitis and even diarrhea. It is reputed to have tranquillizing properties in tincture form.

ADMINISTRATION

INFUSION; TINCTURE; BATH; DOUCHE

Allium sativum

GARLIC

CAUTION

Too much raw garlic taken at once may cause vomiting.

PARTS USED

Bulb

THERAPEUTIC ACTION

Garlic has been used throughout the ages to ward off disease, and has saved many lives in epidemics of infectious diseases. It is antibacterial and can neutralize "unfriendly" bacteria in the gastro-intestinal tract. Garlic provides protection against colds and influenza, and strengthens the chest in cases of asthma and bronchial catarrh. Garlic improves the circulation, lowers blood pressure and reduces cholesterol levels — it is one of the very few plants which is known to do this. This has been verified by controlled clinical studies. Further studies indicate that garlic may have a protective role against coronary heart disease, thrombosis and arteriosclerosis. Scientific studies have shown that it also offers some degree of protection against cancer. Furthermore, garlic has been demonstrated to possess both antibacterial and antifungal properties.

ADMINISTRATION

FRESH CLOVES; POWDERED GARLIC; OIL CAPSULES

Aloe ferox

CAPE ALOE

CAUTION

Do not use aloe during pregnancy or lactation. It should also not be used if you are suffering from hemorrhoids or irritable bowel syndrome.

PARTS USED

Juice of the leaves

THERAPEUTIC ACTION

The juice of aloes has been used both internally and externally since time immemorial. Aloe is one of the oldest recorded medicinal herbs, and one of its ingredients, aloe-emodin, is a powerful laxative (always to be used with caution). It is best used in conjunction with a tincture of caraway seed in order to prevent intestinal cramps and pain. It also has a bitter tonic action on the liver, and it helps to encourage bile flow. Taken in rather small doses, it is an excellent digestive tonic. The fresh juice of the leaf blade can be applied directly to ulcers, burns, sunburn and fungal infections on the skin.

ADMINISTRATION

TINCTURE; CREAM; FRESH JUICE

Althaea officinalis

MARSH MALLOW

PARTS USED

Dried roots, leaves and flowers

THERAPEUTIC ACTION

Long ago marsh mallow was used by the ancient Greeks, and today it is still extensively used by both herbalists and pharmaceutical companies. Primarily it has soothing properties, and a cold maceration of the root will be of help in soothing the digestive tract, as well as for the treatment of gastric ulcers. The mucilaginous element of this plant relieves and heals the "raw" chest which is common in bronchitis and it is also soothing to the ureters and urethra, in the case of kidney stone damage and also cystitis. A poultice of the leaves or the powdered root of this plant can be used most effectively for boils, abscesses, ulcers and any other purulent skin conditions.

ADMINISTRATION

TINCTURE; INFUSION (cold, overnight); POULTICE; COLD MACERATION OF ROOT OR LEAF

LADY'S MANTLE

GARLIC

CAPE ALOE

MARSH MALLOW

ANGELICA

CELERY

ARNICA

WORMWOOD

Angelica archangelica

ANGELICA

CAUTION

Not to be taken during pregnancy or if diabetic.

PARTS USED

Root, seeds, leaves and stems

THERAPEUTIC ACTION

Angelica stimulates both circulation and digestion. It works via the nervous system, and contains volatile oil and bitters. When taken as a tea, the leaves provide a stimulating tonic which cleanses the liver, and it is especially good where illness has left the person feeling weak. It has a calming effect on the digestive tract, eliminating flatulence, easing colic pain or spasms, and improving digestion. It stimulates digestion and is useful for treating anorexia nervosa. Angelica is excellent for bronchitis, strengthening weak lungs by working as a tonic. Angelica tea will help promote perspiration in a fever and is also a useful remedy for cystitis. It acts as a menstrual stimulant and regulator of menstruation, while its antispasmodic action can ease menstrual pain.

ADMINISTRATION

TINCTURE; INFUSION; DECOCTION (roots or seeds)

Apium graveolens

CELERY

CAUTION

Do not take celery seed extract during pregnancy. Celery leaves in salads are safe.

PARTS USED

The seed

THERAPEUTIC ACTION

The volatile oils in celery seeds are responsible for most of its healing effects. Celery seed extract recently became a well-known commercial product, and will help some arthritis sufferers, but not all. It can be used for rheumatism and rheumatoid arthritis. The seeds are diuretic, and also have a carminative function on the digestive tract, relieving flatulence and stimulating the appetite. The leaves are nutritional, providing many vitamins and minerals, and they also act as a nutritive tonic. Celery is a nerve restorer and helps for nervous exhaustion and depression. It acts as a mild sedative.

ADMINISTRATION

INFUSION; TINCTURE

Arnica montana

ARNICA

CAUTION

Do not use arnica on broken skin or internally, as it is a poisonous herb.

PARTS USED

Flowers, root

THERAPEUTIC ACTION

Arnica is the wonder-herb for treating wounds and bruises. Applied directly after an injury, it can prevent a bruise forming. Taken internally, but only in homeopathic form (Arnica D6), for a week before and after an operation, it helps to speed up healing by relieving swelling and bruising. When it is applied to rheumatic joints, it brings relief from pain. For sprains or broken bones, a compress of arnica speeds up repair and also relieves the pain. Apply a diluted tincture (1 tsp/5 ml tincture in 3½ fl oz/100 ml water) to skin ulcers, boils and abscesses.

ADMINISTRATION

TINCTURE (external use only); COMPRESS (for sprains, broken bones, etc.); CREAM (for bruises and sprains); OIL (for rheumatic joints)

Artemisia absinthium

WORMWOOD

CAUTION

The volatile oil is toxic to the nervous system and, when taken in excess, can cause permanent brain damage. Not to be used during pregnancy or lactation.

PARTS USED

Leaves and flowering parts

THERAPEUTIC ACTION

It has a bitter tonic action on the liver, improves the digestion and is used as a good background treatment for ailments of the digestive tract. Treatment with wormwood is best left to a herbalist, but occasional use for one or two days, following the correct dosages (1 tsp/5 ml herb per 8 fl oz/250 ml boiling water), can be beneficial. The leaves can be used in pill form to treat roundworm or pinworm infestation. Wormwood tones a sluggish digestive system and is useful after an operation, when the intestinal tract seems paralyzed.

ADMINISTRATION

TINCTURE; INFUSION; PILLS

Avena sativa
OATS

PARTS USED
Seeds and the whole plant

THERAPEUTIC ACTION
The Scots are often teased for their predilection for oats, but they are right in their choice. Oats are one of the finest foods, giving strength to those who eat them regularly. (The best are rolled oats, which are processed the least.) Oats help a puny child thrive and can be used for weak digestion and intestinal tract disturbances. Oat straw is rich in silica, which strengthens bone and connective tissue. Oats strengthen the convalescent and nourish the nerves. In cases of weak nerves, a nervous breakdown or depression, oats will restore nervous functioning and help relax the overwrought system.

ADMINISTRATION
TINCTURE; PORRIDGE; OATBRAN (reduces cholesterol levels); BATH (in a muslin cloth to give water a creamy texture for soothing eczema); FOOT BATH (regular foot baths of oat straw soothe tired feet and improve the circulation of chronically cold feet)

Berberis vulgaris
BARBERRY

CAUTION
Not to be used during pregnancy.

PARTS USED
Root, bark and stem bark

THERAPEUTIC ACTION
The root is bright yellow and the decoction tastes very bitter as a result of the alkaloid, berberine, which has antimicrobial properties. It is effective against many common intestinal infections and can be used after antibiotic treatment to help normalize gut flora. As a bitter tonic, it stimulates bile flow, tones the digestive system and gall bladder, improves digestion and stimulates peristalsis. It works well in cases of gall-bladder inflammation and can help prevent gallstones. After a bout of jaundice, it can also aid the liver in recovery.

ADMINISTRATION
TINCTURE (as prescribed by a herbalist); DECOCTION (for a hangover); EYE COMPRESS (in the case of eye inflammation and conjunctivitis, use a cotton wool compress soaked in a decoction)

Betula pendula
SILVER BIRCH

PARTS USED
Leaves

THERAPEUTIC ACTION
This herb is a general "spring-cleaner" of the whole system, and will effectively flush out uric acid and other toxic build-up in the body. To treat a person who is listless and constantly sluggish, birch leaf tea taken three times daily for about a week can really work wonders. Because of the cleansing action of silver birch, it can be of help in those types of rheumatism or arthritis which are caused by an accumulation of uric acid in the system. Birch has a diuretic action and is also slightly antiseptic, which can be very useful in cases of cystitis. The bark contains methyl salicylate, which has an analgesic effect.

ADMINISTRATION
ELIXIR (a commercial preparation for detoxifying the system); TINCTURE; INFUSION

Borago officinalis
BORAGE

PARTS USED
Dried leaves, after being picked in the flowering season; seeds

THERAPEUTIC ACTION
Because it is an amazing tonic plant for the adrenal glands, borage provides invaluable support in the stressful lives many people live. It also acts as a nerve restorer. Borage is quite rich in minerals, especially potassium. It can be used as a tea to help reduce fevers and is also very good for chest colds, when it is often used in combination with other herbs such as mullein (*Verbascum thapsus*) or marsh mallow (*Althaea officinalis*). It has a slight diuretic function, combined with its anti-inflammatory properties, which will promote the cleansing of the system in any illness. Borage acts as a galactogogue, promoting the production of milk in breastfeeding mothers. The seeds are a rich source of gamma linolenic acid (GLA) and the extracted oil is used for a number of problems such as eczema, premenstrual tension and joint disease.

ADMINISTRATION
INFUSION; TINCTURE; SEED-OIL CAPSULES

OATS

BARBERRY

SILVER BIRCH

BORAGE

CALENDULA

CAYENNE

CARAWAY

CHICORY

Calendula officinalis

CALENDULA

PARTS USED

Flowers

THERAPEUTIC ACTION

Calendula flowers have been used for healing since ancient times, but these healing properties were only recently substantiated by medical science. Calendula heals wounds, as well as internal and external ulcers. It is an antiseptic, improves blood flow to the affected area and encourages formation of granulation tissue. It is antifungal and can be used to treat athlete's foot, ringworm and candida. The tincture applied neat to cold sores (herpes simplex) hastens healing and it can also improve acne. Calendula has a mild bitter tonic action which improves general health via the liver. It soothes the digestive tract, and can be used for colitis and any ailment infecting the mucous membrane of the intestinal tract. An infusion of calendula can be taken to regulate menstrual and menopausal problems.

ADMINISTRATION

TINCTURE (as prescribed); INFUSION (eyewash for inflamed eyes, mouthwash for ulcers and bleeding gums); CREAM (burns, sunburn, cracked nipples, diaper rash, eczema, ringworm); DOUCHE (vaginal thrush); COMPRESS

Capsicum frutescens

CAYENNE

CAUTION

Not for use if suffering from a gastric ulcer. Excessive use can be harmful. Not to be used during pregnancy or lactation.

PARTS USED

The fruit

THERAPEUTIC ACTION

This pepper, taken medicinally in small quantities, is beneficial to the circulation. It also has a toning and strengthening effect on the blood vessels and heart. It seems to have a general toning effect on the digestive system too, improving digestion and easing flatulence. It promotes perspiration and warms the system in feverish chills or when feeling cold in winter! As a warming agent, it can be helpful in rheumatism, and a cayenne compress relieves joint pains.

ADMINISTRATION

TINCTURE; OINTMENT; DRIED OR FRESH

Carum carvi

CARAWAY

PARTS USED

Seeds

THERAPEUTIC ACTION

The volatile oil which occurs in the seeds of caraway acts as a carminative, thereby easing both griping and flatulence. Its antispasmodic action also goes further than this to ease menstrual pain and it even helps to relieve labor pains. In common with aniseed, caraway can be used to ease a cough, but this is best done in combination with other herbs which are used for coughs. Caraway is a galactogogue, which causes it to stimulate the flow of breast milk, and it also possibly provides a carminative action via the breast milk, to soothe a gassy or colicky baby.

ADMINISTRATION

TINCTURE; INFUSION (to drink or to use as a gargle for laryngitis)

Cichorium intybus

CHICORY

PARTS USED

Roots, leaves and flowers

THERAPEUTIC ACTION

When using chicory, only wild plants are used, or else those which are organically grown. The dried root is mixed with coffee; alternatively it is used by itself as a substitute for coffee. It contains appreciable amounts of inulin, which is an important constituent for diabetes as it helps to lower the blood sugar levels. The bitter action of leaves (freshly juiced), flowers (in an infusion) or root has a cleansing and a stimulating effect on the liver and gall bladder. Chicory is also beneficial in cases of jaundice, gallstones and inflammation of the spleen. It cleanses the blood and helps relieve depression — this is probably a result of the general improvement it brings about to the whole body. It has a diuretic action and it also helps to ease both gout and rheumatism.

ADMINISTRATION

TINCTURE; FRESH JUICE; DECOCTION OF THE ROOT; INFUSION OF FLOWERS; SYRUP FROM THE ROOT (use as a laxative for children; the syrup is not usually made at home, but bought from health-food stores with dosage instructions on the label)

Cimicifuga racemosa
BLACK COHOSH

CAUTION

This herb is not to be used during pregnancy, because it is a uterine stimulant. It may, however, be used during labor.

PARTS USED

Dried root and rhizome

THERAPEUTIC ACTION

This plant comes from North America and Canada, and it was very widely used by the indigenous Indian healers in North America. Although it has several healing properties, the main action is antispasmodic. It is effective for muscle spasm, painful menstruation, bronchial spasm (as in whooping cough), sciatica, rheumatic pain and various complaints of the female reproductive system, with the antispasmodic action relaxing cramps of the uterus or ovaries. It contains hormone-like substances (estrogenic) which help to normalize hormonal irregularities, and it is helpful in menopause. It is a uterine stimulant, and can ease labor contractions, thereby aiding delivery.

ADMINISTRATION

TINCTURE; DECOCTION

Cinnamomum zeylicanum
CINNAMON

CAUTION

Not to be used in large quantities during pregnancy.

PARTS USED

Bark

THERAPEUTIC ACTION

Cinnamon is an aromatic, warming herb, and as such is useful for the treatment of feverish chills and cold conditions. It has a carminative action and it is also an astringent, which means that it is effective for treating cases of diarrhea, as it helps to soothe cramping and flatulence and also slows down peristalsis. Furthermore it can also help to stop vomiting and it relieves nausea. The main medicinal ingredient, cinnamaldehyde, has a hypotensive action and can help to improve peripheral circulation (the warming of cold hands and feet). The oil of cinnamon has antifungal and antibacterial properties.

ADMINISTRATION

POWDERED BARK; TINCTURE; CINNAMON OIL

Citrus limon
LEMON

PARTS USED

Whole fruit

THERAPEUTIC ACTION

The lemon seems to have its origins in India, rather than Greece or Italy like many other herbs. It is antibacterial and stimulates the immune system — hence its use in treating colds. It cools the system, which helps for fever. Lemons help the circulation, strengthen capillaries, improve peripheral circulation, lower blood pressure and have a tonic action on the vascular system. Contrary to what many believe, they have an alkalising effect — they help the body get rid of excess acidity. This is good for hyperacidity of the stomach, rheumatism and gout caused by acidity. They tone the liver and improve digestion. The juice is used externally for skin complaints, as an antiseptic or an astringent.

ADMINISTRATION

FRESH JUICE; DECOCTION (of whole chopped lemon); OIL (of rind)

Echinacea purpurea
ECHINACEA (CONE FLOWER)

PARTS USED

Roots, leaves and flowers

THERAPEUTIC ACTION

Once used by American Indians, echinacea is essential in the herbal medicine chest. At the first sign of a cold or infection, it boosts the defence system by enhancing phagocytic (white cell) activity, and stops the infection. It is an immune system booster, used for infectious problems ranging from colds, boils, cystitis, coughs and influenza, to serious chronic conditions such as neuromyalgia, cancer and AIDS. Though it cannot cure serious diseases, it will assist the immune system in its battle. It helps prevent the spread of infection. It has anti-inflammatory properties, and will support the body during any inflammatory condition. It has the primary purpose of improving the resistance of the body to bacterial and viral infections.

ADMINISTRATION

TINCTURE; DECOCTION (of the root); INFUSION (of the aerial parts); CREAM

BLACK COHOSH

CINNAMON

LEMON

ECHINACEA

HORSETAIL

EYEBRIGHT

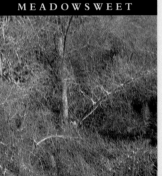

MEADOWSWEET

FENNEL

Equisetum arvense
HORSETAIL

PARTS USED
Needle-like leaves and stems

THERAPEUTIC ACTION
This plant, which has survived as a genus since pre-historic times, has many uses. It is rich in silica, among other nutrients, which has a tissue-strengthening effect on the body. Long-term use can help in cases of bed-wetting and incontinence. It has a good influence on the kidneys and can be used as a diuretic in cases of cystitis. It can stop internal and external bleeding and it also promotes healing. It is very useful in treating the prostate, having an astringent and toning action. Horsetail has proved helpful in treating rheumatism, rheumatoid arthritis and arthritis, mainly due to the action of silica in bone and connective tissue repair, and its diuretic effect. It can be useful in preventing kidney stones, and has a strengthening effect on the tubes and sphincters of the urinary system and the bronchi of the lungs.

ADMINISTRATION
TONIC; INFUSION

Euphrasia officinalis
EYEBRIGHT

PARTS USED
Leaves and flowers

THERAPEUTIC ACTION
This little plant, which generally thrives among the grasses of Britain, has been used for centuries, especially as a treatment for the eyes. There is still no complete certainty as to which one of its chemical constituents is actually the active healing agent, but its actions are both astringent and toning. Eyebright is an invaluable remedy for any form of eye inflammation and eye weakness. It works very well as a mucous membrane restorative, and is also a useful addition to other herbal medicines, such as goldenseal or elder flower, being extensively used in cases of catarrh, hay fever, colds and sinusitis.

ADMINISTRATION
INFUSION (use this especially for an eyewash); EYE-DROPS (these may be purchased from a drugstore); TINCTURE; COMPRESS

Filipendula ulmaria
MEADOWSWEET

PARTS USED
Leaves and flowers

THERAPEUTIC ACTION
This is an astringent herb which also has excellent analgesic properties, because it contains large amounts of salicylic acid (the same substance as that found in aspirin). It is also an excellent remedy for reducing the excess acid in the gastro-intestinal tract, and can be used for the relief of several digestive ailments such as heartburn, ulceration and inflammation of the mucous membrane of the digestive tract. Meadowsweet helps to relieve the pain of arthritis and rheumatism, and, as it does not have the adverse side effects of concentrated salicylates on the stomach, it is completely safe to use. When it is combined with willow bark, it can be used for the relief of headaches, and when mixed with yarrow it can soothe a fever. As it has very good anti-inflammatory effects, it is also useful as an eyewash.

ADMINISTRATION
TINCTURE; INFUSION (to drink or as an eyewash)

Foeniculum vulgare
FENNEL

PARTS USED
Roots, seeds and aerial parts

THERAPEUTIC ACTION
An infusion made from the seeds of fennel is an excellent carminative, especially for babies. Use 1 tsp (5 ml) at a time for soothing colic and reducing wind. The plant contains volatile oils, which have an antispasmodic effect on the digestive tract. Fennel is effective in treating respiratory congestion and it is often found as an active ingredient in cough mixtures and asthma remedies. Tea made from fennel seeds will help to facilitate the flow of breast milk, and in Germany fennel is often mixed with baby formula to use in cases where the baby is not being breast-fed. This makes the milk formula easier for the baby to digest. It can be used as a soothing eyewash. In German folklore it is used for kidney disorders and for menstrual problems.

ADMINISTRATION
DECOCTION OF SEEDS (1 tsp/5 ml of seeds per 3½ oz/ 100 ml of water); INFUSION; TINCTURE

Galium aparine
CLEAVERS (GOOSEGRASS)

PARTS USED

The whole plant when in flower

THERAPEUTIC ACTION

This plant is known to be one of the greatest lymph cleansers and it is indicated for all problems associated with blocked or enlarged lymph glands, fluid retention and toxic build-up. Cleavers can therefore be particularly beneficial in the treatment of cases of tonsillitis, glandular fever and mumps. It has both a diuretic and a cleansing action, and it can therefore be used in conjunction with several other herbs to assist in cleansing the whole system. It is also very good for the treatment of various skin disorders such as eczema and psoriasis. As a supportive medicine, goosegrass can be used in serious chronic diseases to aid the lymphatic function. It has a soothing action on the urinary tract, and it is therefore useful in treating cystitis.

ADMINISTRATION

FRESH JUICE; INFUSION; TINCTURE; COMPRESS (used for the treatment of ulcers and any wounds which are slow to heal)

Gentiana lutea
YELLOW GENTIAN

PARTS USED

Dried root

THERAPEUTIC ACTION

Yellow gentian is one of the most bitter herbs known to us. It is a most powerful and invaluable remedy for strengthening the entire system through internal usage. Since a great many of our health problems are known to originate from faulty digestion and, as a result, poor utilization of the nutrients we take in, yellow gentian helps to stimulate the appetite. It also improves the digestion and helps to invigorate the pancreas. Yellow gentian can also be used for the treatment of jaundice and gall-bladder inflammation. It is often used for treating anemia, as it promotes the production of blood and acts as a general tonic for the entire body, including the nerves (which probably improve as a result of improved digestion).

ADMINISTRATION

TINCTURE

Ginkgo biloba
MAIDENHAIR TREE

PARTS USED

Leaves

THERAPEUTIC ACTION

This ancient "fossil" tree is believed to date back to before the Ice Age, is remarkably hardy and disease-resistant and can live for over a thousand years. The leaves are used in Western herbal medicine, and the main constituents are ginkgolides and flavonoids, which work on the vascular system in several ways. *Ginkgo* improves the circulation, prevents thrombosis (blood clots) and protects against strokes and senile dementia. Research has shown it to have no effect on the memories of normal, healthy people, but it does improve the thought processes of older people with memory problems associated with impaired circulation to the brain. It improves blood flow to the brain and to the peripheries. *Ginkgo biloba* is of immense value in circulatory disorders such as diabetic angiopathy, Raynaud's disease and intermittent claudication. It is an herbal medicine for the middle-aged, to prevent senility and arteriosclerosis, and for the aged, to reduce symptoms like dizziness and forgetfulness.

ADMINISTRATION

TINCTURE; CAPSULES

Hamamelis virginiana
WITCH HAZEL

PARTS USED

Leaves, twigs and bark

THERAPEUTIC ACTION

This herb is well known as an astringent. It constricts the veins and helps stop internal and external bleeding. It strengthens veins, capillaries and varicose veins. It shrinks hemorrhoids as well as easing the pain. Externally it can be used in the form of a compress to treat bruises, sprains, swelling, insect stings and bites. Because it is an astringent, it makes a good remedy for diarrhea, but nowadays it is mostly used for treating external problems in the form of compresses and ointments. A decoction of witch hazel is very soothing, especially used in a compress for the eyes.

ADMINISTRATION

DECOCTION; TINCTURE; OINTMENT; COMPRESS

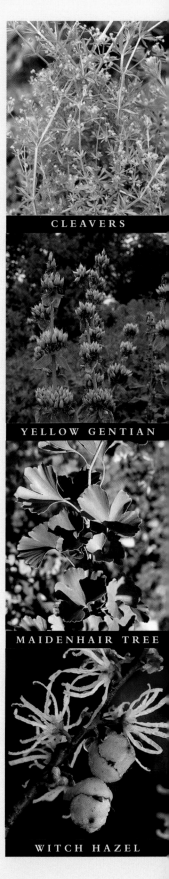

CLEAVERS

YELLOW GENTIAN

MAIDENHAIR TREE

WITCH HAZEL

DEVIL'S CLAW

HOP

ST. JOHN'S WORT

HYSSOP

Harpagophytum procumbens
DEVIL'S CLAW

CAUTION
Devil's claw is not to be used if you are suffering from gastric or duodenal ulcers.
PARTS USED
Dried tuber
THERAPEUTIC ACTION
This plant, which is indigenous to Namibia, is extremely bitter when decocted and, like the other bitter herbs, works on the liver and also the digestive system. It stimulates the appetite, encourages bile flow and improves the digestion. Devil's claw is really best known for its anti-inflammatory and analgesic action in the treatment of certain types of arthritis. In Germany, devil's claw is often used as a supportive therapy in the treatment of cases of degenerative conditions of the motor system.
ADMINISTRATION
DECOCTION; TINCTURE

Humulus lupulus
HOP

CAUTION
Hop should not be used in cases of depression. It should also not be used in a case of impotence.
PARTS USED
The female flower inflorescences (which are also known as strobiles)
THERAPEUTIC ACTION
This plant has a sedative effect and is therefore helpful in treating cases of insomnia. It has a depressant action on the central nervous system, which results in a feeling of relaxation and calm. At the same time it is antispasmodic and can be used in the treatment of stomach cramps and headaches caused by a vascular spasm. The bitter principles in hop stimulate the flow of the gastric juices, thereby improving the digestion. An estrogenic compound has also been identified in this plant, which could adversely affect a man's libido, should he consume too much beer! Tincture of hops also acts as an anaphrodisiac, that is, it suppresses sexual excitement in the male.
ADMINISTRATION
HOP PILLOWS (to induce sleep); TINCTURE; INFUSION

Hypericum perforatum
ST. JOHN'S WORT

CAUTION
This herb can cause photosensitivity in some people.
PARTS USED
Flowering aerial parts
THERAPEUTIC ACTION
This pretty, yellow-flowering plant is generous in its medicinal properties. It is useful as a wound healer, encouraging the formation of granulation tissue and promoting nerve repair. Take the red oil from the flower internally for ulceration of the gastric mucosa. It is anti-inflammatory, has a slightly analgesic effect on wounds and ulcers and will help rheumatism. It strengthens nerves in cases of anxiety and depression, and relieves nerve-related complaints such as neuralgia, sciatica and shingles. It eases menopause and soothes symptoms which can be disturbing at that time. The oil is good for wounds, sunburn, burns and post-operative scars. It is traditionally used in Germany for colic, aches and pains, inflammation of the digestive tract and bed-wetting. A tincture of flowers is effective for rubbing on to rheumatic joints. St. John's wort has been named the "arnica of the nerves."
ADMINISTRATION
TINCTURE; INFUSION; OIL

Hyssopus officinalis
HYSSOP

PARTS USED
Aerial parts when in flower
THERAPEUTIC ACTION
Hyssop has a complicated combination of chemical constituents, which makes it very versatile. It has anti-catarrhal, carminative, blood-cleansing, stimulating, tonic and vasodilating properties. It works well as an expectorant for bronchial catarrh, bronchitis and other respiratory complaints. In a case of weakness or debility during or after illness, it strengthens the system, and its carminative action will soothe colic, improve digestion and eliminate flatulence. It is a good nerve tonic and eases anxiety and tension.
ADMINISTRATION
INFUSION (for colds and flu); TINCTURE; POULTICE OF LEAVES (for bruises and rheumatism)

Inula helenium

ELECAMPANE

PARTS USED
Root

THERAPEUTIC ACTION
Primarily a chest herb, it is good for chronic bronchitis and emphysema and also for ordinary coughs. The complex essential oil (the active ingredient) stimulates the respiratory apparatus as well as being antiseptic, so it promotes the elimination of mucus and kills germs too. It is effective against worms. The root contains inulin, a sugar substitute for diabetics. It promotes sweating in a fever, and acts as a strengthening tonic. It also has a sedative action. As it has a bitter constituent, it aids digestion, and because of its warming action, it will benefit frail, older people with chronic bronchitis.

ADMINISTRATION
INFUSION (in a flask to ensure no evaporation of volatile oil); TINCTURE

Juniperus communis

JUNIPER

CAUTION
Juniper should not be used during pregnancy. Never take it for any longer than six weeks at a time, as it can seriously irritate the kidneys. Because of this, juniper should not be used in cases of kidney disease.

PARTS USED
Dry, ripe berries (dark blue)

THERAPEUTIC ACTION
Juniper is a good medicinal plant for women. It has diuretic properties and is often used in cases of water retention. It is, however, not without dangers, and it must be used with caution, preferably under the guidance of a herbalist. It helps for rheumatism, gout and arthritis. An infusion may help to soothe a case of cystitis, as it is antiseptic and anti-inflammatory, but, because it is quite a strong plant, it is best blended with a herb such as buchu. Juniper berries stimulate hydrochloric acid secretion in the stomach, and people with hyposecretion may chew a few berries before meals.

ADMINISTRATION
INFUSION (keep this in a flask with a lid to ensure that there is no loss of volatile oils); TINCTURE; ESSENTIAL OIL (for arthritic joints)

Linum usitatissimum

FLAX (LINSEED)

PARTS USED
Seeds

THERAPEUTIC ACTION
This is a remarkable seed which can help the body in so many different ways, and inexpensively too. Firstly, linseed is excellent as a bulk laxative — it can be used either whole or freshly ground. It is non-irritating to the mucous membranes of the body and provides a mucilaginous effect (especially if it is ground) which facilitates evacuation. It is completely safe to use for chronic, stubborn constipation and it can also be used for quite a long period of time with no adverse side effects. Linseed tea is also an invaluable remedy for the treatment of coughs, and a poultice of linseed is an excellent remedy for pleurisy. Linseed contains the essential fatty acids which help prevent arteriosclerosis and cholesterol build-up.

ADMINISTRATION
POULTICE (for the treatment of chest problems, as well as for treating boils and inflammation); FRESHLY GROUND SEED (always use it fresh, as it quickly goes rancid); WHOLE SEED; INFUSION

Marrubium vulgare

WHITE HOREHOUND

PARTS USED
Leaves and flowering tops

THERAPEUTIC ACTION
White horehound has a bitter taste and it has bitter tonic properties, so it will be of help in settling the digestion. It is, however, mostly used as an expectorant for conditions such as asthma, dry coughs and chronic coughs. White horehound contains an oil which has a dilating effect on the blood vessels, and it also contains other constituents that can relax the bronchi, which is why it so effectively helps with expectoration. This herb is one of the most widely used plants for the treatment of coughs, and it is included in many of the commercial cough mixtures. The powdered leaves of white horehound can also be used effectively against infestation by worms.

ADMINISTRATION
SYRUP; INFUSION; TINCTURE

ELECAMPANE

JUNIPER

FLAX

WHITE HOREHOUND

GERMAN CHAMOMILE

ALFALFA

LEMON BALM

PEPPERMINT

Matricaria recutita

CHAMOMILE (GERMAN)

PARTS USED

Flowers

THERAPEUTIC ACTION

This flower is commonly used in a tea as a pleasant and soothing after-dinner drink. After having been in use for centuries, its beneficial medicinal properties have recently been verified by research into its chemical constituents. One constituent of chamomile is azulene, used in cosmetics as a healing agent for the skin. It is especially useful for children, as a soothing remedy for restlessness, colic and teething troubles. Furthermore, chamomile has antihistamine, anti-inflammatory and antispasmodic properties which make it useful for treating allergic conditions and digestive problems. In terms of the digestive system, it relieves flatulence, soothes cramps and simultaneously enhances digestion. It is useful for morning sickness during pregnancy, and has a place in the treatment of hormonal dysfunction. It has healing properties, and will speed up the healing of ulcers, wounds and burns. It is effective internally for problems affecting the mucous membranes in the digestive tract, namely gastritis and ulcerative colitis.

ADMINISTRATION

COMPRESS (for external healing); BATH (for babies); TINCTURE; INFUSION

Medicago sativa

ALFALFA (LUCERNE)

PARTS USED

Leaves

THERAPEUTIC ACTION

This plant, used by the Arabs for their prize-winning horses, is valued for its nutrient content, as it contains all the vitamin groups. It acts as a restorative for invalids and convalescents, and it will also help thin people to gain weight. It helps to reduce uric acid, and relieves some forms of arthritis, gout and rheumatism. It is rich in minerals, as its roots penetrate very deeply into the ground and, because minerals are very often lacking in the food of today, it will provide an inexpensive form of mineral supplementation.

ADMINISTRATION

SPROUTS; TEA; TINCTURE

Melissa officinalis

LEMON BALM

PARTS USED

The herb just before flowering

THERAPEUTIC ACTION

This herb has traditionally been used by Germans in the nerve restorer *Melissengeist*. It is a tranquillizer, with scientifically proven effects on the central nervous system. It is invaluable for anxiety attacks, phobias and palpitations with nausea, and also for mild insomnia. It is relaxing and is as effective as chamomile for digestive problems such as "butterflies," flatulence and cramps. Lemon balm can be used as a diaphoretic for fevers and flu. It is a gentle vasodilator, and will stimulate blood circulation. It combines very well with peppermint.

ADMINISTRATION

INFUSION; TINCTURE

Mentha x piperita

PEPPERMINT

PARTS USED

Leaves

THERAPEUTIC ACTION

It is used for indigestion and as a flavoring in toothpaste and mouthwashes. Modern research proves that the choice of peppermint for relieving indigestion and flavoring mouthwashes is a good one. It has about 125 constituents, with only 50% identified, which leaves a lot of research yet to be done. Its carminative action is due to its volatile oil, which is antispasmodic and relieves intestinal colic. It tones the liver and aids digestion. It soothes nerves and relieves pain. It is good for any digestive problem related to tension and stress. It combines well with lemon balm for stress, and with elder flower and yarrow for colds and influenza.

ADMINISTRATION

INFUSION (morning sickness); TINCTURE (digestion); OIL (inhalant for catarrh, or externally for itching)

Oenothera biennis

EVENING PRIMROSE

PARTS USED

Seed

THERAPEUTIC ACTION

Evening primrose has been under the spotlight for many years, but should not be seen as a wonder cure for any problem, as is often claimed. The therapeutic value lies in the main constituent, gamma linolenic acid (GLA), which can be lacking in some people, resulting in problems, especially in bottle-fed infants (breast milk contains high amounts of GLA — absent in cow's milk). The addition of GLA (where it was lacking) to an infant's diet can cure atopic eczema and have other health benefits, especially for allergies. Evening primrose has been shown by research to be of value to sufferers from pre-menstrual tension, and may also help to regulate hormonal disturbances. Some reports of improvement for multiple sclerosis sufferers have been recorded. GLA is an important substance, as it affects enzyme activity and prostaglandin production.

ADMINISTRATION

CAPSULES OF OIL

Olea europaea
OLIVE

CAUTION

Olive leaf infusion or tincture must always be taken on a full stomach to prevent irritation of the mucous membranes.

PARTS USED

Oil of the fruit and leaves

THERAPEUTIC ACTION

Olive oil has appeared on most supermarket shelves since the health benefits have been rediscovered. Many herbal remedies are being scientifically investigated, hence the public demand for them as information is publicised. In ancient times, olive oil was highly prized. Casks were discovered in Egyptian tombs, and references are made to it in the Bible. The best olive oil is labeled extra-virgin and "cold-pressed." It is a mono-unsaturated fatty acid with a complex chemical composition. In countries where a lot of olive oil is used, cancer and heart disease are very much reduced. It is hypotensive (lowers blood pressure) and reduces cholesterol. It also helps prevent thrombosis. Olive oil stimulates bile flow, improves digestion and helps prevent gallstones. Olive leaves have a mild hypotensive action when they are taken as a tea or tincture.

ADMINISTRATION

OIL; LEAF INFUSION; TINCTURE

Panax ginseng
GINSENG

CAUTION

Ginseng is generally a safe herb, but use with caution in case one experiences headaches.

PARTS USED

Root

THERAPEUTIC ACTION

This herb is known for its stimulating tonic action, and is effective for treating exhaustion, debility, ageing, impotence and chronic fatigue. Because of the large number of claims that have been made for ginseng, it has undergone extensive research, and it has subsequently been found to be quite complex in its chemical composition. Its action is mostly the result of the synergistic effect of the chemicals, because the ingredients, when viewed in isolation, are not really significantly potent. Ginseng is a general strengthening tonic as well as a tonic for the central nervous system. It can be effective in treating cases of depression in the elderly, and for lack of concentration. It is useful for older people with low energy levels and low blood pressure, and can aid in boosting vitality in the elderly.

ADMINISTRATION

CAPSULES; DECOCTION; TONIC (commercially prepared)

Plantago lanceolata
RIBWORT (PLANTAIN)

PARTS USED

Leaves

THERAPEUTIC ACTION

This plant, which has been used since ancient times, grows freely in most countries as a weed, and it is a rich source of minerals and has great medicinal value. It has mucilaginous, antiseptic and strengthening properties, which makes it important for the respiratory as well as urinary systems. The silica has a strengthening and healing effect on the bronchi and urinary tubules, and the mucilaginous effect is soothing. It is effective for respiratory and urinary infections, and also for ear infections. French herbalists use ribwort for hay fever, allergic rhinitis and chronic bronchitis.

ADMINISTRATION

TINCTURE; INFUSION; FRESH LEAF (this will stop a cut bleeding); SYRUP

EVENING PRIMROSE

OLIVE

GINSENG

RIBWORT

LUNGWORT

ROSEMARY

RASPBERRY

RUE

Pulmonaria officinalis

LUNGWORT

PARTS USED

Leaves gathered during flowering

THERAPEUTIC ACTION

Traditionally this plant has been used for bronchial complaints, according to the Doctrine of Signatures (*see* page 121), as the leaves were supposed to resemble the lungs. Medical science proved the choice to be correct, as the chemical constituents are soothing and expectorant for the respiratory system. It is also an astringent, which means that it can be used for the treatment of diarrhea and hemorrhoids and also as a gargle for treating hoarseness and laryngitis. It is anti-hemorrhagic and can be used to stop bleeding in the urinary tract after passing stones.

ADMINISTRATION

INFUSION (of dried leaves); TINCTURE (fresh leaf for cuts and wounds)

Rosmarinus officinalis

ROSEMARY

PARTS USED

Leaves and twigs, gathered when the plant is in flower

THERAPEUTIC ACTION

This herb is so familiar, and yet it is hardly understood as a medicinal plant. Rosemary has quite a spectacular chemical composition, much of which is still being investigated. It is a warming and stimulating herb and works on the circulation as well as the nervous system. It strengthens the nerves in cases of depression, and of nervousness which upsets the stomach. Rosemary improves the circulation and it also strengthens the capillaries. It eases rheumatism and arthritis when it is used internally and externally for the joints. The bitter component of this herb improves the digestion. It will raise the blood pressure if it is low, and is an excellent tonic for the weak and aged.

ADMINISTRATION

OIL IN A BASE OIL (improves the circulation, relieves joint pain, stimulates hair growth); TINCTURE (this can relieve the pain of neuralgia when it is applied externally); INFUSION (use this as a hair rinse and also as a tonic tea); BATH (it acts as a tonic, especially when followed by an hour's bedrest)

Rubus idaeus

RASPBERRY

CAUTION

Take raspberry leaf only after the first trimester of pregnancy.

PARTS USED

Leaves and fruit

THERAPEUTIC ACTION

The fruits are used in Europe as juice for fever, as a cleansing tonic, to stimulate and improve the appetite, to tone and cleanse the digestive system, and as a remedy for cystitis. The astringent leaves have traditionally been used to strengthen the uterus during pregnancy and to facilitate childbirth. An infusion is used as a gargle for a sore throat, for mouth ulcers or bleeding gums, and it will also be effective in halting diarrhea.

ADMINISTRATION

INFUSION; TABLETS (for use in pregnancy; these must be taken according to the recommended dosage indicated on the package)

Ruta graveolens

RUE

CAUTION

Not to be taken in pregnancy. Not to be taken in large quantities. Rue can cause contact dermatitis in some people.

PARTS USED

Leaves, gathered before flowering

THERAPEUTIC ACTION

This plant was introduced to Britain from southern Europe by the Romans, and can now be found in most countries. It was prized by Hippocrates. It has a unique aroma, which not many people like. As a medicinal plant it has many uses. It is a powerful emmenagogue, and will bring on delayed menstruation. It stimulates circulation and strengthens capillaries because of its rutin content. It was traditionally used to strengthen weak eyes. It is best used at the first signs of failing sight. Its antispasmodic action makes it suitable for intestinal colic and coughing spasms. It is a nerve strengthener and can be used for anxiety attacks and palpitations. Its bitter action improves digestion. It eases arthritis and rheumatism and can relieve some types of headache. Rue is a whole medicine chest in one plant.

ADMINISTRATION

TINCTURE; INFUSION

Salvia officinalis

SAGE

CAUTION

Not to be used in medicinal applications during pregnancy.

PARTS USED

Leaves

THERAPEUTIC ACTION

Sage is an ancient herb that grew in virtually every garden in Germany in the Middle Ages, and in 1680 a 400-page book on the medicinal values of sage was produced there. Sage contains a volatile oil, the main active ingredient of which is anti-inflammatory and an estrogenic compound. It regulates perspiration and is invaluable for the control of adolescent perspiration, hot flushes, perspiration during menopause, and night sweats. It also helps to dry up breast milk when the time has come to wean the baby. Sage is an antiseptic herb, which makes it an excellent remedy for the treatment of colds and respiratory problems. It is also used as a gargle for the treatment of laryngitis, sore throats and mouth ulcers. It strengthens the nerves. Danish research confirms the traditional belief that sage acts as a sedative, which is also supported by Chinese studies. As an anti-inflammatory, it helps to relieve arthritis and rheumatism.

ADMINISTRATION

INFUSION; TINCTURE; DOUCHE (for leucorrhea); COMPRESS (for healing of wounds)

Sambucus nigra

ELDER

PARTS USED

Flowers, leaves and berries

THERAPEUTIC ACTION

Elder is an extremely useful medicinal plant which can be traced back to Egyptian times. The flowers contain a volatile oil in which over 80 constituents have been identified, as well as many other active compounds and mineral salts. It is an effective diaphoretic which can be used for treating feverish conditions. It is effective for bronchitis, hay fever, flu, measles and scarlet fever. In inflammatory rheumatic conditions, the diaphoretic action is very helpful. A cold strained infusion of the flowers makes a wonderful eyewash or compress. The leaves are cleansing and diuretic and make a valuable

addition to a herbal mixture used for detoxifying the system. The berries of this tree are rich in vitamins and other chemical constituents which have a healing and strengthening effect on the lungs, and are especially beneficial for rheumatism.

ADMINISTRATION

INFUSION (of leaves or flowers); TINCTURE; FRESH LEAF POULTICE (for wounds); OINTMENT (from leaves)

Saponaria officinalis

SOAPWORT

CAUTION

Soapwort is probably best used for external problems as a wash, or otherwise only under your herbalist's directions, as it is a powerful emetic (causes vomiting in large quantities).

PARTS USED

Root

THERAPEUTIC ACTION

Though normally not considered a medicinal plant, soapwort is nevertheless so common and freely available that it can be extremely useful when used instead of soap as a wash for eczema and other irritating skin problems. It is rich in saponins which soothe the skin and the mucous membranes. Internally it is useful for dry coughs and as a laxative.

ADMINISTRATION

DECOCTION OF ROOT (for a skin wash or vaginal douche); TINCTURE

Scutellaria lateriflora

SKULLCAP

PARTS USED

Leaves and flowers, taken late in the flowering period

THERAPEUTIC ACTION

Skullcap is essentially a plant for the nerves. It has a strengthening effect on the central nervous system, and it also has a relaxing action. It is an antispasmodic, which is helpful for nervous tension that affects the digestive tract, or for tension headaches. Its relaxing effect is useful in treating all spasms and even epilepsy. It can be used to wean a person off barbiturates, as it eases seizures and other withdrawal symptoms.

ADMINISTRATION

INFUSION; TINCTURE (fresh plant)

SAGE

ELDER

SOAPWORT

SKULLCAP

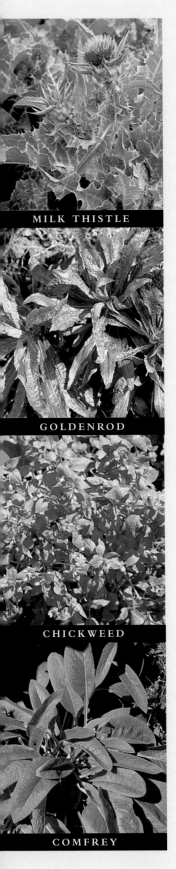

MILK THISTLE

GOLDENROD

CHICKWEED

COMFREY

Silybum marianum

MILK THISTLE

PARTS USED
Seed

THERAPEUTIC ACTION
This herb is a bitter tonic like so many other herbs, but it also has a function that makes it uniquely valuable. This is its hepatoprotective action — it protects the liver. It has its application in cases where chemotherapy is required, because it helps to protect the liver against the damage caused by drug therapy. It is also useful in the treatment of hepatitis and has a healing influence on the liver. Milk thistle increases the production of milk in breastfeeding mothers — hence the name.

ADMINISTRATION
TINCTURE; INFUSION

Solidago virgaurea

GOLDENROD

PARTS USED
Leaves and flowering tops

THERAPEUTIC ACTION
Goldenrod is a plant which is rich in both saponins and tannins, and it also has several anti-inflammatory and antiseptic properties, as well as being a really excellent diuretic. This herb can also be used in conjunction with echinacea for the treatment of nephritis as well as for cystitis. It is also very effective for treating certain conditions of the upper respiratory system, especially where there is a tendency towards post-nasal drip and the overproduction of mucus. Goldenrod contains bioflavonoids, which strengthen the veins and are therefore indicated for those with varicose veins and fragile capillaries. It is a carminative, and will ease the griping of colic and flatulence.

ADMINISTRATION
INFUSION (use for flu, or as a gargle for sore throats); TINCTURE; DOUCHE (antifungal)

Stellaria media

CHICKWEED

PARTS USED
Dried aerial parts

THERAPEUTIC ACTION
Chickweed is a soothing, healing herb and can help to relieve the agony of an itching skin. It is especially useful in the treatment of skin conditions such as eczema and psoriasis. A poultice made from the leaves is excellent for treating conditions such as ulcers, boils and suppurations, and will also help to draw a boil or an abscess to a point. It is mostly used in the form of an ointment for skin problems. When taken internally as a tea or a tincture, chickweed is helpful for treating rheumatism, because it is a diuretic and has cleansing properties. It also has a demulcent action, which makes it a very soothing herb for the urinary system. Traditionally it has been used for weight loss.

ADMINISTRATION
INFUSION; TINCTURE; TEA; POULTICE (made of the leaves); BATH; CREAM

Symphytum officinale

COMFREY

CAUTION
Because it contains pyrrolizidine alkaloids, which may have a cumulative effect in the body and are therefore harmful to the liver, the long-term use of comfrey is not advised. To be on the safe side, use for external applications only.

PARTS USED
Roots and leaves

THERAPEUTIC ACTION
Comfrey is famous for its wonderful healing properties, as well as for the fact that it looks very attractive in the herb garden. The ingredient of comfrey which is mainly responsible for the promotion of healing is allantoin, which stimulates the process of repair by accelerating cell division. Comfrey also has a soothing effect on the mucous membranes, it will soothe a very painful cough, and it helps with the healing of gastric and duodenal ulcers as well as internal suppurations. It is really invaluable in the treatment of arthritis and, when it is applied as a poultice, it will speed up the healing of bone fractures and relieve the pain of joint inflammation. When it is used externally it can heal ulcers, wounds and skin disorders.

ADMINISTRATION
POWDERED ROOT IN A PASTE (use this for treating ulcers, eczema, wounds); LEAVES WRAPPED AROUND A SPRAIN (this is very good for treating dogs and cats);

INFUSION OF LEAVES (for relieving coughs, although it is best when comfrey is mixed with the other cough herbs); TINCTURE (use this externally for arthritis); CREAM (for external use, for the treatment of arthritis and the healing of hemorrhoids)

Tanacetum parthenium
FEVERFEW

CAUTION

Not for use during pregnancy. Tablets or a tincture are the safest, as they ensure controlled dosage. Consult a herbalist for the correct dosage for your particular case.

PARTS USED

Leaves

THERAPEUTIC ACTION

Popularly used for the relief of migraine, this herb has been shown by research to have valuable prophylactic properties: it has an anticlotting function on platelets in the blood, as well as a vasodilatory action. Feverfew can often be very helpful as an anti-inflammatory for some types of arthritis. Its bitterness has a stimulating action on the digestion. It is a tonic for the uterus and it helps with the relief of certain menstrual problems.

ADMINISTRATION

INFUSION; TABLETS; TINCTURE

Taraxacum officinale
DANDELION

PARTS USED

Roots and leaves

THERAPEUTIC ACTION

This common weed is an amazing medicinal plant — it is almost a pharmacy on its own, taking care of just about every contingency. The leaves have a different action to the roots. The leaves are primarily diuretic, containing a rich supply of potassium to ensure that potassium losses (usually experienced when diuretics are used) are obviated. The leaves can be used in kidney disorders, for relief of water retention and rheumatism, and they also have nutritive properties. The young leaves are a tonic, rich in vitamins A, B, C and D. Although the leaves have a mildly stimulating effect on the liver and the gall bladder, it is actually the roots that are really powerful in stimulating bile secretion. They

also have a bitter tonic action, improving the digestion and thereby cleansing the whole system. Dandelion can be used as a background treatment for many skin conditions, as it stimulates excretion of toxins.

ADMINISTRATION

TINCTURE (of the root or leaf); DECOCTION (of the root); INFUSION (of the leaf)

Thymus vulgaris
THYME

CAUTION

Avoid thyme in large doses during pregnancy. Using it in cooking, however, is quite safe.

PARTS USED

Leaves

THERAPEUTIC ACTION

Thyme is another one of those herbs that has been widely and effectively used for centuries, and it certainly holds immense power in its small leaves. An essential oil, thymol, is distilled from its leaves, and this has a great many benefits — especially when it is rubbed into stiff joints and sore muscles. An infusion of thyme is a really excellent treatment for bronchial problems, such as asthma, whooping cough and bronchitis, as this herb is an antispasmodic as well as being an effective expectorant. Thyme is antiseptic and it has antifungal properties if it is used for the treatment of athlete's foot and ringworm. It also has a very good effect on the digestive system and it helps to ease flatulence.

ADMINISTRATION

INFUSION (either to drink or to gargle); TINCTURE; OIL IN A BASE OIL

Trifolium pratense
RED CLOVER

PARTS USED

Flower heads

THERAPEUTIC ACTION

A common problem that is really very upsetting to any parent is a case of childhood eczema. The use of red clover is a completely safe and very effective remedy for the treatment of eczema, and besides this, it can also be used to treat several other irritating

FEVERFEW

DANDELION

THYME

RED CLOVER

FENUGREEK

NASTURTIUM

COLTSFOOT

STINGING NETTLE

skin conditions, such as psoriasis and various skin rashes. This herb also has a cleansing function in the system, and it will provide a good background treatment for several different general health problems. Red clover furthermore has an effective expectorant action, which makes it very good for the treatment of phlegmy coughs.

ADMINISTRATION

INFUSION; TINCTURE; CREAM

Trigonella foenum-graecum
FENUGREEK

CAUTION

Not to be used during pregnancy.

PARTS USED

Seeds

THERAPEUTIC ACTION

The Greeks and Romans in ancient times used fenugreek extensively as a medicinal herb. Fenugreek is probably one of the best herbs to use for a poultice, as the seeds have a softening, drawing and antiseptic action on a boil, ulcer, abscess or otherwise infected flesh. For a poultice the seeds are ground to a powder and mixed to a paste with a little hot water, and this paste is then applied to the affected area. If it is taken internally, fenugreek tea cleanses the whole system and aids the digestion. It is an excellent remedy for chronic bronchitis and emphysema, and it can also be a useful background treatment for many serious diseases where detoxification is required. Fenugreek encourages milk production in breast-feeding mothers. It is usually combined with either fennel or aniseed in order to improve the flavor.

ADMINISTRATION

INFUSION OF SEEDS; POULTICE; TINCTURE

Tropaeolum majus
NASTURTIUM

PARTS USED

Leaves

THERAPEUTIC ACTION

This plant grows well in most places, and is extremely useful in an emergency, as it can nip an infection in the bud. It is a powerful antimicrobial herb, and is best

used fresh. Nasturtium can be eaten at the first sign of a cold or sore throat, and it can also be applied as a fresh poultice to the infected skin.

ADMINISTRATION

FRESH LEAF (chewed); FRESH POULTICE OF THE LEAVES

Tussilago farfara
COLTSFOOT

PARTS USED

Flowers and leaves

THERAPEUTIC ACTION

Since ancient times, this herb has been known to be an excellent therapy for chest problems. It has antiseptic, anti-inflammatory and expectorant properties, which will be of benefit for chronic bronchitis, emphysema and asthma. In common with other herbs that are effective for chest complaints, it is also soothing to the urinary tract, and is effective in treating cystitis. A fresh poultice of leaves is excellent in cases of skin problems such as ulcers, burns and infections. Coltsfoot is a good tonic, with a rich silica and zinc content. It has revealed its stimulating effect on the immune system in research on mice. The fresh juice mixed with honey works very well — take 1–2 TBS (15–30 ml) a day.

ADMINISTRATION

INFUSION; TINCTURE

Urtica dioica
STINGING NETTLE

CAUTION

Do not use stinging nettle for any internal hemorrhage of which the cause is unknown. Allergy-prone people may also be allergic to this plant.

PARTS USED

Leaves, collected during the flowering season

THERAPEUTIC ACTION

One could actually write a whole book about the many different uses of the stinging nettle — which indeed was done by Pharias, a Greek naturalist and philosopher. Nettle is a cleanser as well as a tonic. It is rich in minerals and vitamins, particularly iron and vitamin C, while it simultaneously rids the body of excess uric acid. It has a very good cleansing effect on the kidneys, and it will therefore bring relief in those cases of gout or rheumatism where uric acid is the cause of the complaint. Stinging nettle is hemostatic (which means it can stop bleeding), and so it can be used to lessen the menstrual flow when it is too heavy. Nettle tea is completely safe to take on a regular basis, and it may dramatically improve the energy levels in a tired, anemic person. It improves the milk supply of a breast-feeding mother, and it also helps to revive her strength after the birth of the baby. Nettle can be very effective in the treatment of eczema or urticaria, and it can also be used as a background treatment for several allergic conditions.

ADMINISTRATION

INFUSION; TINCTURE; OINTMENT; FRESH JUICE

Valeriana officinalis
VALERIAN

PARTS USED
Root and rhizome

THERAPEUTIC ACTION
Valerian is the herb which is best known as the great nerve restorer, and it is indicated in the treatment of any disorders of the nervous system which are caused by exhaustion. It is excellent for conditions such as anxiety, excitability, nervous tension and nervous palpitations, and it can also be used effectively in cases of migraine or headaches which are caused by vascular spasm. It is an excellent remedy for any muscular spasm which is caused by tension, and it also works equally well for a bowel spasm. It is also a strengthening herb with very good tonic properties, and it improves the circulation as it tones the heart.

ADMINISTRATION
INFUSION; TINCTURE

Verbascum thapsus
MULLEIN

PARTS USED
Flowers and leaves

THERAPEUTIC ACTION
This plant, which has been used since ancient times in folk medicine, has recently been well researched and scientifically analyzed. The active constituents are mainly expectorant and demulcent, thereby making it

a specific herb for the respiratory system and excellent for the treatment of conditions such as laryngitis, pharyngitis, bronchitis and whooping cough. The demulcent properties of mullein make it a soothing herb for the digestive tract mucous membranes. A few drops of oil infusion are very effective in the treatment of earache, as well as for treating skin inflammations.

ADMINISTRATION
INFUSION; TINCTURE

Vitex agnus-castus
CHASTE TREE

PARTS USED
Berries

THERAPEUTIC ACTION
This herb is especially useful for women. Chaste berry has a toning and normalizing action on the female reproductive system. It helps to regulate the menstrual cycle, and it also has a positive effect when used for treating pre-menstrual acne and pre-menstrual water retention, as well as for pre-menstrual tension. It may also be of great benefit during menopause, as it helps to balance the female hormones.

ADMINISTRATION
INFUSION; TINCTURE

Zingiber officinale
GINGER

PARTS USED
Root

THERAPEUTIC ACTION
This is a most valuable plant, especially in those cases where warming of the body is required. Ginger stimulates the peripheral circulation, it will warm a person who really feels the cold in winter, and it is also very effective in warming a person with feverish chills. Ginger can help to bring a high fever to its breaking point and thereby produce the necessary perspiration to bring down the fever quickly. It is excellent for digestive problems, nausea, colic and morning sickness. Ginger also acts as a carminative, relieving indigestion and flatulence.

ADMINISTRATION
CAPSULES; INFUSION; TINCTURE

VALERIAN

MULLEIN

CHASTE TREE

GINGER

VII

AROMATHERAPY

*"Two liquids are particularly beneficial to the human body —
internally wine, externally oil, both are derived from the vegetable world
and are excellent, but oil is the more necessary."*

(PLINY THE ELDER)

AROMATHERAPY

AROMATHERAPY IS THE USE OF ESSENTIAL OILS COUPLED WITH GENTLE MASSAGE. IT WAS ORIGINATED IN THE 1940S BY MARGUERITE MAURY, AN AUSTRIAN BIOCHEMIST PRACTICING AS A BEAUTICIAN IN LONDON. WHILE HER MAIN FOCUS WAS AESTHETIC, SHE WAS ALSO AWARE THAT THE FRAGRANT OILS SHE USED TO MASSAGE HER CLIENTS HAD A MORE-THAN-PHYSICAL EFFECT. THIS IS WHY AROMATHERAPY HAS CONTINUED TO DEVELOP INTO THE FASTEST GROWING SECTOR OF COMPLEMENTARY MEDICINE.

AROMATHERAPY is fast gaining popularity as a wonderful form of therapy. It is highly versatile and very effective in the treatment of a wide variety of ailments and conditions. It may be used simply to maintain health and a sense of well-being, or else to prevent the stress caused by a frantic life style from turning into a real illness. You may either go to a trained professional aromatherapist, or else blend and use your own essential oils at home. They can be used as body or massage oils, bath oils, inhalations, compresses or to perfume the air.

Plant oils of the highest purity are used in aromatherapy. Fixed oils such as almond or grape seed oil are used as carriers for the volatile, fragrant essential oils. These essential oils have therapeutic and aromatic properties. The science and art of aromatherapy lies in the blending and use of these natural aromatic substances to address not only physical ailments, but emotional ones too. By taking the whole person into consideration, aromatherapy works holistically.

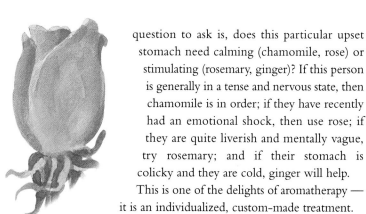

HOLISM

To consider a problem holistically, one needs to take into account other, perhaps minor, ailments as well as the individual's emotional or mental condition. Aromatherapy works entirely symptomatically. All the symptoms seen together form a holistic picture of the individual. Take for example an upset stomach. There are many essential oils which could be used to help solve this problem. The main question to ask is, does this particular upset stomach need calming (chamomile, rose) or stimulating (rosemary, ginger)? If this person is generally in a tense and nervous state, then chamomile is in order; if they have recently had an emotional shock, then use rose; if they are quite liverish and mentally vague, try rosemary; and if their stomach is colicky and they are cold, ginger will help.

This is one of the delights of aromatherapy — it is an individualized, custom-made treatment.

THE ORIGINS OF AROMATHERAPY

Since the dawn of time, man has considered aromatic plants to be more special than others, using them as medicine and in spiritual worship. The best known use of aromatics was in Egypt where the mummies were packed with myrrh and wrapped in cloth soaked in cedarwood oil. This allowed the corpse to be sweet-smelling and also arrested putrefaction. (All essential oils, in varying degrees, are bactericidal.)

There are many beautiful references to several odiferous substances in the Bible. In the Book of Leviticus, for instance, frankincense is used to sanctify sacrifices, the Song of Solomon speaks about the cedars of Lebanon and Mary Magdalene washed the Nazarene's feet with spikenard and then dried them with her hair.

PREVIOUS PAGES **THE LAVENDER FIELDS OF PROVENCE.**

RIGHT **ROSE PETALS FROM WHICH ESSENTIAL OILS ARE EXTRACTED.**

ABOVE **ROWS OF BOTTLES OF ESSENTIAL OILS AT THE FAMOUS FRAGONARD PERFUMERY IN FRANCE.**

Much later on, during the 18th century, the apothecaries wanted to isolate the active components of aromatic oils. Even though it was soon proven that the isolated part did not necessarily work any better than the whole oil or the whole plant, medical science continued to persist in this quest for the next two centuries.

When medicine became more scientific, people became much less confident of healing themselves and gave that responsibility to doctors. We are now experiencing a return to managing our own health. This gives us a responsible attitude towards our health, and also takes some pressure off medical practitioners, giving them scope to deal with serious clinical conditions. Using both systems together is known as complementary medicine.

ESSENTIAL OILS

Essential oils are derived from aromatic plants. *They may be extracted from any part of an aromatic plant:*

ROOTS — ginger, vetiver
STALKS — lemon grass
BARK — cinnamon
WOOD — cedarwood, sandalwood
LEAVES — eucalyptus, tea tree
FLOWERS — orange blossom, ylang-ylang
NUTS — nutmeg
BERRIES — juniper
TWIGS — petitgrain (orange wood)
FRUIT PEEL — grapefruit, tangerine
GUM RESIN — frankincense, myrrh
THE WHOLE PLANT — basil, marjoram

Essential oils come from all over the world. They are sent to central buying houses from which suppliers obtain their stock. Some aromatherapy concerns source their own essential oils. This means that they might have to go to Australia for tea tree, Russia for clary sage, Egypt for geranium, America for grapefruit, South America for palma rosa or the Philippines for ylang-ylang. The most important issue is the purity of the oils. Buy only from a reputable supplier with a rapid turnover of stock, to avoid stale oils, and also because there are oils on the market which have been tampered with, to allow a larger profit margin. Rose, for instance, which is very costly, is often "extended" by geranium, which smells similar but is less expensive. In general, flower oils should be expensive, because their yield is low and extraction is costly.

Most oils are acquired by steam distillation of the plant material. With lavender and geranium, for instance, the whole plant is distilled, whereas sandalwood and cedarwood are broken into wood chips first. Most flowers are far too fragile to be steam-distilled, so they will go through a process of solvent extraction where no heat is involved.

Extraction from any part of an aromatic plant yields the precious, highly concentrated, volatile substance known as essential oil. Depending on which kind of plant is used, these essential oils have varying evaporation, or volatility, rates. Citrus oils are the fastest to evaporate and gum resins the slowest. Gum resins also have the most sustained smell.

Essential oils do not dissolve in water, but they combine well with fats, oils and waxes. They also mix well with eggs, milk or honey. They combine only slightly with alcohol or vinegar. Essential oils may therefore be used in making face creams, body oils and scented candles. They may also be used in combination with some foodstuffs, such as egg whites, avocado or oats, for use as face or hair masks, skin tonics or for an oil-free aromatic bath.

Essential oils, because of their volatility, need to be stored in dark glass bottles with tight-fitting lids. They will not become rancid, but they can lose their potency with time. If this happens, their smell will become faint. Citrus peel oils are considered fresh for six months, whereas other essential oils stored under good conditions are fine for a couple of years. Protect them from extremes of temperature, direct sunlight (the dark glass bottles help here) and being dropped or knocked. Plastic bottles are not a good idea for long-term storage, as the essential oils can act on the plastic. Because of some of their chemical constituents, undiluted essential oils must be kept away from varnished or painted wood surfaces.

Once essential oils have been diluted by mixing into a carrier, their shelf life decreases to about three months.

HOW AROMATHERAPY WORKS

Since the molecules of essential oils consist mainly of carbon, hydrogen and oxygen, our bodies will accept them easily. (We also consist mainly of carbon, hydrogen and oxygen.) There are three main ways in which essential oils can be used to good effect:

OLFACTION

When we sniff any odiferous substance, the volatile particles go up the nose to the olfactory receptor sites which are situated in the nasal cavity, where the messages are passed as neuro-transmissions via the olfactory nerves to the middle of the brain. In the area where we perceive smell, we also have the senses of thirst, hunger, memory and learning — our senses for survival. This is why, when you smell something from long ago, there is an immediate emotional response. (To see exactly how the sense of smell works, please refer to the diagram on page 155.)

INHALATION

Some of the aromatic particles which we inhale go down into our lungs where they combine with the mucous membrane lining them. This is where the oxygen we inhale is transferred to the bloodstream. The essential oil particles do the same and are then carried by the blood to different parts of the body.

DERMAL APPLICATION

The dermal application of essential oils is actually similar to inhalation, as the essential oil molecules are also carried by the bloodstream. With dermal application, essential oils which have been diluted in plant oil are applied or massaged into the skin. The oil sinks into the pores of the skin where the tiny aromatic particles pass through the one-cell-thick lining and are then taken up by the blood and the lymph and carried to the main arteries and the lymph ducts. In this way the essential oil particles travel thoughout the whole body within an hour.

After about 4 or 5 hours, the aromatic molecules have all been used. These molecules are eventually excreted by our bodies, but the beneficial effects of the essential oils have now been triggered and they will last much longer — up to a week.

GENERAL APPLICATIONS OF ESSENTIAL OILS

BATH
DROPS: 6–10
CARRIER: 1 tsp (5 ml) vegetable oil or milk
METHOD: Close the doors and windows of the bathroom. Mix the essential oil with the carrier and add it to the bath. Relax for 10 minutes.
Note: Use a half-dilution for children over the age of four, for the sick or the elderly, and for pregnant women. For younger children between one and four years old, one drop of essential oil will be enough. Be careful with strong oils such as peppermint and black pepper.

STEAM INHALATION
DROPS: 2–4
CARRIER: Hot water (not boiling)
METHOD: Pour the hot water into a bowl and then add the essential oil. Drape a towel over your head, close your eyes and inhale for a maximum of 5–10 minutes.
NOTE: Not for asthmatics.

COMPRESS
DROPS: 6
CARRIER: 3½ fl oz (100 ml) water
METHOD: Use hot water for dull aches and old injuries, or cold water for new injuries. Add the essential oil to the water in a bowl. Place a small towel or soft cloth in the water, wring out and place over the injury. Cover with plastic wrap and a towel or bandage and leave until the compress reaches skin temperature. Renew as required.

BODY OR MASSAGE OIL
DROPS: 15
CARRIER: 2 TBS (30 ml) carrier oil such as almond or grape seed. Do not use mineral or "baby" oil.
METHOD: Mix the essential oil with the vegetable oil in a brown glass bottle with a tight-fitting lid. The mixture can be used daily (as with an anti-cellulite program, for instance), but change the essential oil after a month's constant use to guard against building up tolerance.

UNDILUTED OIL
DROPS: 1
CARRIER: None
METHOD: When it is suggested — in rare instances — that an essential oil may be used undiluted, only one drop is to be used, and only on the specific affected area.

SKIN PERFUME
DROPS: 1
CARRIER: None
or
DROPS: 90
CARRIER: 2 TBS (30 ml) jojoba oil
METHOD: Essential oils may be used either singly or mixed as a perfume. In this case they are applied directly to the skin, but only one drop should be used and be very careful if you have a sensitive skin. Alternatively, add essential oils to jojoba oil and then apply to your skin.

INHALING
DROPS: 2–4
CARRIER: None
METHOD: Put a couple of drops of oil onto a handkerchief. Sniff at intervals during the day, whenever necessary.

DIFFUSION
DROPS: 4
CARRIER: Water
METHOD: Add 4 drops of essential oil to the water in the saucer of an essential oil burner. This will perfume and disinfect the air.

IS AROMATHERAPY SAFE?

Yes, aromatherapy is completely safe, provided you use the essential oils correctly and avoid any oils which might be potentially toxic (*see* page 156).

Essential oils are never to be taken internally. Not only is this potentially dangerous, but essential oils are also more effective when they are applied dermally than when they have to gain access to the system via the gastric tract. It is an excellent idea to test an essential oil first on a smallish patch of skin before use, in order to test for skin allergies.

Because essential oils represent a strong concentration of the plant source, *they must always be diluted before use,* except in the rare instances where otherwise indicated (*see* pages 159–161).

The normal dilution for essential oils is 50 drops of essential oil in 3½ oz (100 ml) of carrier. A half-dilution is 25 drops of essential oil in 3½ oz (100 ml) of carrier.

RIGHT CARRIER OILS SUCH AS HAZELNUT OIL AND CARROT OIL, MIXED WITH A FEW DROPS OF YOUR FAVORITE ESSENTIAL OIL, CAN BE USED AS A SUNTANNING OIL.

THE SAFE USE OF ESSENTIAL OILS

ALTHOUGH IT IS GENERALLY SAFE TO USE ESSENTIAL OILS AT HOME, THERE ARE SOME CIRCUMSTANCES IN WHICH IT COULD BE DANGEROUS TO USE CERTAIN OILS. THESE SPECIAL CIRCUMSTANCES ARE LISTED BELOW, AS ARE THE OILS WHICH SHOULD BE AVOIDED.

SAFE ESSENTIAL OILS

ESSENTIAL OILS WHICH ARE SAFE TO USE IN **PREGNANCY**

✠ *Use the following oils to* ***relieve low immune response, depression, water retention, irritability and anxiety:*** **bergamot grapefruit lemon linden mandarin neroli orange petitgrain tangerine**

All the above oils (with the exception of grapefruit oil) are photosensitizing, and therefore any exposure to the sun should be avoided for at least an hour after these oils have been applied to the skin.

✠ *The following oils are also* ***safe in pregnancy:*** **benzoin eucalyptus frankincense lemon grass patchouli pine rosewood sandalwood tea tree vetiver ylang-ylang**

ESSENTIAL OILS WHICH ARE SAFE FOR **BABIES AND CHILDREN**

✠ *The following essential oils can be used in low concentrations on babies aged 3 months and over (not younger than 3 months):* **chamomile lavender rose**

Use low concentrations for children, about half the usual adult quantities. Remember that essential oils should never be taken internally, so keep them tightly closed and out of reach. Use one drop only, diluted in a tablespoonful of vegetable oil or full cream milk in the bath. Fragrant oils are effective in the nursery for deodorizing, inducing sleep and disinfecting a sickroom. Before adding essential oils to the child's bath, first dilute them in a tablespoonful of vegetable oil or full cream milk to prevent the possibility of undiluted essential oil being rubbed into the eyes.

ESSENTIAL OILS WHICH ARE **POTENTIALLY DANGEROUS**

✠ *The following oils are classified as possible* ***toxins*** *and should be used with great care:* **aniseed hyssop sage**

✠ *The following oils are* **NOT** *to be used in cases of* ***epilepsy:*** **fennel hyssop sage**

✠ *The following oils are* **NOT** *to be used in cases of* ***high blood pressure:*** **hyssop rosemary sage thyme**

✠ *The following oils may* ***irritate the skin:*** **cinnamon leaf fennel fir needle parsley seed pimenta leaf thyme**

✠ *The following oils may* ***irritate the skin*** *when used in baths:* **basil lemon lemon grass lemon verbena melissa peppermint tea tree thyme**

✠ *The following oils are classed as* ***photosensitizing*** *and should* **NOT** *be used before exposure to strong sunlight, sunbeds or other sources of ultraviolet light:* **angelica bergamot cumin lemon lemon verbena lime orange**

✠ *The following essential oils should* **NOT** *be used during* ***pregnancy:*** **chamomile clary sage cypress fennel juniper lavender peppermint rose rosemary**

✠ *The following oils should be avoided by* ***women with sensitive skin:*** **black pepper cardamom coriander ginger**

ESSENTIAL OILS FOR HOME USE

Some oils which are not strictly herbal but are often used have also been included here. Although it is always best to be treated by a qualified aromatherapist, the following essential oils are safe for non-aromatherapists to use. Some of these essential oils should, however, be avoided under certain specific circumstances which are noted in *italics*:

BENZOIN

For dry and sensitive skin, joint pain, problems with respiration and mucous membranes, grief, anger, burnout. It is warming, sedative and protecting.

BERGAMOT

Avoid exposure to sun and ultraviolet lights for one hour after application. For oily skin, herpes, fever, digestive upsets, pre-menstrual symptoms, water retention, sore throat, anxiety, grief, frustration, depression. It has antiviral and antibacterial properties.

CHAMOMILE

Avoid chamomile in early pregnancy or if the pregnancy is unstable. For irritations of the skin, digestive system, female reproductive system, muscles and joints, fever, any inflammation, insomnia, jealousy, fear, panic, anger, hypersensitivity. It has a sedative, calming and soothing effect.

CLARY SAGE

Avoid in pregnancy, but use to ease labor. For oily, inflamed skin, mature skin, baldness, excessive sweating, hypertension, convulsive coughing, stomach cramps, menstrual irregularities, pre-menstrual symptoms, muscle spasms, depression, hysteria, fear, anxiety, paranoia, stress. General tonic and balancer. Euphoric and sedative.

CORIANDER

Stupefying in large doses. Warming to the stomach, muscles, joints, lungs. It revitalises the glandular system, and also improves memory and concentration. Useful for nausea in pregnancy (morning sickness), also for dizziness, exhaustion and being run down. It is a general detoxifier. Stimulating.

CYPRESS

Regulates the menstrual cycle, and should therefore be avoided during pregnancy. Excellent where there is any excess of fluid in the body, for instance mucus, sweating, heavy bleeding, incontinence and edema. Tonic for the circulatory system, helpful for varicose veins and hemorrhoids. Antispasmodic for the chest and also good for muscle cramps. Excellent for relieving the side effects of menopause and for heavy periods. Helpful with skin scarring and oily skin. Calms angry, garrulous people.

EUCALYPTUS

Do not use if you are an epileptic or if you have high blood pressure. Most helpful in the treatment of acne, herpes, neuralgia, boils. Excellent with fever, respiratory infections, catarrh, headaches, aches and pains. Antiviral and stimulant. It helps to clear the head and it also improves concentration.

FENNEL

Avoid if you are an epileptic, pregnant, or if you have sensitive skin. Excellent cleanser for the skin, liver, kidneys, spleen. A diuretic for cellulite and pre-menstrual symptoms. Helps with digestive ailments caused by nervous tension, constipation, nausea. Very good for menopause, scanty periods, insufficient milk in nursing mothers. Aphrodisiac. Gives courage and strength in adversity.

FRANKINCENSE

Good for mature skin as well as oily and inflamed skin. Clears mucus and eases breathing. Helpful with infections of genito-urinary tract. Useful during labor and for postpartum depression. A general tonic and sedative. For anxious, obsessional states.

GERANIUM

Tonic and regulating effect on the whole system. Improves circulation, balances hormones, regulates mood swings. Diuretic. Good for oily and dry skins. Relieves pain.

GINGER

Could irritate sensitive skin. Warming and drying for irritations of the mucous membranes. Helps fever, muscle cramps, poor circulation. Settles digestion, nausea, travel sickness, hangovers. Helpful with joint pain and sharpens the senses. Aphrodisiac.

GRAPEFRUIT

For obesity, water retention, cellulite. It has diuretic properties, helps digestion of fats, stimulates bile secretion. Generally balancing and toning for digestive system. Helps relieve migraine, pre-menstrual tension, discomfort during pregnancy. Mitigates effects of jet lag, stabilizes mood swings, soothes irritability. Euphoric.

JUNIPER BERRY

Avoid during pregnancy. For oily, congested skin and eczema. Detoxifying, stimulates the circulation and appetite. Helps with menstrual irregularities, lymphatic congestion, joint pains, muscle spasms. Stimulant and aphrodisiac. Primarily for nervous disorders and negative states of mind.

LAVENDER

Avoid in early pregnancy. General panacea for balancing most body functions: digestion, menstruation, sebum production. Excellent for respiratory infections, high blood pressure and palpitations, joint pain, muscle spasms. It can speed up labor.

ORANGE

Avoid ultraviolet exposure for about an hour after application. Soothes nervous stomachs, diarrhea, constipation. Aids the digestion of fats. Very good for fevers, colds, flu. It is also relaxing for sore muscles. It aids the repair and healing of body tissues, wounds, scars. Possibly helps lower very high cholesterol. Good for insomnia caused by anxiety. Has an uplifting effect on the mind. Alleviates gloom, depression, lethargy, boredom.

Superb with any skin trauma: acne, eczema, burns, boils, scars. Relieves anger and exhaustion.

LEMON

May irritate sensitive skin. Superb for blood and circulatory system: anemia, varicose veins, high blood pressure. Boosts immune system. It is styptic (contracts blood vessels and tissues). Reduces fever in colds and flu, soothes sore throats and cold sores. Counteracts acidity, balances blood sugar. Helps for cellulite, constipation, dull and greasy skin.

ROSE

Avoid during first trimester of pregnancy. Gently cleanses the body of toxins; calms the stomach during emotional upsets. Good for diarrhea. Has a tonic effect on the heart, both physically and emotionally. Excellent for most female complaints to do with menstruation and menopause, also frigidity. Superb in helping with grief, anger, jealousy, resentment. A feminine oil to soften hardened hearts.

NEROLI (ORANGE BLOSSOM)

Very calming to the nervous system: it relieves insomnia, neuralgia, vertigo, headaches. Soothes irritability, pre-menstrual tension, some menopausal symptoms. It calms nervous stomachs. It is a good skin regenerator. Superb for dark depressions, shock, hysteria. Gives peace.

ROSEMARY

Avoid if suffering from high blood pressure. Wonderful for painful joints and muscles, in cases of rheumatism, arthritis, after-sport muscle stiffness. Revives the senses and clears the head. Helps poor concentration and memory. Eases headaches caused by poor digestion. Clears liverishness and queasiness. It is a stimulant and is good for low blood pressure and respiratory infections. Good for water retention. Invigorating and fortifying for the mind.

SANDALWOOD

Avoid in depression, as its sedative action might depress further. Good for urinary tract infections like cystitis. Aphrodisiac for men and women, cleanses reproductive organs. Soothes sore throats and chest infections. Boosts the immune system. Anti-inflammatory action on the skin. Calms nervous tension, can give peace and comfort to the dying.

TEA TREE

Superb for any fungal infections: thrush, skin rashes, athlete's foot, nail bed infection. Antivenomous on insect bites. Quells viral infections like chickenpox and cold sores (herpes). Boosts the immune system. A highly antiseptic oil.

YLANG-YLANG

It balances excited states, slows down rapid breathing or heartbeat. Has a balancing action on the hormonal system, especially the reproductive system. It is an aphrodisiac and an antidepressant, as well as an antiseptic for intestinal infections. It eases panic, shock, hysteria, fear. It balances the sebum secretion of the skin.

LEFT **A COUPLE OF DROPS OF ESSENTIAL OILS ADDED TO WATER AND HEATED GENTLY OVER A FLAME IN A DIFFUSER WILL SCENT A WHOLE ROOM.**

TABLE OF AILMENTS AND SUGGESTED OILS

THIS INFORMATION IS GIVEN AS A GENERAL GUIDE FOR PEOPLE WITH SOME KNOWLEDGE OF ESSENTIAL OILS. IT DOES NOT REPLACE PROFESSIONAL MEDICAL CARE. IT MUST ALSO BE STATED THAT A SMALL PERCENTAGE OF PEOPLE ARE ALLERGIC TO ESSENTIAL OIL.

ACCUMULATION OF TOXINS
OILS: fennel, juniper
METHOD: massage, bath, compress

ACHES AND PAINS
OILS: chamomile, coriander, eucalyptus, ginger, lavender, rosemary
METHOD: massage, bath, compress

ACNE
OILS: bergamot, chamomile, tea tree, geranium, lavender, rosemary
METHOD: massage

ALLERGIES
OILS: chamomile, lavender
METHOD: massage, bath, compress

AMENORRHEA
OILS: clary sage, fennel
METHOD: massage, bath

ANXIETY
OILS: bergamot, frankincense, lavender, neroli, ylang-ylang
METHOD: massage, bath, inhaling, diffusion

ARTHRITIS
OILS: benzoin, chamomile, ginger, eucalyptus, rosemary
METHOD: massage, bath, compress

ASTHMA
OILS: benzoin, frankincense, lavender
METHOD: massage, diffusion

ATHLETE'S FOOT
OILS: lavender, tea tree
METHOD: massage, bath, compress, undiluted

BALDNESS
See Hair Care

BRONCHITIS
OILS: benzoin, eucalyptus, frankincense, sandalwood

METHOD: massage, steam inhalation, bath, diffusion

BRUISES
OILS: fennel, lavender
METHOD: massage

BURNS
OILS: geranium, lavender
METHOD: compress, undiluted (apply directly to the skin)

CANDIDA
OIL: tea tree
METHOD: massage, bath

CATARRH
OILS: eucalyptus, frankincense, lavender, tea tree
METHOD: massage, bath, steam inhalation

CELLULITE
OILS: fennel, geranium, grapefruit, juniper
METHOD: daily massage, bath

CHICKENPOX
OILS: bergamot, lavender, tea tree
METHOD: massage, bath, compress, undiluted (swab the skin with a little oil on a wet cotton ball)

CHILBLAINS
OILS: geranium, lemon
METHOD: undiluted

CHILDBIRTH AID
See Labor Pain

CHILLS
OILS: benzoin, ginger
METHOD: massage, bath

CHRONIC COUGHS
OILS: frankincense, sandalwood
METHOD: massage, bath, steam inhalation

COLDS
See Influenza

COLD SORES
See Herpes

COLIC
OILS: chamomile, fennel, ginger, lavender
METHOD: massage, bath

CONSTIPATION
OILS: fennel, orange
METHOD: massage, bath

CRAMPS
OILS: clary sage, ginger, lavender
METHOD: massage, bath

CUTS
OILS: chamomile, lavender, tea tree
METHOD: compress

CYSTITIS
OILS: bergamot, chamomile, lavender, sandalwood
METHOD: massage, compress

DEPRESSION

OILS: bergamot, lavender, neroli, sandalwood, ylang-ylang

METHOD: massage, bath, inhaling, diffusion

DRY SKIN

See Sensitive Skin

EARACHE

OILS: chamomile, lavender

METHOD: massage

EDEMA

OILS: fennel, geranium, grapefruit, orange, rosemary

METHOD: massage, bath

EXCESSIVE MENSTRUATION

OILS: cypress, rose

METHOD: massage, bath

EXCESSIVE PERSPIRATION

OIL: cypress

METHOD: massage, bath

FATIGUE

OILS: benzoin, eucalyptus, ginger, rosemary

METHOD: massage, bath, diffusion

FEVER

OILS: eucalyptus, rosemary, tea tree

METHOD: massage, bath, compress, steam inhalation, diffusion

FLATULENCE

See Indigestion

FRIGIDITY

OILS: clary sage, rose, ylang-ylang

METHOD: massage, bath, skin perfume, diffusion

GASTRIC SPASMS

See Cramps

GOUT

OILS: benzoin, juniper, rosemary

METHOD: massage, bath, compress

GUM INFECTIONS

See Mouth Infections

HAIR CARE

OILS: chamomile, lavender, tea tree

METHOD: massage, bath

HALITOSIS

OILS: bergamot, fennel

METHOD: massage (massaging is best done to the stomach and throat — the oils will penetrate the skin and work from the inside)

HEADACHES

See Migraine

HERPES

OILS: bergamot, tea tree

METHOD: undiluted

HIGH BLOOD PRESSURE

OILS: lavender, ylang-ylang

METHOD: massage, bath, inhaling, diffusion

HOARSENESS

See Laryngitis

HYPERTENSION

See High Blood Pressure

INDIGESTION

OILS: chamomile, fennel, ginger, lavender, orange

METHOD: massage

INFLAMED SKIN

OILS: chamomile, lavender, rose

METHOD: massage, compress

INFLUENZA

OILS: bergamot, eucalyptus, frankincense, lemon, tea tree

METHOD: massage, bath, steam inhalation, diffusion

INSECT BITES

OILS: chamomile, lavender, tea tree

METHOD: massage, undiluted

INSECT REPELLENT

OILS: geranium, lavender, rosemary

METHOD: massage

INSOMNIA

OILS: chamomile, lavender, neroli, rose

METHOD: massage, bath, diffusion, undiluted (on pillowcase)

IRRITATED SKIN

See Inflamed Skin

ITCHING

OILS: bergamot, lavender, tea tree

METHOD: massage, bath, compress

LABOR PAIN

OILS: clary sage, lavender, rose

METHOD: massage, compress, diffusion

LACK OF NURSING MILK

OILS: fennel

METHOD: massage, compress

LARYNGITIS

OILS: benzoin, lavender, sandalwood

METHOD: massage, compress

LOW BLOOD PRESSURE

OILS: coriander, eucalyptus, ginger, rosemary

METHOD: massage, bath

MATURE SKIN

OILS: frankincense, neroli, rose, sandalwood

METHOD: massage

MEASLES

OILS: eucalyptus, tea tree

METHOD: massage, bath, compress, undiluted (swab on a wet cotton ball)

MENOPAUSAL PROBLEMS

OILS: fennel, geranium, rose

METHOD: massage, bath, diffusion

MIGRAINE

OILS: chamomile, lavender

METHOD: massage, bath, compress, diffusion, undiluted (on temples and occiput)

MOUTH INFECTIONS

OIL: fennel

METHOD: massage

MUSCLE CRAMP
OILS: lavender, rosemary
METHOD: massage, bath, compress

NAUSEA
See Vomiting

NERVOUS EXHAUSTION
See Fatigue

NERVOUS TENSION
See Stress

NEURALGIA
See Sciatica

OBESITY
OILS: fennel, juniper
METHOD: massage, bath,
steam inhalation

OILY SKIN AND SCALP
OILS: bergamot, cypress, geranium
METHOD: massage, bath

PAINFUL MENSTRUATION
OILS: chamomile, clary sage,
frankincense, juniper, lavender
METHOD: massage, bath, compress

PALPITATIONS
OILS: neroli, orange,
ylang-ylang
METHOD: massage, bath,
inhaling, diffusion

PILES
OILS: cypress, juniper
METHOD: massage
(lower abdomen and back)

POOR CIRCULATION
See Low Blood Pressure

PRE-MENSTRUAL SYMPTOMS
OILS: chamomile, lavender
METHOD: massage, bath,
diffusion

RASHES
OILS: chamomile, lavender
METHOD: compress, massage

RHEUMATISM
OILS: chamomile, eucalyptus,
juniper, lavender, rosemary
METHOD: massage, bath, compress

RINGWORM
OIL: tea tree
METHOD: undiluted

SCANTY PERIODS
See Amenorrhea

SCARS
See Stretch Marks

SCIATICA
OILS: chamomile, eucalyptus,
lavender, rosemary
METHOD: massage, bath, compress

SENSITIVE SKIN
OILS: chamomile, lavender,
sandalwood
METHOD: massage, bath

SHOCK
OIL: neroli
METHOD: inhaling, massage, bath

SINUSITIS
OILS: eucalyptus, ginger
METHOD: massage, bath, inhaling,
steam inhalation, diffusion

SLUGGISH DIGESTION
See Constipation

SNORING
OIL: eucalyptus
METHOD: undiluted (on pillowcase)

SORES
See Cuts

SORE THROAT
See Throat Infections

SPRAINS AND STRAINS
OILS: chamomile, lavender
METHOD: massage, compress

STIFFNESS
See Muscle Cramp

STRESS
OILS: benzoin, bergamot, chamomile,
clary sage, frankincense, lavender,
neroli, rose, sandalwood, ylang-ylang
METHOD: massage, bath,
diffusion, inhaling

STRETCH MARKS
OILS: frankincense, neroli, sandalwood
METHOD: massage

TEETHING PAINS
OIL: chamomile
METHOD: massage

THROAT INFECTIONS
OILS: eucalyptus, geranium, tea tree
METHOD: massage

THRUSH
See Candida

TONSILLITIS
OILS: bergamot, geranium, lemon
METHOD: massage, diffusion

TOOTHACHE
See Teething Pains

VARICOSE VEINS
OILS: cypress, lemon
METHOD: massage

VERTIGO
OIL: lavender
METHOD: inhaling

VERUCCAE
See Warts

VOMITING
OILS: chamomile, fennel,
lavender
METHOD: massage, bath,
inhaling, diffusion

WARTS
OILS: lemon, tea tree
METHOD: undiluted

WATER RETENTION
See Edema

WRINKLES
See Mature Skin

VIII

HERBAL
HOME
COSMETICS

*"Anoint thy face with goat's milk in which violets
have been infused, and there is not a prince of earth
who will not be charmed with thy beauty."*

(OLD CELTIC SAYING)

HERBAL
HOME
COSMETICS

For centuries, women have been making their own cosmetics using ingredients from their kitchens and gardens. Turning back to nature is a perfect way of keeping your own natural beauty. As the recipes given contain no preservatives, make only small quantities and, preferably, keep them in the refrigerator. Be sure to label your containers clearly in case they are inadvertently used as a salad dressing.

SKIN CARE

The secret of having good skin is keeping it clean. There are three methods of doing this: steaming (which is the most thorough), washing and using creams and lotions.

STEAMING

This method is beneficial to all types of skin. It cleans the skin of surface dirt, stimulates the circulation and unclogs blocked pores. If you have dry, sensitive skin, don't make the steam bath too hot, and limit yourself to 5 minutes. For normal skin, apply the steam for up to 7 minutes and for oily skin, up to 10 minutes.

Bring water to the boil, pour the boiling water into a bowl, lean over it and cover your head and the bowl with a towel so that no steam escapes. Your face should be 12–18 in (30–45 cm) from the water. To make the steaming more beneficial, add 1 TBS (15 ml) of dried herbs or a handful of fresh herbs to the water. Use rosemary, sage or mint for a stimulating cleanse; use thyme as an antiseptic; use lavender and chamomile for

soothing the skin and comfrey for healing. After steaming your face, splash it with cool water or apply a mild skin toner.

CLEANSING

Cleanse your skin twice a day to remove dirt and old make-up. Cleansing also removes dead cells and softens the skin. Spread a suitable cream or lotion lightly over the skin, leave it on for a few minutes and tissue off. Use a pH-balanced soap and rinse with lukewarm water. Follow cleansing with a toner and moisturizer.

To make herbal cleansing oil which is most suitable for dry skin, *see* instructions for herbal bath oil on page 114.

FACIAL COMPRESS

A facial compress stimulates and moistens the skin. Cleanse the face before applying a compress. Pour boiling water over herbs of your choice, leave to draw and let the water cool a little, then strain the liquid. Put a small clean face cloth into the liquid, wring out lightly and apply to your face. As the compress cools off, repeat the process.

Herbs for steaming or facial compresses are marigold, elder, parsley, yarrow, fennel, lemon balm, pelargonium and roses.

RIGHT **THE SECRET OF HAVING GOOD SKIN IS USING A CLEANSER, TONER AND MOISTURIZER. STEAMING AND FACE MASKS ALSO HELP TO REMOVE IMPURITIES.**

SKIN TYPES

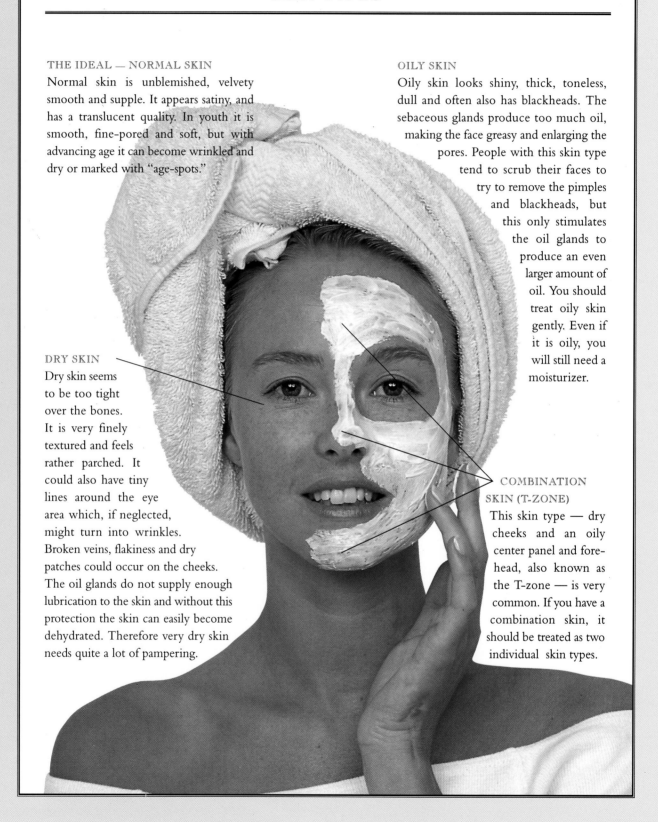

THE IDEAL — NORMAL SKIN

Normal skin is unblemished, velvety smooth and supple. It appears satiny, and has a translucent quality. In youth it is smooth, fine-pored and soft, but with advancing age it can become wrinkled and dry or marked with "age-spots."

DRY SKIN

Dry skin seems to be too tight over the bones. It is very finely textured and feels rather parched. It could also have tiny lines around the eye area which, if neglected, might turn into wrinkles. Broken veins, flakiness and dry patches could occur on the cheeks. The oil glands do not supply enough lubrication to the skin and without this protection the skin can easily become dehydrated. Therefore very dry skin needs quite a lot of pampering.

OILY SKIN

Oily skin looks shiny, thick, toneless, dull and often also has blackheads. The sebaceous glands produce too much oil, making the face greasy and enlarging the pores. People with this skin type tend to scrub their faces to try to remove the pimples and blackheads, but this only stimulates the oil glands to produce an even larger amount of oil. You should treat oily skin gently. Even if it is oily, you will still need a moisturizer.

COMBINATION SKIN (T-ZONE)

This skin type — dry cheeks and an oily center panel and forehead, also known as the T-zone — is very common. If you have a combination skin, it should be treated as two individual skin types.

CLEANSER

TONER

STEAM

CLEANSING CREAM

1 oz (25 g) each lanolin and cocoa butter

4 TBS (60 ml) each almond oil and strong herbal infusion

COLD CREAM

¾ oz (20 g) beeswax

4 TBS (60 ml) peanut oil

¼ tsp (1.25 ml) boric acid

4 tsp (20 ml) rosewater

COCONUT OIL CLEANSING CREAM

4 TBS (60 ml) sweet almond oil

2 TBS (30 ml) coconut oil

1½ tsp (7.5 ml) beeswax

1 TBS (15 ml) emulsifying wax

2 TBS (30 ml) strong herbal infusion

¼ tsp (1.25 ml) boric acid

1 TBS (15 ml) witch hazel

Use the same method to make all three cleansing creams. Heat the oils and/or waxes and herbal infusion separately over two water baths or *bains-marie*. Where boric acid (a powder) is used, first dissolve it in the infusion. When the waxes have melted, blend the infusion with the oils. Whisk by hand or with an electric mixer until the mixture has cooled and blended. Pour into a jar and shake before using.

✠ *To make a strong herbal infusion, pour 8 oz (250 ml) boiling water over a handful of fresh herbs or a tablespoon of dried herbs. Cover and stand for 20–30 minutes. Strain.*

✠ *Herbs for cleansing creams are rosemary, lady's mantle, lavender, chamomile, dandelion, marigold, nettle and violet.*

BUTTERMILK AND ELDERFLOWER LOTION

Heat 8 oz (250 ml) buttermilk with 3 TBS (45 ml) of elderflowers. Simmer for 30 minutes. Cool, strain, bottle and refrigerate. Apply to spotty, oily skin with a cotton ball. Allow to dry on skin, then rinse with lukewarm water. Use the remaining curds in a mask. Add fuller's earth or kaolin to thicken the mixture and spread over the face, omitting eye area. Cover eyes with eye pads or with cotton balls dipped in a herbal infusion for eyes (*see* page 169), put your feet up and relax for about 20 minutes. Rinse off mask with lukewarm water and follow this with a toner and a moisturizer. The kaolin and fuller's earth have drawing properties, which make them an excellent addition to all your face masks.

To make cleansing milk lotions, heat 8 oz (250 ml) milk and 3 TBS (45 ml) of your favorite herb until milk smells strongly of the herb. The milk should not boil or form a skin. Cool, strain, bottle and refrigerate.

SOAPWORT LOTION

Simmer a handful of soapwort leaves and stems in enough water to cover for 10 minutes. Cool and strain. This is good for skin rashes and eczema.

YARROW LOTION

Make a strong yarrow infusion, strain and bottle. Good for oily, spotty skins.

✠ *Strain herbal infusions and herbal oils through a coffee filter. When making herbal oils or infusions, steep the herbs in glass or earthenware containers. Never use aluminum or metal containers, because of possible contamination of the oil or infusion by the metal.*

TONERS

A toner freshens the skin and removes residual soap or cleanser. Soak cotton balls in toner and wipe over the skin.

Rosewater is one of the oldest and best skin toners. Make your own by placing 2 handfuls of heavily scented rose petals in a pan and covering with distilled water. Cover pan and bring water to the boil. Simmer for 30 minutes. Strain. Add more petals and repeat until water smells heavily of roses. Bottle in sterilized bottles and leave for a week before using. You need many roses and a lot of time, so if you would like some immediately, go to your drugstore. For oily skin, make up a toner of 1 part witch hazel to 3 parts rosewater.

Make simple toners from infusions of herbs or flowers. Use 1 tsp (5 ml) dried herbs or 1 TBS (15 ml) fresh herbs to 8 oz (250 ml) boiling water. Stand for about 30 minutes. Strain, bottle and refrigerate. This will last for a few days.

For toners, choose from the following herbs and flowers:
CHAMOMILE (flowers) — healing, soothing; softens wrinkles.
COMFREY (foliage) — healing; clears pimples.
DANDELION (foliage) — full of vitamins; for sallow skin.
ELDER (flowers) — refines, softens and whitens the skin.
LAVENDER (flowers and foliage) — healing and soothing; good for sunburned skin.
MARIGOLD (flowers) — it helps to clear blemishes and pimples; it is also claimed to be rejuvenating.
MINT (foliage) — stimulating and cooling.
PARSLEY (foliage) — helps spotty skins and helps to fade freckles; it contains vitamin C.
PELARGONIUM (foliage) — antiseptic; helps sagging skin.
ROSEMARY (foliage) — tonic for tired skins; astringent.
SAGE (foliage) — astringent; good for oily skin; closes pores.
THYME (foliage) — antiseptic; for problem skin.
VIOLET (flowers) — clears pimples and blemishes.
YARROW (foliage) — useful for oily skin.

For oily skin and larger pores, make toners more astringent by adding witch hazel. Mix equal parts of witch hazel and herbal infusion.

✠ *After straining liquid from herbs, liquidise remaining herbs. Add 1 tsp (5 ml) honey and sufficient fuller's earth to thicken to a paste. Use as a face mask.*
Apple cider vinegar is an ideal toner as its acidity restores the acid mantle to skin. Use 1 TBS (15 ml) vinegar to 1¾ pints (1 liter) water. Make aromatic vinegar toners by following the instructions for Vinegars for Baths on page 114. Use flowers like roses, marigolds or elderflowers. Always remember to dilute before use.

MOISTURIZERS

Moisturizers keep skin moist and can also attract moisture from the atmosphere. The combination of oils, waxes and water keeps skin smooth, soft and flexible. Moisturizers act as barriers between skin and harmful bacteria and harsh elements. Apply, leave to absorb for 20 minutes, then wipe off excess to prevent attracting dirt which could clog the pores.

The simplest moisturizers are made of herbal infusions and glycerine. Add 1 TBS (15 ml) strong herbal infusion to 1 TBS (15 ml) glycerine. Bottle and refrigerate. Shake before use.

GENTLE MOISTURIZER
2 tsp (10 ml) beeswax
1 tsp (5 ml) emulsifying wax
4 tsp (20 ml) almond oil
1 tsp (5 ml) each wheatgerm oil and honey
4 TBS (60 ml) strong chamomile and lavender infusion
3 drops lavender essential oil (optional)

MOISTURIZER FOR DRY SKIN
4 tsp (20 ml) each beeswax and lanolin
1 tsp (5 ml) avocado oil (or calendula oil)
2 tsp (10 ml) each wheatgerm oil and glycerine
4 TBS (60 ml) almond oil
3 oz (90 ml) comfrey and calendula infusion
½ tsp (2.5 ml) boric acid

MOISTURIZER FOR OILY TO NORMAL SKIN
2 TBS (30 ml) each emulsifying wax and almond oil
4 oz (120 ml) strong herbal infusion (yarrow and sage for oily skin, rosewater for normal skin)
½ tsp (2.5 ml) boric acid
1½ tsp (7.5 ml) witch hazel
1 tsp (5 ml) glycerine
3 drops rosemary oil (optional)

Use the same method to make all three moisturizers. Heat waxes and oils in a *bain-marie*. In a separate bowl, heat infusion and honey, glycerine and/or witch hazel over another water bath. If using boric acid, first dissolve it in the infusion. When the waxes melt, add heated infusion, stirring until mixture thickens and cools. Stir in essential oil (if using) when cool.

FACE MASK

MOISTURIZER

EYECARE

FACE MASKS

A mask cleanses, nourishes and rejuvenates your skin. First cleanse face and neck. Apply mask, avoiding lips and eye area. Protect eyes with cotton balls soaked in witch hazel, water or herbal infusion for eyes. Leave for 10–30 minutes, then rinse off. Pat face dry and apply moisturizer.

AVOCADO MASK FOR DRY SKIN

Mash 2 TBS (30 ml) avocado, add 1 tsp (5 ml) rosewater (or herbal infusion) and 1 tsp (5 ml) honey. Apply. Leave for 20 minutes and rinse with tepid water.

MASK FOR BLEMISHES AND BLACKHEADS

Mash up a small ripe tomato and add 4 tsp (20 ml) kaolin and 1 tsp (5 ml) strong comfrey infusion. Mix this to a paste, adding more kaolin or infusion if necessary. Apply to your face and leave on for about 10–15 minutes. Rinse off with tepid water.

✠ *Press juice from comfrey stems; apply to painful pimples.*

CHAMOMILE AND YOGURT MASK

Make a strong chamomile infusion. Add 1 TBS (15 ml) infusion to 1 TBS (15 ml) yogurt, 1 TBS (15 ml) oatmeal and 1 tsp (5 ml) honey. Apply the mask to your face. This will help to clear blemishes. The oatmeal has a cleansing effect and the honey has antiseptic qualities.

THREE GREENS HEALING MASK

Place a large comfrey leaf, a small handful of dandelion leaves and a small bunch of parsley in water to cover. Simmer for 10 minutes, liquefy and strain. Add kaolin to thicken to a paste and apply to skin. Leave for 15 minutes, then rinse off with lukewarm water.

CREAM AND CALENDULA MASK

Add 1 tsp (5 ml) calendula oil to 1 TBS (15 ml) fresh cream. Apply. Leave for 30 minutes, then rinse off the excess. This is good for dry skins. Pour the remaining cream into a bottle, label and refrigerate.

To make your own calendula oil, steep calendula petals in a good quality oil. Place petals and sufficient oil to cover in a glass jar and leave in a sunny position for three weeks. Strain and bottle.

BUTTERMILK, ELDERFLOWER AND OATMEAL MASK

Mix 1 TBS (15 ml) buttermilk with 1 TBS (15 ml) oatmeal and add 1 tsp (5 ml) of a strong elderflower infusion. Add 1 tsp (5 ml) honey for extra vitamins. Apply to face, leave for 20–30 minutes, then rinse.

EYES

Herbal compresses soothe, tone and brighten the eyes. They are applied to closed eyes and are not to be used as eye baths. If you think you have an eye infection, consult a doctor.

To make compresses, cut two layers of lint cloth for each eye. Dip into cold infusion, squeeze lightly and cover closed eye. Replace as compresses become warm. Rest 10 minutes.

Herbal infusions must be fresh (discard after 12 hours).

Elderflowers are a mild stimulant and brighten the eyes. Chamomile flowers are soothing for tired eyes. Keep your used chamomile tea bags — they are the perfect shape for your eyes. Just dampen and use.

Infusions of the following herbs also make good eye compresses: fennel (good for tired eyes), horsetail (good for redness and swollen eyelids), parsley and lemon verbena.

BATHING

To help you unwind after a busy day, have a relaxing bath. To make a bath bag, *see* page 114. *Use the following herbs:*

SOOTHING — lavender, chamomile, valerian root and linden flowers (a cool lavender bath takes the sting out of sunburn).
TONING — rosemary, nettle, comfrey, mint and juniper.
REFRESHING AND DEODORIZING — lemon verbena, lemon balm and lovage leaves. If you prefer, you could also use a strong infusion of these herbs.

AFTER-BATH BODY SPLASHES
Use fragrant herb-scented water as a refreshing splash after bathing. Herbs to choose from are: lavender, scented rose petals, rosemary, lemon balm, lemon verbena, lemon thyme, eau-de-cologne mint, violet, lovage and chamomile.

PEPPERMINT SPLASH
    1¾ pints (1 liter) distilled water
    17 oz (500 ml) white wine vinegar
    3 handfuls of peppermint leaves

Bring to the boil. Simmer for 10 minutes. Strain and bottle. If it is too strong for your skin type, dilute before applying.

SPICY SPLASH (ESPECIALLY FOR MEN)
    Steep 1 tsp (5 ml) crushed coriander seeds and 3 bay leaves in 2 oz (50 ml) pure alcohol (from your drugstore) for 3–6 weeks. If scent is not strong enough, strain and add fresh coriander seeds and bay leaves. Strain, add 8 oz (250 ml) distilled water and bottle.

HANDS AND FEET

We often neglect our hands and feet. Before working with detergents and hot water, use a barrier cream to protect your hands. Rinse your hands in a herbal infusion after washing them. Leave your hands in the infusion for a few minutes before drying them. Suitable herbs are chamomile, comfrey, fennel, lavender and lady's mantle.

Soak your feet in a foot bath. Use strong infusions of comfrey, sage (for sweaty feet), lavender (soothing), chamomile (calming), marigold, rosemary (for toning and stimulating) or mint (for tired feet). A mustard bath warms you if you have a cold. Soak feet for 20 minutes, pat dry, then massage.

RICH HAND CREAM
    4 tsp (20 ml) emulsifying wax
    1 tsp (5 ml) each beeswax and cocoa butter
    2 tsp (10 ml) lanolin
    1¼ oz (35 ml) almond oil
    1 tsp (5 ml) wheatgerm oil
    2½ oz (70 ml) strong marigold infusion
    ¼ tsp (1.25 ml) boric acid
    4 drops each lavender oil and benzoin (optional)

Melt waxes and oils in a *bain-marie* and heat infusion with boric acid over another water bath. Add infusion to oils and stir until cool. Massage cream into hands, especially cuticles. It is also good for dry feet.

BARRIER CREAM
    1 TBS (15 ml) each petroleum jelly and lanolin
    2 TBS (30 ml) strong comfrey infusion

Melt petroleum jelly and lanolin in a *bain-marie* and add the heated infusion. Mix to a thick cream.

HAIR

Your hair indicates your state of health. Improve your hair by following a well-balanced diet. A scalp massage also improves hair. Using herbs to treat your hair restores its condition, strengthens it, stimulates growth and intensifies the color.
Use the following herbs for hair:
CATMINT — promotes shiny hair.
CHAMOMILE — lightens and conditions; stimulates growth.
MARIGOLD — for shiny highlights.
NETTLE — conditioner, improves color and texture of hair and helps with dandruff (rub a strong infusion into scalp daily).
PARSLEY — gives lustre, stimulates growth, helps dandruff.
ROSEMARY — darkens, conditions, tones, stimulates growth.
SAGE — helps darken hair.
THYME — rub strong infusion into scalp to help for hair loss.
YARROW — greasy hair (rub strong infusion into scalp daily).

Use oil conditioner for brittle, dry hair and split ends. Mix 1 TBS (15 ml) almond oil with 1 TBS (15 ml) jojoba oil (a liquid wax, excellent for hair). Steep the herb, depending on hair type and color, in almond oil for three weeks in a sunny position, or heat herbs and oil over a water bath and simmer for an hour, topping up the water when necessary. Cool and strain. Press oil from herbs. Repeat until oil smells strongly of the herb.

Massage 1 TBS (15 ml) conditioner into scalp, then work oil into hair 1 TBS (15 ml) for short hair, 2 TBS (30 ml) for long hair). Cover hair with plastic wrap and a warm towel. Sit in a warm sunny place for 30 minutes to one hour, then wash hair. Apply shampoo to make an emulsion, then add water. Depending on condition of hair, treat once or twice a week. If jojoba oil is unobtainable, use almond or olive oil.

Make a mild shampoo from soapwort. Make an infusion from a handful of soapwort to 17 oz (500 ml) boiling water. Add a handful of herbs (chamomile for blond hair, rosemary for dark) to the soapwort before adding the water. Leave for 20–30 minutes. Strain. Use 8 oz (250 ml) to wash hair. It will not foam like commercial shampoos. To add shine, add 1 TBS (15 ml) gelatin to the above recipe or to 3 TBS (45 ml) of your normal shampoo. Make sure it dissolves before using.

Prepare a simple shampoo by adding a cupful of the strong infusion of the herb of your choice to your shampoo.

After rinsing your hair, give it a final rinse in diluted apple cider vinegar — 1 TBS (15 ml) vinegar to 1¾ pints (1 liter) water. As the vinegar is herbal, your hair won't smell of pickles! This rinse removes all traces of calcium and soap residue from your hair, it stimulates the scalp, and treats dandruff and an itchy scalp.

Use an infusion of herbs, by themselves or mixed, as a final hair rinse. Rinse your hair over a basin in order to catch the liquid. In this way you can keep pouring it over your hair to rinse it thoroughly.

ABOVE **YOU WILL HAVE LOVELY HEALTHY HAIR IF YOU USE HERBAL SHAMPOOS AND CONDITIONERS.**

RHUBARB AND CHAMOMILE DYE

To lighten blonde hair, simmer a rhubarb root and stem in white wine for about 30 minutes. Allow to stand for approximately 30 minutes and then strain. Mix in equal proportions with a strong chamomile infusion and add enough kaolin to thicken to a paste. Leave the paste on your hair for 20–60 minutes, depending on the degree of lightness you want. Rinse off and shampoo hair. Instead of chamomile, use a paste or rinse of rosemary and sage if you wish to darken your hair.

INDEX

Page numbers in **bold** refer to the main herb entries in *A Directory of Herbs*, the alphabetical listing in *Herbal Healing*, and the list of essential oils in *Aromatherapy*.